Cooking Without Recipes

Unleash your creativity and prepare
meals your friends and family will love!

CHERYL SINDELL

KENSINGTON BOOKS
http://www.kensingtonbooks.com

KENSINGTON BOOKS are published by
Kensington Publishing Corp.
850 Third Avenue
New York, NY 10022

Cover design by Annmarie Dalton.
Illustrations by Mona Daly.
Kensington and the K logo Reg. U.S. Pat. & TM Off.

ISBN 1-57566-142-X

First Printing: March, 1997
10 9 8 7 6 5 4 3 2 1

Printed in the United States of America

Cooking Without Recipes

Cooking without Recipes *is dedicated to my loving husband, Robert Heller, and our sweet daughter, Chelsea Leigh.*

This book is also dedicated to every man, woman, and child who loves to eat, and who wants to put food back into its proper perspective by having more fun in the kitchen, and by giving mealtime the attention it deserves.

"I feel a recipe is only a theme, which an intelligent cook can play each time with a variation."

—Madame Jehane Benoit,
author of *Mme. Benoit Cooks at Home.*

"*Cooking without Recipes is* a recipe for greater enjoyment of the cooking process. I hope it makes its way into every home in America."

—Dean S. Edell, M.D.
Syndicated medical reporter

CONTENTS

FOREWORD
by
Joachim Splichal

I always add an element of play to the food I serve, whether I'm cooking at home or at one of my restaurants. I let fantasy take over, let myself dream up new dishes. I find ingredients that make cooking more interesting. I also like to include some humor and some entertainment in the menu descriptions, and to surprise my customers when the food actually arrives in front of them. This gives life to the table, gives people something to talk about. It's what I love to do, and it makes my customers happy.

Sometimes when I tell people I improvise, they're shocked: "Wow, he cooks without recipes! How can that be?" My answer is that my instincts are a better guide than a recipe. I might start by looking at suggestions in a magazine, but then I give it my own interpretation by changing it around and adding a little of this or that. That defines your character in cooking, your personal style. And, anyway, most recipes are confusing and time-consuming. Why would anyone bother with measuring a quarter teaspoon of salt?

When you want to create a dish, just start with a feeling. Then from there you have to see what ingredients are available, and what's fresh. Go to the fridge, or go to the farmer's market; let your imagination explode, let yourself play: Do a corn risotto, where the corn becomes the rice. Or do a lasagna with potatoes instead of noodles, or gnocchi with polenta instead of potatoes. And why not throw in some caramelized onions or grilled shiitake mushrooms. I call that the Cracker Jack, or surprise, factor; I do that in every dish. It's a very simple process, but you have to take that leap, you have to trust your intuition. This is exactly what Cheryl captures in *Cooking without Recipes*!

The most important thing is for *you* to like the food you're cooking. When you prepare food for your guests, pick ingredients that *you* feel like eating that day. And when the dish comes out onto the table, if you're proud of it and it's tasty to you, then you've succeeded.

I cook with a lot of vegetables and potatoes, grains and beans because *I* like to eat that way, and a lot of those foods are ignored. A lentil is a lentil, but if it's prepared well it can be fantastic! Cheryl Sindell shows you that healthy ingredients are often the most exciting ingredients.

Cooking without Recipes also emphasizes the importance of having fresh-cooked meals at home, of sharing time and conversation with those you care about. In America, we're always on the run, but in Europe families sit down to dinner for at least an hour or two, which allows them to gather and talk about the day and what's happening in their lives. Fresh-cooked meals also provide the opportunity for children to taste and become familiar with a variety of vegetables and other nutritious foods. Of course, my twins were just born, so we haven't been able to sit down together around the table yet!

The bottom line is people get together for meals to interact, to laugh, to have fun. There's a lot of passion and love at the table, and you can enhance that by serving delicious food. *Cooking without Recipes* simplifies the art of getting a great meal on the table. Cheryl believes, as I do, that you know how to cook once you let your imagination come out and play.

—Joachim Splichal
(owner of several California-French restaurants, including Patina and Pinot Bistro)

PREFACE

When I was eight my family moved from Cincinnati, Ohio, to California. When we first came to Los Angeles, we moved in with my grandparents for seven months, and that's when I became particularly close to Grandma-ma Sultana. I often called her Grandma-ma, because although she was only five feet, six inches tall, she appeared bigger than life to me. I think it was because her long, gray hair was usually piled high on top of her head.

I loved sitting on her comfortable lap whenever I could, but when she was busy cooking I'd sit on a high stool near the warm stove and watch her every move. She had an uncanny knack for turning everyday ingredients into original dishes that were absolutely scrumptious. Like most cooks from her generation, Grandma-ma cooked without recipes, adding a bit of this and a bit of that, but how she did it was a mystery to me.

One day, as she was giving me tastes of little meatballs stuffed with potato and leek, which I ate as quickly as she could make, I asked her how she learned to cook without recipes.

"Break the rules, honey, and your creative juices will tell you what to do." She told me to look at the colors that exist together in nature, and to savor the taste of the dishes I enjoy eating most. When cooking, she said to think back on what I liked eating and improvise along those lines.

"Use only the ingredients you enjoy," Grandma-ma emphasized. "Omit every herb, spice, and ingredient you don't like, and infuse the dishes you make with spirit!"

Grandma-ma promised me that if I smelled, felt, and tasted my favorite ingredients—really examined them—they'd practically jump up and tell me what to do. She was right! Boiling spiral noodles instead of curved hollow ones, and adding a little of this and that, together we made a cheesy noodle dish that turned out better than my favorite traditional macaroni and cheese.

I asked Grandma-ma to explain how she started cooking creatively. She said it happened in an instant one day after an artist had told her how he had created his painting. This piece, the artist explained, started out with a splash of white that asked to be red. Then it solicited a black line through its center. The painting was finished when it didn't ask for anything more.

Grandma-ma told me that cooking, painting, music, writing—and all other forms of art—are about making choices, and that the ingredients you decide to leave out are just as important as the ones you put in. An original dish is nothing more than a composite of choices a cook has made. And a recipe is a cook's choices written down.

"But how," I asked, "do you decide?"

"Listen to your instincts, sweetheart, really listen with your eyes and all your other senses, and you'll know what to do. Your creative voice is always there, inside, chatting away, trying to get your attention."

"But what if I don't hear it?"

Grandma-ma looked at me, smiled, and said, "Take your time, sometimes you need to walk away for a while. Have some milk and cookies, or go outside and play, and within a short time you'll know what to do. I know you'll always be a great 'cooker,' honey."

Eleven years later, when I was nineteen, my grandmother died. I was devastated and thought of her often. But it wasn't until I had a full-time job, married, inherited my three teenage stepchildren, and gave birth to a daughter, that I realized the influence my grandmother had on me, my life, and my cooking. In addition to working full-time, a large instant family made streamlined cooking procedures absolutely essential.

My first creative experience in the kitchen occurred one night when I was tired and didn't feel like going to the market. I wanted to make a salad, but didn't have any lettuce in the house.

I sat down at the kitchen counter and thought about Grandma-ma and her gentle ways. I closed my eyes, felt her presence, and could almost taste and smell the macaroni-type dish we had made together when I was a child. But just thinking about cooking without her, and experimenting on my own, was terrifying. I thought about how Grandma-ma had encouraged me to think of myself as the facilitator of what the food wants to become, and used that as a starting point.

I looked in the refrigerator, found three foods I enjoy—an avocado, a cantaloupe, and a tomato—and imagined their flavors united. I cut and tossed them together in a bowl, tasted the combination, and decided to add a little salt and pepper. This unusual salad turned out to be one of the most sensuously satisfying and healthful dishes my husband or I had ever tasted.

Another unusual salad followed. I mixed together a package of frozen baby peas, a small slab of low-fat cheese (cut into quarter-inch cubes), two large handfuls of raw sunflower seeds, and the leaves from a large bunch of watercress. I topped this colorful side-dish salad combination with a ready-made olive-oil-based red-wine vinegar dressing and served it to a group of friends.

From that time on, I always thought of infusing my food with spirit, and began creating entire meals without using recipes. My loving husband, Robert, and all my wonderful children and friends are supportive and always amazed when I come up with something different, especially when they think there's no food in the house. Some dishes have been more memorable than others, but since there's a way to fix most mistakes, I haven't had many failures. Plain and simply, cooking creatively brings pleasure to my life on a daily basis.

Cooking without Recipes was written out of my desire to pass the same enjoyment on to you—the reader. To the main ingredient—fun—I've added my knowledge of the creative process, a subject that has held my interest since I was a young girl. I sautéed my creative juices with information I've learned as a nutritionist, regarding health-related food issues, and sprinkled in valuable cooking principles and techniques. Finally, I peppered in anecdotes about my personal life and quotes from other people who inspire me.

The ideas and innovative cooking methods, offered under the **Try This** headings, are the up-to-the-minute suggestions I've created for my clients as a clinical nutritionist over the past sixteen years. My clients have inspired me to share the information with you, because without writing a single word down, they'd translate what I'd say into homemade pizza, creamy pasta, delicious spreads, sauces, dips, incredible soup, salad, grain, veggie, and dessert dishes—all guilt-free. And, they began entertaining more often because cooking got easy. This book will change your way of cooking, eating, and entertaining, too.

My grandmother knew that creative juices fly when you don't follow rules, so she gave me permission to experiment. With this book, Grandma-ma Sultana Sadacca and I are passing the same permission on to you, with two words of caution: Watch out! *Cooking without Recipes* will spur your creativity and it will even change your life, causing you to do wild and wacky things both in and out of the kitchen.

In *The Artist's Way,* Julia Cameron says, "When you begin unlocking your creativity it doesn't just unlock in the desired area. You will find yourself reorganizing your living room furniture, painting your house a different color, changing your wardrobe, cooking something different on Thursday. It's a very multifaceted thing."

While writing this book I decided to paint over the existing wallpaper in my guest bathroom, which eventually led to experimenting in just about every area of my life. So, buyer beware!

Cheryl Sindell
Brentwood, California

Introduction

How many times has a recipe left you in the lurch? It says you need some exotic, esoteric item. You run around to find it. You buy it. And then the recipe never mentions the ingredient again! It rots in your cupboard because you're not sure what it is, or what to do with it.

I remember following a recipe that called for a *salamander.* Was I supposed to go out and buy a lizard? Finally, I discovered that it's a costly cooking utensil I'd never use again. I didn't buy it, but still felt confused about what to make, so I decided to give other recipes a try.

Mouthwatering Cookbooks

One day, on my way out of the supermarket, I bought one of those $1.95 Dell recipe books called *Easy Gourmet*. It was lying between *Removing Wrinkles with Home Remedies* and *Flatten Your Tummy in 30 Days*. As soon as I read this little cookbook, I realized that most of the recipes called for fattening, fatty ingredients, and that if I cooked with them I'd be in desperate need of that tummy book in less than thirty days!

1

Since it had always been important to me to remain lean and healthy, I began omitting the unhealthful ingredients immediately. The results, however, tasted terrible.

Then I tried recipes from the so-called "health cookbooks," but they didn't provide satisfying answers, either. The nutritional breakdowns that accompanied those recipes were incomplete, astonishingly inaccurate, and the results turned out worse than the recipes from that first little book.

Next, I began accumulating best-selling cookbooks. I read the recipes in the kitchen and followed their directions, but too many of the dishes I made didn't turn out to my liking, or anyone else's. I still liked eating, but I started to hate cooking! So for company, I'd purchase restaurant meals and try to fool everyone by putting them into my own pots and pans. The cleanup was just as time-consuming, and I'm not a good actress, so entertaining wasn't much fun. I continued to read and enjoy cookbooks, but I decided to start reading them in the bedroom—for information, pleasure, inspiration, and ideas.

Fortunately, it didn't take long before I realized it would be easier to reacquaint myself with the chef inside me than to revamp other people's recipes. And, just knowing I could make delicious meals without running around for specific items made cooking more enjoyable.

Although cookbooks are great sources for ideas, it takes a great deal of time and energy to follow them. I found a trip to some exotic food market makes a dish more difficult instead of more delicious, so I'd rather spend my time at the farmer's market. In addition, most recipes require special equipment, exact measurements, tedious directions, and marathon preparations that torture both the food and the cook.

Recipes Aren't the Gospel

Most food is overhandled, overcooked, oversauced, and overdone. With many recipes, hard work is created, the cook is overworked, and valuable nutrition is destroyed.

"Steam the broccoli, put it in a food processor, add cream, salt, sherry, and tomatoes, beat the mixture, pour over pounded chicken, and bake for fifty-five minutes at 350 degrees." Too many specific steps can bog you down, and make you wish you'd ordered out instead of eating some caloric conglomeration.

One time, when I still didn't trust my creativity enough to make meals for company, I followed a recipe I had for spanakopita—spinach casserole baked in filo dough. The directions said to keep adding melted butter, to keep the sheets of dough together. I had used almost a half pound of butter to prevent the dough from drying up; glue would have worked better. When it was time to sit down and eat, all I could think about was that fat going straight to my thighs. Everyone said the dish was delicious, but I felt guilty watching them eat and wished we'd gone out to a restaurant instead. I promised myself never to cook that way for anyone again!

The next day, I made a similar dish using an aerosol *nonstick* spray. It was easier and it tasted better. Coming up with that simple technique encouraged me to begin cooking creatively again.

Recipes might tell you to mix the dry ingredients together in a particular order when it doesn't make a bit of difference how the ingredients are combined. Why should it matter if two, four, or six cups of water, broth, or juice are added to the soup pot? The type and amount of liquid used determine the desired flavor and thickness.

And, who's to say which vegetables go best in soup? It's a matter of preference. Recipes provide ideas, but they needn't dictate our every move.

Recipes tell how many people a dish serves. But that changes with the guests' appetites, and the number of other dishes available. I don't know anyone who wouldn't welcome smaller portions when served a seven-course meal.

COOKING WITHOUT RECIPES IS NECESSARY

But, you may ask, if all I have to do in order to create original dishes is cook whatever I please and still use cookbooks for ideas, why is this book necessary?

Although entertaining without recipes is freeing, it's also intimidating. Having *Cooking without Recipes* beside you is like having a true kitchen-friend who shares ideas with you about creativity, food, nutrition, and entertaining. It provides the confidence you need, and means never having to feel intimidated about getting a meal on the table again.

How to Use This Book

Simply turn to the chapter dealing with the subject you're interested in. There's no need to start at the beginning, or read the book straight through.

The first chapter inspires you to entertain creatively, while the second one encourages your creative instincts to run wild. The remaining chapters show you how to mix and match your favorite ingredients and cuisines because—as far as I'm concerned—food, like language, evolves according to people's needs.

Soon you'll be eating sinfully delicious meals without gaining weight: dishes that rely heavily on beans, grains, pasta, fresh fruits, vegetables, and lean meats. Pairing grains with beans yields complete protein while eliminating fat, so bulgur, couscous, quinoa, and rice share top billing with all types of vegetables and beans. Since I'm a clinical nutritionist, healthy food choices are always important to me, but I *never* sacrifice taste!

When you want to cook, I recommend that you think about what type of dishes you're interested in eating. Then read that particular food chapter for practical advice, important nutritional information, and quotes that will inspire you.

The ideas under the **Try This** headings in each chapter provide strategies, cooking methods, tips, and ideas instead of recipes to get your creative juices flowing. Most of the time you won't need measuring cups and spoons, but don't worry; you won't be floundering around. I talk about procedures and suggest approximate amounts, whenever you might need direction, but most of the time I provide less explicit explanations so you can improvise.

In no time at all, you'll cook to the beat of your own pulse, ad-libbing from the refrigerator's contents or planning your menu at the market after seeing which seasonal foods look best. Ultimately, you'll be spending less money to prepare more delicious dishes, because the naturally ripened, seasonal foods I recommend are more flavorful and less costly.

When you stop depending upon recipes, there's no item you absolutely need. So if you're at the market and the produce looks limp and wilted, put it back. If the mushrooms look mushy or shriveled, don't buy them. Tomatoes should smell like tomatoes, so if there's no aroma put them back. If the salmon is overpriced, or smells fishy, don't buy it. If the packaging of any item costs more than the product inside, who needs it? Even while placing items on the conveyor belt at the checkout stand, you can comfortably change your mind about purchases.

Let Your Creativity Run Wild!

Cooking without Recipes brings out your confidence by encouraging you to take off on simple ideas, make up your own dishes, and do things your way. Leftover beans can be used to create soup, burritos, or pasta bean salad. Tomatoes, onions, olives, and bell peppers could be the inspiration for a sautéed garnish over fish, a pizza topping, chopped salad, or an omelet filling.

Imagine what a confident cook could do with leftover cooked rice. Reheated with raisins, milk, and cinnamon, it makes a delicious hot cereal. Improvise rice pudding, or your version of refried rice. Think about pouring curry sauce, marinara, ragout, or stew over it. There's no need to get overambitious, because you'll discover that simple, identifiable, every-day foods turn out better than fancy special-occasion dishes. And, they're appreciated by guests who don't have to ask, "What's this?" Good cooking doesn't need a name or an explanation.

With your creative impulses brought back to life, you'll create delicious dishes faster and with less work than it takes to stop for takeout.

No two people have the exact same tastes, so when a cook puts together the foods he or she enjoys in the quantities preferred, it stands to reason that an original dish results. Each of us has the ability to create new dishes from the many ingredients available in the marketplace.

And, once you become accustomed to cooking like an artist rather than a technician, you'll rarely make the same exact dish twice. With a vivid imagination like yours, you may find yourself putting a surprise ingredient in each dish.

On the other hand, if you don't express your creativity, predictable cooking results. We've all known repetitive cooks who have a repertoire of six to ten dishes. They make them over and over again.

Knowing what you're going to eat at Aunt Sally's house before you get there may feel comfortable, but being fixed in her ways makes it impossible for Sally to use ingredients with a fresh approach. People like Aunt Sally get stuck on the same few dishes, simply because they lack the confidence to ad-lib and allow a true cooking style to emerge.

As a creative cook, you'll still make dishes repeatedly, but it won't be because you don't know how to make anything else. It'll be because they're your favorites. And, for variety or convenience you may improvise a bit each time.

Use Convenience Items

Although most top chefs add convenience items such as ketchup, mayonnaise, and salsa to some of their most famous dishes, most cookbook authors suggest that it means a loss of integrity to use them. But, if you're like me, you don't always have the time to make everything from scratch. To make cooking easier, quicker, and sometimes better, I recommend purchasing certain types of healthful convenience items that aren't highly processed, and using them when needed.

Convenience pays off, but since we're all in a hurry these days, figuring out what—and what not—to buy is difficult. It takes a lot of time, energy, patience, and a great pair of eyes to wander the market aisles in an investigative mode. So, to save time at the market and in the kitchen, I've read the labels for you.

In addition to a variety of methods that require cooking from scratch, I recommend delicious ready-made spaghetti sauces, mixes, seasonings, salad dressings, and other convenience items. None of the products suggested contain synthetic sweeteners, alcohol, caffeine, hydrogenated (or saturated) oils, tropical oils, cottonseed oils, or an abundance of sugar or salt. Although they're all healthful and good, some taste better than others, so Best Tasting Bets (***, **, *) are listed. Three stars is the highest rating, and one star is still good.

It's much more difficult to ad-lib breads, because they require exact measurements. So, to save you time and energy, I suggest you pick up a fresh, special loaf of bread at your local bakery when you need it. For irresistible desserts, why not mix and match fruits and ready-made bakery items? Shortcuts make cooking and entertaining more enjoyable. When you haven't made everything from scratch you'll feel relaxed and energized, not beaten down, when it's time to sit down. It's common for restaurateurs to have outside sources make some of their breads, rolls, and desserts. So, don't feel guilty. If famous chefs can do it, you can, too!

Eat What's Right for You

Most cookbooks are designed for either meat-eaters or vegetarians, which implies that there are only two ways to eat. Nu-

trition in the real world, however, is not that definitive, and neither are we.

In this book, I take into account that everyone is different.
Everyone thinks differently and has unique nutritional needs,
depending upon their constitution and how they're feeling at
the time. Meat-eaters often eat vegetarian-style meals several
days a week. And, people who generally don't eat animal protein may occasionally do so.

I have a tennis partner who considers herself a "most-of-the-
time vegetarian." In other words, mostly she eats vegetarian-
style meals, but when she's in the mood she enjoys a tuna melt
at her favorite restaurant.

As children, my brother Barry and I ate whatever was provided, because we weren't as aware as we are today. My fa-
ther was a "meat, salad, beans, and potatoes man." He didn't
like chicken, fish, or vegetables much, so my mom accommo-
dated his tastes by serving steak most nights with a big tossed
green salad and beans or potatoes of some sort. One of the
ways my dad showed love was by giving me his steak bone to
chew on, and I remember enjoying it immensely.

Now, when I think about the starving people in the world
and the space it takes to raise enough grass to feed one cow,
I realize that more than flavor matters. The same amount of
land, planted with grain, could feed more people than a cow
could feed, assuming every part of the animal was eaten. Therefore, the trend toward eating *less* meat and animal fat is a
healthful one. By eating leaner protein, less fat, and more fruits
and vegetables, experts say that by the next millennium we
could cut the cancer rate in half and significantly lower the oc-
currence of heart disease. That doesn't mean you must eliminate meat or dairy products from your eating plan. If you feel
better including some animal protein in your diet, use it as a
condiment. Only purchase nonfat or low-fat dairy products, and
try to find out if hormones have been added to the meats or
dairy products you're considering.

Wouldn't it be wonderful if we knew which dairy owners and
ranchers add hormones to their feed and which do not, so we

could make an informed decision? Let's write letters to the FDA, and put pressure on them to provide better labeling than what's available at this time.

All suggestions and recommendations should be addressed to:

Food and Drug Administration
5600 Fishers Lane
Rockville, MD. 20857

It's possible to be healthy on a vegetarian diet, but if you want to include animal products in your diet, I recommend skinless, white meat poultry, or lean beef (hormone-free).

Although certain types of seafood are healthful options, too, I'm concerned about the possibility of hepatitis when mussels and oysters are eaten raw or undercooked. The possibility of getting parasites from sushi also concerns me, so be careful about where you purchase your fish and which restaurants you select. And, because of the possibility of salmonella and Listeria bacteria, I suggest you avoid eating raw or undercooked eggs alone or in foods such as protein drinks, eggnog, and Caesar-salad dressing.

Remember, there's no perfect eating plan. Even if your way seems contradictory or doesn't conform to tradition, choose what you want to eat, and eat it the way you want! Never eat something simply because it's plopped down in front of you in a restaurant, on a plane, or at someone's home. It's always important to be aware of your thoughts, beliefs, feelings, tastes, and nutritional needs. And then give yourself unconditional permission to change your mind as you and your body change!

Make Mealtime Special

Not long ago, my husband and I were invited to our friends' home for dinner. I was really looking forward to going, because this couple usually cooks wonderful dishes for us. But, since neither of them had enough time to cook that day, they brought in restaurant food. It was wonderful being there, with them, but I missed the home cooking, the aromas coming from the kitchen, and the conversation with my friend about how each dish was made. Cooking takes a lot of effort, but like a strong magnet, home-cooked meals draw families and friends together. As Julia Child once said to me, "We must all do whatever we can to bring home cooking back to the family table."

A few days ago I had the privilege of counseling Sam, an astute ten-year-old boy who has two younger brothers. He explained that most nights his mom serves dinner to him and his brothers while Dad is still at work. About a half an hour after the boys finish, Mom and Dad sit down to eat. More than anything, Sam wants the entire family to eat together. "How else can we talk," he asked, "without repeating everything twice?"

I totally agree with Sam. Two paychecks, two cars, two bathrooms, two televisions, and even two dogs may be necessary, but two dinner hours? They don't provide the love, emotional support, or sense of security every person needs! In fact, some of the world's problems would be solved if we'd simply invite family and friends to sit around our dining room tables more often. It would decrease our sense of isolation and increase our feeling of connection and communion in the privacy of our homes. There is no better time to sit down and express our feelings than over a delicious, hot, home-cooked meal. So, cook for the people you care about whenever you can, because giving is the secret to leading a happier life!

At my home, mealtime is usually the only time my family has to laugh and talk about the day's events together. It's sacred to us, so my husband and I have established three requirements: Everyone has to show up on time—hands washed; the T.V. is turned off; and the answering machine must answer all calls during our dinner hour. I hope this book encourages you to cook often, and make mealtime a special time in your home, too!

CHAPTER 1

◆

Entertaining with Ease

"For a single woman, preparing for company means wiping the lipstick off the milk carton."
—Elayne Boosler

Not long ago my family and I were invited for dinner at the home of a couple we had never met. It was a bon voyage party in honor of our mutual friends who were moving to Seattle, Washington. Six other adults and their children also attended the dinner my husband and I later dubbed, "The Dinner from Hell."

THE DINNER FROM HELL

When we arrived, Janice, the hostess, was up to her elbows in flour, and her face was buried in a cookbook. She barely said "hello" as she excused herself for not being able to shake our hands, or hang up our coats. Her husband, David, attempted to introduce everyone.

After putting two vegetable dishes and a pie into the oven, Janice ran around serving the children hamburgers and fries while getting the salad on the adults' table. The other guests and I offered to help, but Janice said she'd prefer doing it herself, since she worked full-time and didn't get a chance to entertain often.

It was obvious Janice had worked hard to prepare for this party. Her house was immaculate, two elaborate centerpieces were on the table, and fresh flowers were in every room— including the guest bathroom.

While Janice transferred the cooked vegetables onto serving plates, and placed them on the adults' table, the children were complaining that their burgers weren't cooked enough. Janice smiled, she put the hamburgers back on the grill, and urged us to begin eating our salads.

We sat down—without Janice—and ate quickly, realizing the vegetables were getting cold. Some of the other women and I got up to clear the plates, just as Janice sat down to eat. We sat down to keep her company, but two minutes later we heard a buzzer go off, and Janice sprang to the kitchen to bring out the entrée. It looked spectacular but no one, including Janice, knew whether or not to shell the soft-shelled crabs. The two side vegetables—now cold—were passed around, along with the crab, but everyone just stared at their plates.

Janice barely finished her salad before she had to begin making dessert with the children. They oiled Pyrex pans before adding chocolate and butterscotch chips, in addition to every other type of candy imaginable.

The other guests and I began clearing our plates. I think everyone wanted to escape the boring small talk that was going on, because even the men were getting up to help.

Janice was busy placing the children's creations, one by one, into the microwave for three minutes, and then into the freezer for another fifteen minutes to harden. She washed and arranged berries, and then she smelled something burning and let out a scream. After taking the cherry pie out of the oven, and scraping off the top, she prepared coffee twice, since most of the guests wanted decaffeinated instead of regular. Janice then put coffee cups and dessert plates on the table, and kept popping up and down to serve the children milk with their lovely creations.

By the time Janice had an opportunity to sit down with a cup of coffee, she looked exhausted. She never ate dinner, and since all the kids had school the next day, everyone had to leave.

Later that evening, I thought about Janice and the exhausting dinners from hell I myself had created in the past. When the house would finally grow quiet I'd feel like climbing into a hot bath and then immediately into bed, but no, there was food to put away and there were dishes to rinse. And if I didn't soak the pots and pans, I'd have a bigger mess in the morning that no detergent could solve.

Then, the next day, I'd wash dishes, put everything away, and recover from what was supposed to be enjoyable. I would realize—as I have many other times—that I had worked my tail off for days on a meal that took less than half an hour to eat. And, since there wasn't much about entertaining that I interpreted as fun, only the pain was memorable. Nightmarish dinners like that encourage everyone to pick up the phone for restaurant reservations rather than face entertaining at home.

COOKING, THE LOST ART

After years of exhausting experiences I finally realized that there needn't be a difference between party meals and family meals. I finally figured out that my family deserves those special little extras I prepare for friends, and my company merits the casual home cooking I fix for my family.

There's a woman I know who entertains often, and in addition to the salad and dessert, she never makes more than two dishes. It's nice, because everything's good and we always feel comfortable leaving her house. I used to feel that if I'd made chicken, I better serve beef, too. And if I cooked string beans, I needed an alternative for people who might not like them. I'd end up with at least two entrées, two vegetables, and two desserts. I don't have the time, energy, or desire to put parties together like that anymore. In fact, I'm convinced that unless you're the ultraenergetic Martha Stewart, simplicity is always best!

If I see a picture of a dish that looks good in one of those big, beautiful, glossy coffee-table cookbooks, I use it for inspiration, and imagine how I'd do it more creatively and simply, yet still elegantly. People want to know what they're eating, and get excited about recognizable food when it's done correctly. And, in case you haven't noticed, stuffy, overdone, gourmet parties are out, because no one—not the hostess or the guests—has enough fun.

The idea is to enjoy the preparation of a meal, without worrying, and then remarkably everything turns out perfectly!

When a host tries too hard to be perfect, with the "in" foods, desserts, and floral displays, everything says "exotic and difficult," but nothing says, "I made this especially for *you.*" Let's bring back *simple* home cooking, and entertain more often!

BRING BACK HOME COOKING

Wouldn't cooking be fun if you could implement a memorable meal in less time than it takes to eat it? Nothing's better than a hot meal customized with the ingredients you enjoy. And once you have a clear idea of what you want to make, and you're not bound to recipes, you're able to free your inhibitions and cook quickly. Soon you'll find yourself spending more time talking with your friends than in the kitchen preparing for them.

A memorable dinner has a distinct concept, and if you trust the creative process, your unique party idea reveals itself. Each of us has a unique style of entertaining, but don't expect to understand yours immediately. Take some time to figure it out.

Your Style

Trust and accept yourself, and your taste—your way of entertaining will naturally evolve, but it does require time. It's a little like finding your voice when you write.

If you write enough, and you trust the creative process, your style appears. If you listen carefully, you hear a little inner voice revealing the truth about what you feel, and then you write it down. Your rhythms assert themselves. A writer edits, reedits, and then reedits—just as a cook seasons, tastes, and readjusts a dish.

The same voice that tells you what to write tells you what type of party you'd like to create. Some people don't hear the message, but see it instead in their vivid imagination or mind's eye. Then, adjustments are usually needed, depending upon practicality, finances, and availability.

You may envision everyone at a swim party, but that's difficult without a pool. Unless, of course, you want to bring in a port-a pool. If you visualize twelve people seated around a large table and you only have six chairs, you could rent more. If your house is too small, ask a friend—a close one—if you can use her house.

The idea is to take risks with the environment and your cooking. You'll see, your way of doing things is always better than someone else's recipe that may cause trepidation in the kitchen, and embarrassment at the table.

The Style Maker

My style of cooking began to emerge when I started experimenting and realized that I don't enjoy eating the same vegetable, or any other ingredient for that matter, in every course or even twice in the same meal. So now, when I plan a menu, I choose dishes that complement rather than mimic each other.

For my taste, bruchetta, tomato salad, and spaghetti, all with tomato-based sauces, would clog my palate; the entire meal would taste like one giant tomato. None of the dishes would seem special. But since you may not like what I enjoy, and what bothers me may not bother you, pay close attention to your own likes and dislikes, and take off creatively from there.

To learn how to cook, experiment. And, to entertain with ease, take calculated chances instead of classes. If you want to take cooking classes, however, do it to pick up ideas, and because you think they're fun, but not necessarily to imitate everything the teacher does. With or without formal training, it's easy to develop your unique style.

The next time you have fifteen minutes to shop and twenty minutes to cook, buy a few ingredients, go into the kitchen and ask yourself, "What's the worst thing that can happen if I make something horrible?" You can always give it to the dog. Or, throw it away and what have you wasted? A few dollars and a little time.

From using your sense of smell, taste, and sight, you develop intuition, or a sensibility for cooking. You acquire a knack for putting ingredients together creatively. Cooking more often enables you to understand food in the same way that you realize a plaid shirt doesn't look good with checkered pants. You become instinctively aware of what tastes good, and unequivocally know that lemon juice and milk don't go together.

The Matchmaker

"Mix and Match cooking" (putting together a bit of this ingredient with that) is similar to "Mix and Match dressing." Just as some people feel uneasy cooking creatively, others feel insecure assembling their wardrobes. For example, some men feel unsure about what to wear unless they buy particular shirts and ties to match each sport jacket and suit they own.

My husband, on the other hand, buys accessories he likes on sale whenever possible. When shopping, he doesn't know which tie he's going to wear with each jacket or shirt he buys, yet he has an easy time putting together fabulous-looking combinations when dressing, simply because he has the confidence to follow his instincts.

Shana, my friend Leslie's daughter, is in a class of her own when it comes to both dressing and cooking. Have you noticed that these areas, like music and language, often feed one another creatively? Shana cuts interesting holes and jagged edges

into unusual garments such as ironworkers' suspenders, fireman's shirts, and police jackets. She builds her style of dress around accessories she acquires that can't be purchased in any store.

Because Shana also follows her instincts regarding food, she is equally talented in the kitchen. I've seen her add a little milk to root beer, fruit spread to cottage cheese or plain yogurt, and Cajun vegetable seasoning to popcorn. Once you become more creative in the kitchen, you'll experience creative crossover in other areas of your life, too.

After cooking without recipes, and entertaining improvisationally, I remember figuratively carrying my creative voice into the computer room to write this book. I began painting rainbows, flowers, angels, and hearts on my jeans, and I designed a mat for my front porch that says, "WELCOME: Heller Dining Hall." (My married name is Heller.) The mat has a red background, with a big aqua plate in the center, and yellow silverware on both sides.*

While writing this book I experienced creative crossover in other areas, too. I designed a pair of stingray cowboy boots, began wearing shiny navy-blue nail polish, and began breaking rules I'd previously obeyed when dressing. I had heard that pink shouldn't be worn with red, black shouldn't be worn with brown or navy, and that silver jewelry should *never* be worn

*(B.F. Hurley Mat Company will make any design for you too—and it won't fade since it's made of plastic—800-274-6287.)

with gold. Little by little, I broke all those rules and now have a great time mixing and matching my clothing. Yet, before tapping into my cooking creativity, I didn't feel comfortable buying a blouse without a skirt, or a blazer without the perfect pin, so I'd look for salespeople with good taste to put me "together." Now I feel comfortable selecting terrific-looking tops and bottoms and assembling fabulous-looking outfits at home to suit my casualness and comfort level. Cooking without recipes, you'll find, helps you understand your style both in and out of the kitchen.

To become a pro at Mix and Match cooking, and dressing, shop sales for items you like, and follow your instincts. You'll end up with innovative, inexpensive dishes—or outfits—put together with elements you may never have thought go together, but do. With a little experience, you'll put a surprise in every dish, and in everything you do!

Experience Matters

I'm certain that everyone is busier than ever these days, but I'm convinced the main reason most people don't cook has less to do with lack of time and more to do with fear of failure. Many people feel frightened about experimenting with food, because as children they were never taught their way around the kitchen. But if that happened to you, be courageous and get into the kitchen anyway. Remember, no one is born a cook, or a non-cook. It's what you get used to doing. A habit. And, the more you do anything, the better you get at it!

That reminds me of what Richard Nixon once said during one of his addresses, "The greatest sadness is not to try and fail, but to fail to try." I couldn't agree more! I was talking with a thirty-something woman around Thanksgiving last year, who's an extremely capable and talented television producer, and I asked her if she enjoyed her Thanksgiving dinner.

"It was great," she responded. "I made it through another

year without cooking. I don't know what I'd do if I ever had to face that bird. Someday, when I'm eighty, I just know I'll have to do it, and I'll be terrorized!"

In the movie *Kramer vs. Kramer,* we saw how cooking is merely a function of experience. Remember the scene where Dustin Hoffman makes French toast in a glass for his son? He can't get the bread in, it breaks in several places, ingredients are strewn throughout the kitchen, and then the broken pieces of bread stick to the pan. The lack of kitchen experience says a lot about this man and his ability to care for his son!

Later on, in one of the last scenes, Hoffman makes French toast again, but this time he uses a whisk and a metal bowl to beat the egg. The toast turns out great, and Hoffman proudly sprinkles powdered sugar on his finished product!

As you cook more often, entertaining becomes second nature, and you actually crave cooking for your family and friends. What better way to transform a day into a celebration than by inviting people you care about to your home for dinner? There's (almost) no art form more loving than cooking. And, there's no better way to stimulate intimacy than with a home-cooked meal, where there are second servings instead of second seatings, and no bill to pay when you're through.

DESIGNING THE PARTY

Get Comfortable

For me, planning my wardrobe is almost as much fun as planning the dinner, so I start there. After I decide what to wear, I can more easily visualize myself having fun at my own party, and then it's easier to plan.

At my party it's important for me to look good in something comfy, so I'm always interested in wearing comfortable shoes (high heels are out), along with flattering clothing I can move around in easily, which don't require dry cleaning if I spill. You, on the other hand, may prefer dressing up in clothes you ordinarily don't get a chance to wear. Remember, it's your party and you can wear what you want to. Anything goes!

Invite an Eclectic Mix of People

The most important part of a party is not what's on the table, but who's on the chairs, so I suggest you make up a guest list before doing anything else. Just thinking about the people you'd like to entertain will inspire you to plan a menu that will be remembered the next day. Invite a variety of people, and, whenever possible, only invite people you truly care about. Personally, I don't want to share good food with people I wish I'd never met.

For me, there's nothing more miserable than spending time with guests out of obligation rather than connection. It's easier for most of us to cook for people with whom we feel close. You don't have to love your guests, but it's best if you like them, at least. Small talk, when there could be meaningful talk, feels empty and lonely.

It's not necessary that all your guests previously know each other, and the number of people you invite, of course, is up to you. But if you're planning a sit-down dinner, make sure you have enough chairs!

Ask yourself these questions as you're completing your guest list:

- Do the people I'm entertaining prefer formality or casualness? (Tell your guests "how" you're dressing.)
- Do I want to invite their children?
- Are there particular foods or drinks I'd like to serve because of upcoming celebrations or holidays? Anything I want to avoid?
- Do my friends eat meat?
- Will my guests prefer the party inside, outside, or both?
- What kind of music would they enjoy? Or would they prefer silence?
- What method of cooking would best set the tone I want to cre-

ate? For example, for some people you might want to barbecue salmon, and for others you'd poach it to create a more formal atmosphere.

CULINARY SECRET #1: **The key to successful entertaining is to invite a good mix of people who are interested in having fun! If the company is good, the meal is automatically special.**

Planning the Menu

To figure out what you want to prepare, think about non-threatening easy-to-prepare dishes you enjoy eating. Think about what you particularly liked or disliked about meals. Go to the market, see what's available, and listen to your instincts. But, whatever you do, make something that everyone is at least somewhat familiar with. And, if you want to stay sane, never prepare one meal for the kids and another for the adults! The following suggestions may be of help when planning your menu:

- Make only a few dishes.
- Use ingredients in each dish that complement rather than mimic each other, so everything tastes different instead of the same.
- Balance the menu. In other words, if the entrée is going to be heavy, serve a lighter first course.
- If you want to serve a rich dessert, it's best to do so after a light meal.
- If you want to prepare healthful food, choose healthful ingredients.
- Be true to your taste. Do you feel excited just thinking about the foods you're planning to cook? If not, what *would* tickle your gastronomic taste buds?
- Do you get nervous thinking about the menu? (Yes!) Then improvise dishes you've made and liked before, instead of making something totally new.

The Structure

If you think about it, the people you invite and the food you decide to serve help you determine the structure of your meal. Do you want to serve many small courses, set up a buffet table, prepare a plate for each person (restaurant style), or invite your guests to help themselves at the table, (family style)?

You could set up a sandwich, salad, taco, or sundae bar. There are many options, but remember the food you make and the way you serve should accommodate your guests, without compromising your style.

Organization Is Essential

It really is possible to spend time with your guests at your own party if you've assembled the ingredients, prepared the food (including dessert), and set the table in advance. Before your guests arrive, take out the serving dishes you're going to use, making sure you know what's going to go in each one, and place the best utensil to serve the food near each dish.

Set everything up to make freshly brewed coffee (at night, most people prefer decaffeinated), so all you have to do is plug it in about fifteen minutes before you want to serve dessert. And, never, never, never again will you have to spend the evening in the kitchen while your friends sit around having a good time without you

Cooking As a Spectator Sport

Sometimes I prefer *not* to have everything all ready-to-go when my guests arrive because I consider cooking a spectator sport, and I like showing off my cooking skills a bit. I like to stir-fry, grill, make surprise packages, or prepare make-ahead dishes, such as lasagna, that need impressive last-minute finishing touches such as fresh basil leaves and tomato slices.

It's also fun to talk with your friends while grilling in the kitchen, or barbecuing in the backyard, mindlessly flipping, stirring, or turning while sipping a margarita, dark beer, or whatever you enjoy. Of course you still have to be organized and prepare ahead, so you won't have to spend your time searching for ingredients, utensils, and serving dishes!

My house lends itself to these casual styles of spectator cooking because the backyard, kitchen, and family room all flow into one another. They're the pulse or spirit of our home, or that comfortable place people "hang out" when they come over.

Where's the pulse of your home? Is your house formal, or—like mine—does it lend itself to a more casual down-home style of entertaining? Perhaps you prefer getting *almost* everything ready—except last-minute touches—so you have time to strut your stuff as you prepare fresh guacamole, salsa, or eggless Caesar salad in front of your guests right at the table. Check out the trouble-free, spectacular spectator-cooking ideas that follow.

STIR-FRYING

One of the best techniques to showcase your cooking in front of company is stir-frying. It means quickly cooking diced, minced, or sliced food in a wok or skillet over high heat while stirring it frequently. And, since it's a rapid process, it's best to have all of the ingredients you're planning to use prepared ahead of time and cut into uniform pieces to ensure quick and even cooking. (I like diagonal cuts because food looks prettier that way.) And, the smaller or thinner the pieces, the quicker they cook.

To stir-fry, you begin by putting a little oil in the wok, which will seal in the juices of the ingredients you're cooking and keep them tender. You don't need a lot of oil, but if you want to use even less, or eliminate it completely, substitute broth or cubes of frozen stock for some or all of the oil (see chapter 7, page 178 for details). The full flavor, color, and texture of a stir-fried dish make up for any fat that's removed!

Stir-frying also assures that vegetables remain crisp (just barely tender), so the results are fresh, and since the food isn't overcooked, most of the nutrients are retained.

If I'm adding chicken, shellfish, or meat, I usually cook it first two thirds of the way, and then add the tougher, higher-moisture vegetables because they take two to three minutes longer to cook than the more tender ones. For example, if I wanted to stir-fry carrots, mushrooms, broccoli, onion, garlic, asparagus, red pepper, and bok choy I'd start (as I always do) sautéing the onion and garlic in a little oil to release their flavors; then I'd add the ingredients in approximately the order that follows:

1. carrots   2. broccoli   3. asparagus
4. red pepper   5. mushrooms   6. bok choy

Remember, there are no rules, because you may prefer a particular ingredient crisper, or more tender. Add soy sauce and peppery hot spices. Grated fresh ginger is always welcomed. Do whatever makes your heart sing.

I played around stir-frying those ingredients for guests—substituting fresh spinach for the bok choy—and added some grated (or sliced) ginger, honey, a little fresh orange juice, and finally some soy sauce. Since the dish was slightly runny, I thickened it with a little cornstarch: I made a paste in a separate little bowl by mixing a couple teaspoons of cornstarch with some of the hot juices that had collected at the bottom, and returned the mixture to the wok. Then, I tossed the vegetables some more, the dish thickened, and I served them over noodles I had cooked, rinsed, and tossed in a little oil. Everyone liked it!

Play around; in this case it's not only allowed but recommended. Swap ingredients. Now that you have this basic stir-frying technique under your belt, you can't go wrong!

Cook It Simple

To make another scrumptious improvisational stir-fried dish, begin by heating some oil in a wok or skillet. Add fresh onions, garlic, mint, and ginger—the fire should be high enough for them to sizzle. After they're browned, add chicken, shrimp, scallops, strips of flank steak or a combination of them all.

Add snow peas or snap peas, spinach (or bok choy), bean sprouts, frozen veggies (to save time), or anything else you can think of, adjusting the heat higher or lower as you see fit. Continue tossing and flipping in front of your guests until the food is cooked to your perfection.

Add chicken broth if you need more liquid, and thicken with cornstarch if the dish needs to be thicker (see procedure above). Season to taste with soy sauce, and serve this with your favorite type of rice.

WAISTLINE TIP

You'll be glad to know that removing the skin from chicken eliminates three quarters of the total fat and cuts the calories by half.

Try This

Your family and friends will love this. I could eat variations of this simple-to-make meal once a week. Heat a skillet or wok, add some oil, and sauté onion and garlic. It doesn't matter if they're cut beautifully. After you've stirred it a little while, add boneless, skinless, chicken that has been packaged and cut for fajitas. (If you can't find that, ask the butcher to thinly slice boneless, skinless chicken breasts to eliminate some of the work!)

Add lots of juicy, red, ripe, diced tomatoes—you'll need lots of juice. Add a big handful of snipped cilantro, and save some to sprinkle on this dish at the end. Serve this stir-fry over rice or pasta, or to make a side dish for your guests, stuff it into baked potatoes.

VALUABLE TIP

When you're cooking, remember, taste only minuscule amounts of the dish you're making to discover if the flavor is on track. If you taste too often you can overwhelm your discriminating tongue (and gain weight).

My Favorite Chicken Stir-Fry

My stepdaughter, Laura, makes variations of this dish for our family often, because it's a wonderful meal that's fresh and light. She's made it with chicken, and combinations of snow peas, broccoli, water chestnuts and canned button mushrooms, but I like this variation best:

To start, she heats oil in a wok, and sautés lots of minced garlic. She adds bite-sized pieces of chicken breast—marinated for several hours in sherry—and cooks them two thirds of the way. She removes the chicken from the wok, so it doesn't over-cook, and sets it aside.

She takes the wok off the heat for a moment, adds a little more oil and about three cups of seeded green bell pepper that has been cut—like the chicken—into bite-sized pieces. When the peppers turn a brighter green, Laura adds back the chicken, and a little cornstarch—mixed with the juices in the wok (see the procedure that describes this above), and tosses everything together. She seasons the dish with soy sauce, and serves it over hot, short-grain sticky rice. Mmm, I love it when someone else cooks for me the way I like to eat!

Grilling

When the weather is warm, I'm sure you'll agree, there's nothing more delicious than grilled food. (See chapter 6, page 158, for ideas on marinating—and for safety's sake, remember not to baste meat with the same mixture you used to marinate them.)

Invite your guests to join you while barbecuing, so you can

visit with them. In fact, serve drinks and appetizers outside, and your guests will automatically congregate there.

Just make sure to start with a clean grill, oil the rack before starting the fire, and preheat the grill so the heat is even when you put on the food. And, when you think the meat is cooked, insert a knife into the thickest part to see if you've guessed right.

MEAL ON A SKEWER

Marinate chicken, scallops, shrimp, or cubed New York or sirloin steak in a ready-made sauce (see page 74), and string the meat on bamboo or metal skewers alternating between pearl onion, yellow neck squash, zucchini, mushrooms, green peppers, and potatoes. (The peanut dressing in chapter 4, page 98 is great for dipping.)

I turned this concept into a vegetarian dinner once with purple and Yukon potatoes and served artichokes and grilled shiitake mushrooms on the side. Choose whatever vegetables are special to you and your guests. I always enjoy a grilled meal!

QUICK GRILL

Brush some chicken or turkey breast slices with a bottled sauce (try Bullfighter, Escoffier, or White Wine Worcestershire) and grill about four minutes on each side, or till browned and cooked through. Or, if you want it to cook even faster, pound the chicken or turkey slices between two sheets of waxed paper and they'll take less time on each side. Serve on a bed of your favorite type of steamed rice or vegetables, or pop the chicken or turkey into a grainy or sourdough roll, and serve outside with some spicy salsa and coleslaw.

NUTRITION TIP

Turkey is leaner than chicken, and white meat is leaner than dark meat.

FRUIT AND VEGETABLE GRILL

I love this technique! Brush delicious, whole, organic veggies with a little olive oil and garlic that have been mixed with Tamari or soy sauce, and grill. (Use a ready-made barbecue sauce, or make one similar to Paula's in chapter 6 on page 157.) Zucchini, onion, corn on the cob, peppers, and Japanese eggplant are perfect for grilling. Grilled fruit such as pineapple, oranges, grapefruit, and pears taste amazingly good!

COOKING *EN PAPILLOTE*

Next time you're in the stationery store, pick up some parchment paper to cook *en papillote*. I like to cook food in parchment or aluminum foil, so I can watch my guests' faces as they open these interesting surprise packages. (In addition, there are no pots to scrub!)

Cooking *en papillote*, or cooking in paper, usually entails cooking delicate items such as fish, shellfish, or strips of chicken. But no matter what you put inside, the aromas, juices, and flavors are retained inside the package until it's carefully slit open right before your guests' eyes.

This method of cooking originated in France and is especially good for people on low-calorie diets; little or no oil is necessary because the food is actually *steamed* inside the wrapping. Food wrapped in parchment bakes in the oven, foil-wrapped foods steam in the oven, or they both cook beautifully on the grill.

COOKING IN PARCHMENT PAPER

Cut a piece of parchment paper into a large heart shape, about two inches larger than the food you're going to cook, fold the heart lengthwise, and, on the folded side, spray or brush the paper with canola or olive oil.

Place a fish fillet, or whatever you're cooking, on half of the paper heart, season the food with flavors you like—herbs,

lemon juice, wine—and fold the paper together securely, beginning at the top of the heart. Once the paper is sealed at the edges, fold it again to make certain it's secured, and then give the end a firm twist. (Do *not* puncture the paper, or the juices will run out.)

Now, so it doesn't burn, brush or spray the outside of the package with a little oil. Most items will cook in a 350-degree oven within fifteen to twenty-five minutes (fish takes a little less time). You can usually tell it's done when the package puffs up and the paper turns brown.

SENSATIONAL SEAFOOD WRAP

Your guests will love eating fish if you cook it this way. Place a skinless white fish fillet or deveined shrimp in oiled parchment paper, or foil. Add chopped onion or shallots, sliced mushrooms, peppers, and a few tablespoons of soy sauce, white wine, or some other liquid. Bake each package at 350 degrees for approximately fifteen minutes for each inch of thickness.

BRISKET COOKED IN FOIL

To make an incredibly tender and tasty brisket, trim all visible fat from the meat. Place on a large sheet of heavy-duty aluminum foil, and sprinkle a package of Lipton onion soup on top. Seal the foil leaving air at the top, and place the package into a roasting pan or dish to bake in the oven, approximately one hour at 350 degrees. Throw in some baked potatoes at the same time, and voilà, you've made a tasty meal.

SAFETY TIP

Whenever possible, use a marble or plastic cutting board, instead of wood, when trimming or cutting raw meat, poultry, or fish.

If you must use a wooden board, wash it right away with hot, soapy water, and run it through the dishwater occasionally. (You can also turn the board over and use the other side.)

Try This

To make this easy foil-wrapped chicken dish, put chunks of your favorite veggies, such as potato, tomato, onion, zucchini, and crookneck squash, in a piece of foil. Place chicken breasts or strips of chicken on top of the vegetables, and add seasonings such as rosemary, a blend of Italian herbs, garlic, a little olive oil, and vinegar. For variety, you might want to add your favorite ready-made pasta sauce.

Fold the tin foil together at the edges, bake for about thirty minutes at 350 degrees—and surprise, a wonderful dish will be inside!

Foil-Wrapped Vegetables

Place your favorite veggies onto a large square of foil—slices of potatoes, onion, garlic, whole cherry tomatoes, crookneck or butternut squash, and so on. Sprinkle them with water or wine, add garlic, basil, kosher salt, pepper—or your favorite seasonings to taste. Roast the veggies in the oven for about thirty-five minutes at 350 degrees, or grill them for the same amount of time. Tell your guests to open their packages slowly and carefully at the table, allowing the steam to escape.

Sea Bass in Foil

I love Chilean sea bass made this way, and it's simple to make. Place the fish in a sheet of foil. Add lemon juice, diced tomato, seeded jalapeño pepper, Maui onion (or whatever kind you have on hand), plus frozen lima beans and peas (you don't need to cook them first). Season with salt and pepper to taste, and bake on a cookie sheet at 350 degrees for about thirty to forty minutes.

Showstoppers

Sometimes deciding what to make is the most difficult part of entertaining. But, with these versatile "showstopping" techniques, you'll always have ideas to build upon. Never again will you feel like a writer staring at the blank page. We're capable, creative individuals and there's a little Julia Child in each of us waiting to express herself.

Dishwasher Method

The dishwasher method is unusual, easy, and a good conversation piece. The steam from the dishwasher is perfect for steaming tasty fish without adding fat, or making a mess in the kitchen. Think of it as a self-cleaning cooking utensil, but you must run it through, without soap, before beginning.

Wrap your favorite type of fish fillet in foil—one for each guest you're serving. I enjoy orange roughy or salmon. Add slices of lemon and your favorite fresh herbs—dill, basil, thyme, cilantro, kosher salt, freshly ground pepper—anything that suits your mood. Place the packets on the top rack of your dishwasher and again (*without* adding soap) run the full cycle.

NUTRITION TIP

Try to serve salmon, trout, tuna, and other deep-sea fish at least once a week. They are excellent sources of fats known as omega-3 fatty acids, which help to reduce the risk of heart disease and cancer.

COFFEE-CAN LOAF

This is a distinctive way of cooking because the loaf can be sliced into perfectly round pieces, and guests always want to know how you did it. Oil the inside of a one-pound coffee can, or line it with aluminum foil. Fill the can with a combination of lean ground meats (turkey, beef, or chicken), chopped onion, garlic, and scallions, along with your favorite seasonings and ready-made sauces.

Cook as you go. I like to add a little Worcestershire, A-1 Sauce, and top the loaf with a little ketchup. Fill the can only three fourths of the way full to allow for expansion. Bake at 350 degrees for one hour. Tap the can with any utensil, and the loaf will slide out easily onto a plate.

SAFETY TIP

To determine whether or not meat is done, check the color of the meat's juices rather than merely looking at the color of the meat. When the meat is fully cooked, the juices run clear and show no pink color.

PAULA'S CHICKEN TONATA

My dear friend Paula loves to eat delicious healthful food, yet hates to cook. She still cooks for her family often, but probably wouldn't care if she were banned from the kitchen permanently. Although Paula has her Ph.D. in both art and psychology and is a college professor, who teaches art full-time, she becomes so frazzled in the kitchen, she forgets to add common sense to her dishes.

Paula called me recently to say she made this dish for her family, and that it was so good she wanted to make it for me. The moment I tasted it, I asked if I could pass the technique on to you.

Paula said to grill or sauté enough chicken breasts for the number of people you're serving, taking care not to dry them out. Then blend the following ingredients together in your Cuisinart, after your company arrives. For every small can of water-packed tuna, add three dashes of olive oil, the juice from half a lemon, and about three tablespoons of capers.

Cover the chicken with the mixture, and place thin slices of lemon, capers, and pitted Greek kalamata olives on top.

When Paula made this showstopper dish for me, she had already prepared the chicken, and then did the rest while we talked. She garnished the plate with parsley, and served the chicken at room temperature with a crisp salad. The meal was delicious, but a bit treacherous, because Paula accidentally left the pits in the olives; she took one bite and chipped her front tooth!

SAFETY TIP

White-meat chicken is done when the color becomes opaque, the juices run clear, and the temperature reaches 140 degrees. Dark meat should reach 165 degrees.

Try This

Don't wait for Thanksgiving to cook a turkey! At our house I'm sure we eat turkey in one form or another as often as chicken. Sometimes I rub a whole turkey with olive oil and a marinade (See chapter 6, page 160 for ideas), then, loosening the skin with my fingers—the best cooking tools—I place fresh herbs underneath the skin, next to the flesh. I particularly like the appearance and flavor of sage, basil, and thyme. Mix and match them, depending upon what you have on hand. (Not trussing, or tying up the bird, allows the turkey to cook more evenly and quickly.)

As the bird cooks, the skin becomes transparent, and a beautiful pattern reveals itself. As you place the hot turkey on the table and slice through the leaves, you'll notice how quiet everyone becomes.

QUICK TIP

My family likes their turkey *hot,* so instead of letting it sit around, my hubby—the doctor—puts on surgical gloves and slices it at the table straight from the oven. Most drug stores sell these handy gloves. (You'll find a lot of uses for them.) See page 168 for stuffing ideas, and check the chart below for approximate cooking times with and without dressing.

ROASTING TIMES FOR TURKEY

Poultry Weight	6 lbs.	10 lbs.	12 lbs.	20 lbs.
Stuffed	3 hours	3¼ hours	3½ hours	4¾ hours
Unstuffed	2¾ hours	3 hours	3¼ hours	4½ hours

Remember, roasting times are only approximate, a thermometer in the thickest part of the thigh should register 180 to 185 degrees. The leg will also wiggle fairly easily.

IT'S SHOW TIME!

Timing Is Crucial

Every good cook knows that timing is essential to a successful meal. There are people who were once good cooks but stopped, for one reason or another, and now feel they can't do it any longer simply because their timing is off. They're afraid of preparing multicourse meals, meant to be served on one plate, for fear that everything won't be ready at the same time. Timing does take practice, but with planning it's easy to serve every dish cooked to perfection, at the right temperature, *every time*. (And if you mess up, there's always the microwave!)

Let's say you want to sit down to eat at 7:00 P.M., and the chicken you're making takes one hour to cook, the baked potatoes take forty-five minutes, and the spinach casserole takes thirty minutes. You're also serving salad, as a first course, so you must add the estimated amount of time it takes to eat that dish to the cooking time.

It's just a matter of counting backwards. If you estimate fifteen minutes for the salad, you want the cooked items to be ready by 7:15 P.M. That way, you'll have enough time to eat the salad while everything else is still in the oven. Therefore, put the chicken in the oven at 6:15 P.M., pop the potatoes in at 6:30 P.M., and begin cooking the casserole at 6:45 P.M. By doing that, everything will be thoroughly cooked and hot when you're ready to serve.

After everything is under control, take about an hour to relax before your guests arrive. Take a bath or shower. Spend at least twenty minutes meditating (you'll feel as though you've had a two-hour nap), take your time getting dressed, and be sure to be ready by the time your guests are due to arrive.

Greeting Your Guests

People can feel good or bad about coming to your home from the moment they walk through your front door. So, *please* be on time to greet them. If you're excited to see them, they'll feel it, and if you're not, they'll know that, too. There's nothing worse than sitting alone while the host is getting dressed.

Comforting Your Guests

As your guests walk in, introduce everyone, mentioning connections or interests people might have in common. With certain friends you might invite everyone to take their shoes off (you'll be surprised how much more relaxed people become). Serve their favorite beverages, and if there are children, set up a room where they can play.

When my daughter Chelsea was about four, some dear friends invited our family over, along with several other couples with children, and a baby-sitter greeted us at the door when we arrived. Believe me, I was impressed and enjoyed the time with my husband!

If you think about the comfort level of your guests, without trying to impress them, they'll feel relaxed and touched by what you've done.

The Music

I suggest you select the music you want to play, maybe a recently released CD, something you'd like to share, and start playing it before the guests arrive. It'll get you in the "mood," and you won't have to fumble around with electrical equipment when you could be spending time talking with your friends.

Match the music to the mood you want to create. Put on some soft jazz or mellow rock if you want a relaxed atmosphere (make sure it's low enough for people to talk). And if you want people to dance and get wild, put on a little heavy metal, rock and roll—or perhaps you'd prefer something in between—or no music at all.

(If You're the Guest)

Have you ever noticed how people generally remember to send flowers to funerals but often forget to take them to the living? Personally, I'd rather have flowers at my dinner parties than at my funeral.

So, if you're lucky enough to have been invited to someone's house, *never, never* go empty handed. It's an honor to be invited, so take something wonderful to that special person who's been kind enough to entertain you. What you take doesn't have to be exotic, or expensive. A fragrant oil or cologne, a special CD, a book would be fine! Any unusual little gift the host will appreciate that says, "I thought about you!" Once, a group of friends chipped in and bought my husband and me a gift certificate to a day spa and we savored every moment.

A Table As Creative As Your Meal

As you know, the concept for the beautiful food you create results from using the right side of your brain in a free-form, nonrestrictive manner. Now, to match your table setting and style of presentation with the food, you need to unlock yourself from conventional thinking again.

When setting the table, you may hear a voice in your head saying: What side does the napkin go on? Do I have enough of the same plates, silverware, napkins, glasses? Or, do you remember why I got myself into this mess? Quiet that voice by trusting your creative process. Make sure each item in each place setting complements the others, but it doesn't all have to look the same. Why not put a different colored napkin in each person's glass, or at the top of their plate? Your table setting, like the food you serve, is more exciting when it's creative. Sometimes I use a variety of dinner plates that are various shades of pastels. Don't doubt yourself or become self-conscious just because you haven't done everything like everyone else. Be proud!

I ran into a woman recently who remembered being at a party at my house ten years ago because I served a meal consisting entirely of finger foods, and we ate off paper plates. Ask any toddler, there's something about the tactile stimulation of eating with your fingers that makes food taste better. Be creative; do what you want. Remember, there are no rules! Why not decorate your table in three shades of one color, or two unusual colors?

I once went to a baby shower where everything—the balloons, the table settings, the food—was black and white. The
hostess served dark beer, black bean soup topped with plain
white yogurt, and fettuccine pasta with a black olive sauce. For
dessert we had white cake topped with bittersweet chocolate
and vanilla ice cream, along with black coffee and whipped
cream. You don't have to go that far but that shower was a
refreshing break from the traditional baby pink or pastel
blue.

Alternative-Use Tableware

Just as you don't have to follow Emily Post's rules of etiquette
for setting the table, you can use alternative-use tableware. Your
silverware, plates, napkins and glasses can be made from the
finest silver and china, or you can use jars for water, and juice
goblets for wine. In fact, without going to lots of trouble, over-
sized goblets and dishes create a playful, dramatic atmosphere
to match the relaxed, fun ambiance of your party.

Turn coffee cups into dessert dishes, or dessert cups into coffee mugs. Each item should complement the others, but nothing needs to match perfectly. Set each place setting with a knife
and a spoon, or only a spoon and a colorful napkin if those
are the only utensils your guests will be needing.

A myriad of fancy silverware and glasses can make anyone
feel ill at ease, not knowing what to use. Your guests will feel
excited eating and drinking from alternative-use tableware, but
be sure to set your table at least the day ahead; taking something that's used for one function and turning it into something
else takes thought, and a little time.

Centerpieces

Unless you have a favorite candle you'd like to light, drop
any old-fashioned notions you may have about centerpieces,
because you don't need them! Most centerpieces, especially the

tall ones, are best for inhibiting the conversation with the person across from you. Because you're inviting people you care about, a chilled bottle of wine or a crusty fresh bread—off to the side—will grace your table just fine!

It was while baking potatoes that, by accident, I baked a whole bulb of garlic and learned of its buttery flavor. That evening garlic turned into the centerpiece and incredibly delicious spread on bread. A centerpiece, I believe, is anything that draws people in, not some object that you'd rather move off to the side. (Take a look at the spreads on page 148, in chapter 6, for other useful centerpieces.)

Presenting the Meal

Whether you're serving restaurant style, or putting the food into serving plates and bowls family style, take the time to make each dish stunning, because the way food looks on a plate is almost as important as how it tastes. When food looks exquisite, when it looks visually delicious, people feel fussed over. So visualize in your mind's eye how the food is going to look on each plate, considering the color and composition of each item you've prepared. See if it's appealing, because a beautiful dish is always more impressive than a difficult one. Sometimes it's fun to assemble food as though it were a mosaic, combining unrelated foods.

But don't worry about arranging food perfectly. The beauty of Mother Nature is in her imperfections. Think of each dish as a piece of art, a handsome still life you're setting up for a photoshoot, and as you play with the design, your instincts will tell you what to do. To receive that message, relax and trust yourself!

Seating Your Guests

When you want your guests to be seated, guide them. Tell them to take a seat wherever they please, or explain where you want each person to sit. Sometimes it's a good idea to put place cards out, and at other times it's more fun to add a little mystery and excitement.

At a dinner party I attended, there was a drawing to determine where everyone should sit, and a single woman, Paulette, drew the number of the seat next to a man named Brad. The hostess asked everyone to join hands at the table, and there was "electricity," or a strong current of energy, between Paulette and Brad. Last I heard, they're still happily married.

Let's Join Hands

I think of Mother Nature whenever I see food. And when I get closer to nature in some way, by taking a hike in the mountains or walking through a garden, I always think of the godliness inside each and every one of us, because everything that's alive is part of nature. So at our house, before dinner, we like to say thanks, or a little prayer of gratitude, for the people at the table, the food, and the people who planted, harvested and prepared the food. This simple gesture provides us with a moment to reflect on the important issues in life, rather than dwelling on the inconveniences and problems we all face day to day.

Joining hands, with our right palms up, and our left palms down, we feel a chain of energy, and someone elects to speak from the heart using words that are comfortable.

I might say, "Thank you dear God for the people who are sitting around this table, and for the delicious-looking food we're about to eat. . . ." Someone else may then join in to express whatever he or she is feeling at that time.

If the same food were served to the same people on two consecutive nights, I'm sure each evening would still be unique. Because, saying a prayer of thanks gives everyone an opportunity to feel "where" they are at that particular moment.

Accept All the Help You Can Get

At every dinner party, there are usually two or three guests who want to help you serve and clear the table. Let them! In fact, to have a successful dinner party, solicit all the help you can get.

Or, if you don't want your guests to help, hire someone to help you clean up. And, if you can afford it, have that person come early to prep the food, and help you serve it, too. It's so much more enjoyable when you don't have to do all the work yourself.

And, if you can't hire someone to clean up, and no one offers to help, put away the perishables and then finish at your leisure. After all, is there anyone who has more right to have fun at your party than you? Have the time of your life!

Dessert

Wait awhile after dinner to serve dessert, or even move to another room to give everyone a chance to stretch, and the evening will be more relaxing.

Dessert doesn't need to be exotic or difficult; frozen yogurt with a fancy store-bought Italian cookie, or a baked apple with coffee and steamed milk will end the meal beautifully. See chapter 11 for more ideas, and always remember, there's no need to get too fancy. Overdoing is passé. Creating a simple, tranquil ambiance matters most!

KITCHEN BLOOPERS

Mistakes happen. Everyone makes them. In fact, no one throws a dinner party (or gets through life) without them, but the more errors you make, the more creative you become. Mistakes are the beginning of invention, so don't stop trying simply because you've misjudged something.

Cooking involves pleasing other people, so even when you're following your instincts, you'll always get a little nervous before entertaining, particularly when it's for people you want to impress.

Recently I had my editor over for dinner and, wouldn't you know, my dog got sick, all over the floor, just as she was walking in. Then, the oven-roasted potatoes I've made hundreds of times—that have always turned out perfectly—weren't quite done when I was ready to serve them. And although the phone usually never rings on Saturday night, I had to unplug the kitchen extension to shut it up!

Annoyances can usually be alleviated, and most bloopers can be salvaged, but if there's one the dog won't even eat (a real flop), throw it away and don't worry. Remember, famous chefs do it all the time.

The incredibly funny comedienne Rita Rudner tells the story of the cake she threw away. Her mother once made a carrot cake and didn't grate the carrots. She put them in whole, and didn't even cut off the green things. She called them "cake handles."

Some cooks accidentally ruin dishes by adding too many ingredients, too much or not enough liquid, following too many procedures, or cooking the food too long or not long enough. But, as you'll see, there are easy solutions to common disasters:

STALE BREAD.

If your bread, chips, or crackers are becoming stale, sprinkle them with a little water, then place them uncovered in the oven at about 350 degrees for about seven or eight minutes, or until they taste fresh again. Or, use the stale bread to make homemade croutons, see chapter 4, page 93.

TOO RUNNY.

If a dish is too thin, take out the meat or vegetable so they don't overcook and allow the dish to reduce or continue to cook uncovered, until some of the water evaporates, before replacing the meat and veggies. If you don't have the time to do that, mix about one tablespoon of cornstarch or flour in a small bowl with some of the simmering liquid, stir it back in, and the dish will thicken.

TOO DRY.

If poultry or meat is too dry, add some type of low-fat sauce or water to the dish while it's cooking, or right before serving.

TOO THICK.

If a dish is too thick and gummy, add some liquid—water, wine, beer, juice, milk, or broth—depending upon the kind of dish you're making.

TOO SALTY.

If soup or some other dish tastes too salty, increase the volume of the liquid and add slices of potato, carrot, or a small handful of rice. Or you could drain and rinse a can of beans, add them to the pot, and they'll absorb some of the salt. Or, if you'd prefer, increase the ratio of solid to liquid ingredients instead.

NEEDS SALT.

If a dish needs salt, but you don't cook with salt for health reasons, add a little lemon juice or vinegar instead.

TOO SPICY.

If a dish turns out too spicy, make a second one without seasonings and combine the two batches.

BLAND TASTE.

If fruit doesn't have much taste, add a pinch of sugar. When a dish tastes bland or boring, add red-pepper flakes, RedHot Cayenne Pepper Sauce, Tabasco sauce, or any other spicy seasoning you prefer.

UNDERCOOKED.

If poultry is undercooked, place it in a microwave-safe dish, without a cover, and cook it in the microwave until done. Put it back into the oven, or cut it into chunks and stir-fry.

OVERCOOKED.

If the veggies in your soup are overcooked, turn it into a pureed soup, and no one will ever know that it was meant to be a chunky one.

IF THE FOOD STICKS.

If food is sticking to a pan, transfer it to another one, but first spray it with a little olive or canola oil.

STICKY PASTA.

Pasta sticks together after removing it from the water, so if you have leftovers, submerge it in ice water for a few minutes before putting it in the fridge. Or toss it with a little olive oil and that will work, too.

BURNT TASTE

- If a dish tastes burnt, remove it from the pan, and add a little lemon juice to the food.
- If broiled or grilled meats are burnt, scrape or cut off the scorched parts.

- If your pie or any other type of dessert burns, serve the good part in little cups with frozen yogurt on top, cobbler style.
- (Burnt pans can be cleaned more easily after soaking them in water containing a few shakes of dishwasher detergent.)

MELTED YOGURT.

If you have frozen yogurt that has melted, turn it into a sauce. Go with the flow and make a plain cake more delicious by pouring the yogurt sauce over the top. (See chapter 11, page 276 for more unexpected dessert ideas.)

You Deserve Applause

It's important not to judge yourself too harshly when cooking (or any other time for that matter), because creativity responds more favorably to encouragement. So, even if you make mistakes, here are a few tips to remind you to always applaud yourself for entertaining.

- If you forget to serve one course, no one will ever guess.
- If a similar dish turned out better last month, no one will compare.
- If a dish is a little underdone or overdone, it won't matter. (Perhaps your guests prefer it that way.)
- Forgive yourself, love yourself, laugh at your mistakes, and everything will get better!
- Never apologize for your cooking, if everything isn't exactly as you planned, no one will know.
- No one can predict what's going to happen at a dinner party. It's your attitude and how relaxed you are that matter most, anyway. If you're having a good time laughing, and eating with a smile on your face, your guests will have a good time, too!

THE PARTY'S OVER

Postparty Creative Repercussions

We've talked about the preparty planning and the party it-self, but let's not forget the important afterparty events, because no matter how great the party was, most hosts become inse-cure afterward.

Some people have a relatively objective opinion about their own party, and they can judge accurately whether the food they prepared was delicious, or if it left something to be desired.

Others always feel that what they made was not good enough, no matter how delicious everything was. But that's the nature of creativity. At one time or another, all artists feel that way, because by the time they've completed a work, they've already grown from the experience and it's no longer their best. For that reason, most actors and actresses find it difficult to watch their performances on TV or the big screen.

Beethoven, as you know, was talented beyond belief, and in a class by himself. Yet, on his death bed, what he said re-flected the feelings artists often go through when judging their work: "I did have a knack for music, didn't I?"

(If You're a Guest, You Can Help)

The guests make the host feel more secure. So, if the party was a blast, *shout it from* the rooftops! You know the time, ef-fort, and money that go into entertaining, so compliment your host enthusiastically on your way out the door. Then your friend will entertain more often and you'll get invited again! I bought a cute card the other day that I'll send the next time I get invited. It says, "Thanks to a great host and hostess. From your grateful guest and guestess."

And, the Next Day . . .

Even if you send a card, call the day after the party to express what a nice time you had. I always give a big thanks to my dear friends Maxine and Eliot, who entertain my husband and me often. But it blows me away when she calls to say how much fun she and Eliot had entertaining us. And, even if we haven't invited them to our house recently, they invite us again. They never stand on ceremony.

Let's take a journey now into the creative process, so you can develop your unique style of cooking and entertaining.

CHAPTER 2

◆

The Creative Process: Cooking "By Ear"

"In creating, the only hard thing is to begin; an oak is no harder to make than a blade of grass."
—James Lowell

Self-expression is one of our most basic needs. Who hasn't asked him or herself at one time or another, "If I have a special talent, what is it?" There are seminars and counselors everywhere trying to help us discover our passion, our gift, our life's work, or our life's mission. We feel creativity running through our blood, and yearn to cultivate it.

Marianne Williamson, author of *A Return to Love,* says, "Each of us was born with imagination, and each and every person is coded for brilliance. The talents we're born with we never lose. Everyone deserves to shine!"

As infants, our creativity was obvious, because each situation was new and needed to be handled in an original way. I'm enamored with my daughter because, like most children, she has a seemingly effortless, inexhaustible way of doing the unexpected. When she was six, I gave her cardboard cylinders from several empty rolls of toilet paper, some glue, string, and paints to play with. From this, she created one of the most unusual, not necessarily gorgeous, puppets that I've ever seen. It resembled Pinocchio's sister. Broadly defined, creativity means coming up with something different; seeing life from a different perspective, perhaps upside down or inside out so you can come up with a new slant or idea.

Unfortunately, as we grow older, some people forget how good it feels to be original. We refuse to experiment because the thought of being mediocre is frightening. We follow recipes to the letter, merely to get the job done, even if that means cooking with ingredients we don't love.

Just think how much more fun it would be to "cook by ear," allowing your creative juices to fly. Creative cooking is a hobby anyone can master, one that brings a lifetime of enjoyment on a daily basis. And, if you follow your heart, cooking is as easy as child's play. Even if your creativity was stifled as a child, be audacious! The kitchen is your playground.

WHAT STIFLES YOUR COOKING CREATIVITY?

When you were a child did you hear messages such as these? "Pickles and peanut butter don't go together." Or, "Don't eat spaghetti with fries." Well maybe those don't seem like the best combinations, but who knows? Maybe one day some manufacturer will make a fortune from marketing microwavable spaghetti-fries.

Cooking is learned like language—by observation, participation, and experimentation. And creativity is fostered by encouragement, but negative comments asphyxiate the fire. Few children are encouraged to cook creatively, or are taught to use the stove properly, because many parents feel it's easier to keep the kids out of the kitchen and away from the stove.

In some homes, there's still a double standard: Boys are told one day they'll have a girlfriend or wife, who will know her way around the kitchen, so there's no need to bother learning. Many girls are discouraged, too, but for a different reason. They're taught that there's already a good cook in the family, so why should they try?

Jello Biafra, the leader of the defunct punk band Dead Kennedys, said in an *L.A. Weekly* interview, "Hang onto your mind. I mean a lot of people start out really creative when they're little kids, then slowly but surely, their schools, their coaches, and their churches chop away all the creativity to a point where they're scared to actually think for themselves."

My friend Beth, on the other hand, gets lots of encouragement from her folks to express her creativity. Her mom is a writer, her dad an actor, so they understand just how important it is to encourage creative efforts. But Beth rarely cooks today, because several years ago, when she spoke of attending chef's college, her parents refused to support her endeavors. "We didn't raise our daughter to be a cook!" they said. Creative cooking takes a backseat for many creative people, because they feel it isn't important, and wastes too much time.

My neighbor says that every time he gets creative in the kitchen, a little voice in his head speaks out, saying, "Neil, what about your screenplay?" But I tell him writing a screenplay is no more or less important than building a terrific pot of stew.

THIS BOOK WILL CHANGE YOUR LIFE

From cooking without recipes and coming up with creative cooking solutions, you'll be able to solve other problems in your life creatively, too. Creative juices never compartmentalize themselves because there are no walls between creativity for music, cooking, writing, painting, drawing, or building.

Rex, an architect and client of mine, had never cooked anything more than a can of soup, yet wanted to lose weight by eating low-fat dishes. Once he started creating delicious, healthy meals, and losing weight, he discovered other benefits, too. Without any effort, he began seeing old problems in a new light. He explained that he was adding garlic to a pot of soup one time, and the solution to a design he'd been contemplating for months popped into his head. "It's refreshing," he said, "and sometimes productive, to be distracted by something other than our same old problems."

When it comes to food, creatively means going somewhere

unexpected and doing something you don't usually do without losing the integrity of the dish. Change two or more significant ingredients in a recipe and it becomes your own.

A young woman, Felicia, who interned with me while she was in chef's school, complained that her creativity was being stifled by instructors who constantly reiterate that there's only one way to cook. So, I sent her to the market to look at fruits, vegetables, and other ingredients as though she'd never seen them before. She returned from her journey and said she felt like a kid again, one who was on an outing, in awe after turning rocks over and seeing the burgeoning life beneath them. As a result of her adventure, she made fat-free brownies, substituting prune puree for butter. (Look for her innovative method in chapter 11.) Although Felicia was learning the basics in school, she craved opportunities to do the unexpected, and try out new cooking methods. We all need creativity in our lives! In *Picasso, An Intimate Portrait,* Picasso said, ". . . the important thing is to create. Nothing else matters; creation is all."

CREATIVITY INVOLVES ACTION

For creativity to cook, you need more than just an idea. You need to follow through with a plan step by step, doing whatever you love with passion, and allowing your heart to sing. I know it's scary to begin, but try to remember, everything is easier once you get started!

It's a lot like getting up to give a talk, or introduce a speaker at some important event. You're not sure the words will come. You get up anyway, take that leap of faith, and end up knowing exactly what to say. It's strange; we talk all day long, and then wonder if we can.

When I began doing cooking segments on KABC, *Eyewitness News,* in L.A., I was so nervous my thumbs would shake. In a short period of time I collected tons of videos with the camera focused on my quivering thumbs, but I didn't give up! Sometimes, perseverance is all you need to succeed.

Today, when I do radio shows, or cook on TV, my hands are steady, but I'm still hoping I'll find the words I need to answer the interviewer's questions. The words always do come, and I find the more intent I am on my message—instead of on myself, or the outcome—the more conversational I become.

Innovative, creative cooking takes the same leap of faith, and is just as rewarding, once you listen and learn to trust that soft voice inside your head. But, take your time! Ideas must percolate, and then simmer, for the creative process to work. Cooking without recipes is anything but a connect-the-dots, paint-by-the-numbers game!

You won't choose to follow through with all of your ideas, and every idea you try won't work out perfectly. But remember, mistakes are the by-product of being an inventive risk-taking person, and fixing whatever you don't like is usually easy. When you make a mistake, simply take a new direction.

Benjamin Franklin wrote in his autobiography, at the age of seventy-eight, ". . . on the whole, though I never arrived at the perfection I had been so ambitious of obtaining, but fell far short of it, I was, however, by the endeavor made a better and happier man than I otherwise should have been, if I had not attempted it." It's crucial for each and every person's development to try her hand at whatever she yearns to do.

Go Wild!

While I was writing this book, I got the urge to paint over the existing wallpaper in my guest bathroom, but my left brain, or critical voice, warned, "That's a stupid idea. Don't begin, you can't paint over wallpaper, you don't have spare time, the supplies you need are costly, and you don't even know how to paint!"

As I listened, my desire to paint began to wane, so I decided to shop for new wallpaper instead, but couldn't find my colors. I also realized that I'd need to hire a paperhanger, and a painter to paint the baseboards, and I still wouldn't have exactly what I wanted.

Then my creative voice, or right brain, jumped in and said, "It's not the fear of failure holding you back, but the failure to begin. The hardest thing is to begin! Put on some old clothes, take out the paints and brushes you have in the garage, blast some upbeat rock-and-roll music, and paint!" "If it looks bad," my critic agreed, "we'll cover it with paper."

I gathered my materials and allowed my instincts to take over. It was as if the paints told me where to begin. Using a can of Rust-Oleum, I sprayed black stripes on the walls. When the work needed to dry, I decided to stop for the day.

The next day, I put on my grungy outfit again, walked into the bathroom, and after looking at the walls and paints for a short while, I knew what to do. Using turquoise, the color of my kitchen, I painted over parts of the black stripes with upward happy strokes to the accompanying music. I knew it was time to stop for the day and let the paint dry when I began to feel the work would get worse, not better, if I kept going. As the paint was drying, I thought about other colors that would complement what I had done and decided to paint my entry hall purple with the same upward motions.

The next day I added some irregular white lines that looked terrible, so I covered them up with the turquoise I had used the day before. The work was finished after I sprayed dots of silver paint, and the walls didn't ask for anything more.

Now I have the wildest, wackiest bathroom that ties in colors from the rest of my house exactly the way I want. Ultimately, by painting over paper, and mixing enamels with Rust-Oleum, flats, and sprays, I broke every painting rule I had ever heard. And I had an absolute ball!

Just as there are many ways to paint a bathroom, or a picture —unless you're painting by the numbers—there are many ways to combine foods. There's no need to be in a rut. Baked chicken and potatoes have been made millions of times. It's more exciting to try something new!

You won't find rules in this book, because rules discourage creativity. To cook creatively, *break the rules, and use your cooking sense.* It's not for the sake of breaking the rules that you break them; you avoid following rigid rules because you want to experiment and come up with something new and different.

Think of something unusual you'd like to do regarding food. Anything! Start by merely changing the order in which you eat your food. Perhaps you'd like to eat dessert first. During a long writing day not long ago, I ate leftover pizza for breakfast, cereal and fruit for lunch, and pancakes for dinner.

I promise that once you begin eating and cooking the way you want, you'll miss it when you can't. Creative cooking takes you into another realm of consciousness, a new world, one you don't want to leave. It's both relaxing and stimulating—a little like making love. When you put your creative talents to use, your critic—that inner voice that sounds off like the meanest, most antagonistic person—quits giving you a hard time. And without the judgmental mental chatter, beginning becomes easier!

So, let go, make something exciting. PLAY! You're in competition with no one, and you can work at your own pace. Time becomes meaningless in the face of creativity, because the more you cook the more enjoyable it becomes, and the easier it gets.

SIMPLE FOODS ARE BEST

I agree with Alice Waters's philosophy about food. She's the restaurateur and chef at Chez Panisse and Cafe Fanny in Berkeley, California. Alice says, "We all try too hard. Just be simple. We come up with an idea, and right away think that it's too easy, but it never is."

When cooking, don't get too complicated. There's no need to think about style or making foods fancy. Diners don't mind if there's some secret ingredient in a dish they can't put their fingers on, but they want to know what they're eating. It's comforting to identify a dish and call it by a familiar name. Wolfgang Puck, renowned restaurateur, has established his fine reputation by using flavorful secret ingredients and cooking simply.

Personally, I don't like foods when they're loaded with greasy sauces. Recently, I stayed at a hotel where every dish on the menu was so rich that nothing sounded appealing. My daughter was ordering from the children's menu, so I asked the waiter if I could, too.

COOKING ISN'T ROCKET SCIENCE

When you're cooking, it's important to remember that everything has already been done by someone else, so don't take yourself too seriously. At best, all you're doing is making a pot of soup, not building the Taj Mahal.

Anne Lamott, in her book *Bird by Bird,* says, "Life is like a recycling center, where all the concerns and dramas of humankind get recycled back and forth across the universe. But what you have to offer is your own sensibility."

The most famous cookbook authors tour the world for ideas and then turn whatever they loved into something distinctively their own. Adding your love, personality, and spirit is what makes your cooking special.

Believe in yourself, and the dishes you make will be unique. Fearless cooking is an act of faith in your own creativity. But give yourself a lot of leeway, because trying to do something perfectly will make you feel tense and paralyze your efforts.

I was trying to ski without falling during a recent vacation in Telluride, Colorado, when a ski instructor said to me, "Don't focus on your feet to see if you're doing it right. Look up at the mountains ahead and become the skis!"

Perfection is an illusion. Drop your preconceptions about how the food is going to turn out, or you'll lose the sense of what you're doing and the pure pleasure cooking brings. To come up with original dishes that have flair, you can study nature, and look in cookbooks, magazines, and newspapers for pictures of dishes that look appealing. Study the nuances. You may like the spirit of a recipe but not all of the ingredients, or the recommended cooking techniques.

A client of mine once gave a party based on a glorious display of foods she saw in a glossy magazine, piling huge serving trays high with appetizers. The party was a hit.

Following Rituals

Some people feel more creative when they signal their "muse" or unconscious mind with a ritual. Ian Fleming sat beside the ocean and listened to the crashing waves before writing. Bach poured cold water over his head before playing. I need a mug of plain hot water at my desk before I begin writing. Certain cooks feel more creative with a large glass of ice water at their side. Perhaps water is associated with creativity because it's fluid. Other cooks, however, simply walk into the kitchen and begin improvising dishes immediately.

WHAT ENCOURAGES YOUR CREATIVITY?

What enhances your creativity, and what stifles it? Do you like music in the background when you're cooking, or do you prefer quiet? Do you like to do one task and finish it, or several things simultaneously? When have you felt the most creative? What were you doing? Was it before or after sex, or eating tiramisu? Where were you? Who was with you? What were you wearing, or not wearing?

Now, take some quiet moments to discover ways of cooking that set *your* creativity into motion. Maybe some aromatherapy, a poem, or silent prayer would help. Setting up a noncritical, comfortable environment is important, so pay close attention to your likes and dislikes.

It's essential for me to surround myself with supportive people, so to remind myself of that I have a little newspaper clipping, from the *Los Angeles Times,* tacked on my bulletin board with a quote by the late agent to the stars, Irving Lazar. He said, "Try to stay away from annoying people and places that cause you pain or make you feel disagreeable."

How To Cook without Recipes

For inspiration before cooking, I always ask myself what I feel like eating. What will make me feel good? What's my heart's desire? Wanting to eat, of course, is always the best reason to cook!

Then, I look at the foods I have on hand to see what's practical, and place the items I'm thinking of using on the counter while interviewing them in my mind's eye, as if they were people. I ask them what they'd like to become. In other words, I see the ingredients without a preconceived notion of how the foods should be used, until they come together in a fresh way. Thomas Merton once said, "Everything will speak to us if we let it and do not demand that it say what we dictate."

There are two main ways to create things. With sculpting, for example, you can either select a block of matter and shape it into something, or, the matter selects you, tells you what to take away, and the artist in you exposes what's already inside.

With cooking it's similar. You can flavor a dish with combinations of seasonings to make it Italian, Mexican, or Asian. Or, you can look at ingredients and listen to your instincts before deciding what you're going to create.

CULINARY SECRET #2: To create, you must respond to your inner voice without censoring anything it says. If you hear a critical voice proclaiming, "You should follow the rules," or, "You mustn't think for yourself," ignore it. The voice you're listening for is a positive, supportive one that will be softly whispering something like "Invite some friends over, prepare dinner for them, it'll be easy." Then, your mind may give a "hint" of an idea about how to execute it. Remember, though, you must be quiet enough to hear it. (Unfortunately, the positive voice usually doesn't speak as loudly as the critic.) Trust the simple, confident statement, or feeling, and you'll have a direction. Welcome it. Don't think too much, or get too logical, because analyzing is damaging to the creative process. Your only job is following through!

Cook Often

Creativity is similar to a muscle that must be exercised. Without regular workouts it atrophies, yet never dies. It's nice to cook for others when you feel relaxed and want to cook but—like having a baby—there's never a perfect time! Don't wait for an idea to surface in perfect form, or to have the perfect ingredients or utensils. If you want to cook, just get in the kitchen and do it. Doing something for pure pleasure stimulates creativity.

Your Kitchen

When you begin cooking without recipes, your kitchen may feel like a cross between an artist's studio and a science lab. It's important to feel comfortable in your kitchen, so make it a room you will enjoy.

My kitchen is bright, airy, and cozy. It isn't what I'd call big, or state-of-the-art, but it has everything I need. Knowing I don't need to go through extensive planning and list-making has made the kitchen a more comfortable place, a welcomed change of pace after a hectic day at work or school.

After school each day, my daughter Chelsea does her homework on our long, white Formica counter, next to my "third" desk. She says she feels more comfortable and warmer there than anywhere else in the house. When my husband comes home, he always gives everyone a kiss before stopping by the kitchen to see if anything is on the stove. When he lifts the tops off the pots and pans, it gives me a warm feeling knowing he's looking forward to dinner. Lee Iacocca writes that he "doesn't consider a man successful unless he goes home for dinner every night."

The kitchen, for me, is the perfect place to let go of tension. I enjoy messing it up in a way that's not too hard to clean up. When I'm cranky, feeling rotten, pessimistic, dissatisfied, or generally miserable, I cook. It's restorative to handle nature's gifts, unwind, nourish my body, and offer good food to friends and family. Food soothes!

Essential Equipment

You probably already have most of the essential items you'll need to cook well. It's helpful to have a couple of nonstick saucepans, two skillets of varying sizes, or a wok, and a large soup pot. That's all you need because if your equipment is too fancy you'll find yourself washing your many utensils when you put them away, and then washing them again when you take them out since you haven't used them for so long.

My utensils are *well-seasoned* (well-oiled), because I use them often, but when I need new ones I purchase heavy iron skillets (they have them at Sears). I also like *Calphalon* cookware because heat distributes evenly in them.

As far as tools are concerned, it's helpful to have a pastry brush, a blender, a mini food processor, a slotted spoon, a steamer, a ladle (a spoon with a deep bowl), a spatula (pancake turner), peeler, paring knife, and a chef's knife.

Mary Sue Milliken and Susan Feniger, the owners and chefs at Border Grill in Santa Monica, California, recommend using knives made out of high-carbon stainless steel, and I agree, since they stay sharp. So, now all you need to do is purchase a few of your favorite ingredients, and you're ready to bring drama into your kitchen!

Your Well-stocked Pantry

Depending upon what's available, fresh-looking, and well-priced, I strategically stock the following ingredients because they're my favorites. Take a look at my list, but only purchase ingredients *you* enjoy, depending upon availability, freshness, and price.

PANTRY ITEMS

- Dried pastas, beans
- Several kinds of rice—white, brown, wild, etc. Grains such as couscous, bulgur, kashi, kasha, and other favorites.
- Canned beans, Italian tomatoes, pureed tomatoes, tomato sauce, spaghetti sauce, and both beef and chicken broth
- Dried herbs (turmeric, oregano, cumin, thyme), packaged taco and chili seasoning, Italian crushed red pepper
- Freshly ground pepper, and kosher salt (a little salt added to strategic dishes is fine, unless you have high blood pressure, but be judicious!)
- Fresh onions, potatoes, and garlic
- Water-packed canned tuna, canned anchovies, capers, artichokes, mushrooms, Greek Calamata olives, hearts of palm
- Chocolate chips, graham crackers

REFRIGERATED ITEMS

Check the temperature of your refrigerator. The fridge should be 40 degrees Fahrenheit, or colder.

- Fresh fruits and vegetables, sun-dried tomatoes
- Potatoes—red, Yukon Gold, sweet
- lemons
- Olive and canola oil, salad dressing, and various types of vinegar
- Nonstick cooking spray (PAM)
- Pickapeppa Sauce, A.1. Sauce, Worcestershire, Masterpiece Barbecue
- Bullseye Grilling (Spicy Hot Cajun, teriyaki, and roasted garlic with herbs, tamari, or soy sauce, Tabasco Sauce, or Frank's Original RedHot Pepper Sauce (my favorite), escoffier Robert Sauce, bullfighter steak and burger sauce
- salsa
- minced garlic
- poultry, lean meat, fresh fish
- eggs

- low fat and nonfat dairy products (mozzarella cheese, milk, sour cream, and plain yogurt)
- flour, cornstarch, baking soda and powder (keep these in the fridge to avoid those little black pesky bugs)
- fresh herbs, quick-rise powdered yeast, or whatever kind you prefer
- mustard
- catsup

THE FREEZER

Your freezer should be zero degrees or colder. Freeze left-over meals, and keep a supply of the following items:

- bread or baguettes for croutons and stuffing
- homemade stock
- frozen vegetables
- Nonfat frozen yogurt
- frozen blueberries and strawberries for desserts

COOKING, A SKILL YOU CAN LEARN

Almost every baby loves to drink from a bottle, but no one is born loving to cook. Cooking is what you get used to doing. A skill you learn, practice, and improve over a lifetime. And the more you do it, the better you get. As cooking becomes a habit, almost second nature, you'll want to cook for your family and friends more often. You'll even feel upset when you don't have time to spend in the kitchen.

When you cook a delicious dish, one you really enjoy, remember the things you did that worked out well. Then, the next time you cook, improvise upon those techniques.

Great Chefs

I've had the pleasure of working with several famous chefs over the years, developing restaurant menus, and have maintained friendships with many of them. Unanimously, they've told me that after they learned the basics from instructors in the best culinary schools, they learned to cook by experimenting.

Most people may think that chefs automatically know how to create dishes, but the most famous chefs in the world also build upon old ideas by trying various restaurant dishes, reading cookbooks, and comparing notes with other cooks. They create culinary art, as you and I do, by breaking the rules. And every chef I know has felt growing pains at one time or another while experimenting in the kitchen.

Chef Joachim Splichal, owner of Patina restaurant in Los Angeles, told me that when he's cooking, there's often a point when it feels as though a dish is falling apart—when it's not going to work—but then it usually does. This is a phenomenon that's experienced by most creative artists. It's also how successful recipes are developed.

A dish becomes a recipe when chefs or home cooks combine ingredients that go well together and write down what they did. Menus are created when chefs or home cooks make a list of their favorite dishes that go well together.

Rocky Kalish, a comedy writer and fearless-cook friend of mine, invents new dishes all the time. He made Chinese potato latkes (pancakes) by grating daikon radishes instead of potatoes. They turned out great. Another time he made latkes with yams, then pumpkin, turnips, and finally zucchini. They were all delicious! His secret, he says, is to *think* taste.

Think Taste, and Taste Food

Artists mix paint on their palettes as they see what their paintings need, and cooks think of their palates when deciding which herbs to add to their dishes. When you're cooking, taste the food, look at it, smell it, and add a pinch of this or a dash of that depending upon what you think it needs.

When making salad dressing, taste it on a slice of cucumber or lettuce leaf so you can taste it the way it's going to be eaten. Taste your dips on chips. If you're making a soup, imagine eating a whole bowl, and try sauces on the foods you're planning to serve with it.

We Learn through Trial and Error

The tortilla was invented two thousand years ago when lime was accidentally mixed with ground corn. And only sixty-two years ago, Ruth Whitman, proprietor of the Toll House Inn, chopped semisweet chocolate and added it to butter cookies, thinking it would melt. Instead it just softened in place. Bingo! Toll House cookies, otherwise known as chocolate chip cookies, were invented.

Remember, it was quite by accident one evening, a long time ago, that I baked a whole bulb of garlic. Whenever I turn my oven on to bake a casserole, or potatoes, I try to use it to the max by baking whatever else I have on hand at that time. That particular day, I was rushing to get an extra eggplant and a foil-wrapped beet into the oven. Accidentally I put some garlic wrapped in foil in the oven, too. When I unwrapped it and discovered its buttery flavor, I knew, from that moment on, I'd be baking garlic often.

When entertaining, don't be afraid of running out of a particular item, or not having enough food. Being flexible goes hand in hand with cooking. If you haven't made enough, you can always expand the meal the way the Chinese do with another dish.

Toy with the size pans you use, as well as your presentation. Why not bake a casserole or even a cake in a skillet or oven-proof bowl? You have the ability to improvise new dishes during the entire cooking process. Mistakes are the beginning of inventions. Try substituting chestnut puree for fat and Pam for butter when making anything with filo dough, or adding fat-free ricotta cheese when you want to make any dish taste creamy. New ideas always come from building upon old ones.

THE POWER OF THE KITCHEN

No one understood the power of the kitchen more than the prime minister of Israel, Golda Meir. She wanted more fighter planes for her country from a United States dignitary who was on an official visit, so Golda invited him to her home.

As he sat in the living room, Golda came in from the kitchen saying, "Taste my strudel, and you'll discover my real claim to fame." He loved the pastry; they chatted; and by the end of their meeting Golda had all the MIGS she had wanted.

KNOW WHEN TO STOP

An original meal is like a story that can have numerous endings. A meal can go in a million directions, and they'll all taste good. All art is about perceiving. Culinary art is about seeing, smelling, and tasting. Trust yourself. Trust your nose. Trust your taste buds. And, trust the creative process.

Most important, learn when to put a dish aside and go on to another. Some cooks ruin a dish by adding too many ingredients, following too many procedures, or cooking it too long. Knowing when to stop is just as important as knowing how to get started! A dish, a painting, a song, or a book is finished when it doesn't ask for anything more.

THE MOST LOVING ART FORM

Remember, there is no better way to stimulate intimacy than with a home-cooked meal, where there are second servings instead of a second seating, and no bill to pay when it is through. What better way to transform an average day into a celebration than by inviting people you care about to share food in your home? Cooking truly is one of the most loving art forms I know.

Cooking without Recipes

The chapters that follow show that gorgeous and delicious pizza, salads, pasta, "go withs," soups, stews, chili, veggies, grains, beans and dessert dishes can be prepared easily and quickly without recipes, making it easy to entertain. Just as endless possibilities result when good jazz musicians sit together and make music, you can create an infinite number of original dishes when you "cook by ear."

Your creative cooking talents become one of your most valuable assets, nourishing others while feeding your soul. Offer the food you make with love, everyone will love your food, and you'll become even more large-hearted.

Now, once again, take a minute to remember yourself as a child and how good it felt to be spontaneous. Did you build sand castles at the beach, with lots of rooms and secret passages, or did you make caramel-fudge mud pies at school in the sandbox? We all started out creating freely, and the exciting part is that you still have the ability to be original today.

Last week, my daughter and I bought some brightly colored beads, thin leather cord, and colored string to make good-luck anklets and friendship bracelets. After we finished, we went into the kitchen, took out some of our favorite ingredients, and made a delicious lunch together. Then we just talked. Chelsea brings out the creativity in me, because she continues to have that seemingly effortless, inexhaustible way of doing and saying the unexpected, whether using string and glue, beads and cord, or food. If you want to get creative in the kitchen, go into the kitchen with your favorite child and cook.

Ready ... Set ... Go!

Now, wash your hands and prepare yourself for a lifetime filled with enjoyable cooking experiences. Ready? Sure you are. Roll up your sleeves, turn the page, and we'll make pizza!

CHAPTER 3

◆

A New Spin on Pizza

"The perfect lover is one that turns into a pizza at 4:00 A.M."

—Charles Pierce

I've cooked for a lot of people for a lot of years. With my extended family, grandparents, aunts, uncles, all the kids and all our friends, there's often a large crowd around our table at mealtime.

I cook all types of food, but, prior to writing this book, when my family got their weekly pizza urge, I never made it at home. We'd go out for it, or have it delivered because the thought of making homemade pizza intimidated me. Like most people, I believed culinary classes were practically a necessity to make a good pizza.

My family's *"pizza-tooth"* is not unique. Everyone enjoys pizza because, like a G-rated movie, it has something for everybody! Just last year, four billion fresh and 1.1 billion frozen pizzas were sold. Some people, especially kids, would like to eat pizza every day!

The term *pizza* was first used in Naples in the eighteenth century, meaning flat bread with cheese, herbs, or oil. It wasn't until the 1890s, when Mediterranean cookery came into fashion, that pizza rose to center stage and became the all-American passion. Today, pizza is requested more often than any other single food, so over 43,000 pizzerias have sprung up in the United States alone.

The only problem is that most restaurant and store-bought pizzas contain unhealthful oils in their dough. Finding that out didn't make me happy, but it did provide me with the impetus to experiment. Within a short time, I learned that making a delicious pizza is not as difficult as it's cracked up to be! As you're about to discover, you don't have to leave your house for the best pizza you've ever tasted.

Homemade pizza is almost impossible to mess up, even without formal training or recipes. *Not* being schooled allows you to feel more independent and to find your own way creatively, so you can veer from traditional toppings and make the type of pizza you enjoy most. You'll make it often, because nothing else can take its place! Don't worry, this doesn't mean that you can't call "pizza man" anymore, or that you can't frequent Italian restaurants. Order out when you want, and when you make your own pizza, it will be appreciated even more!

FORGET TRADITIONAL PIZZA RECIPES

To come up with innovative ideas, it's a good idea to browse through Italian cookbooks and compare pizza recipes; they're loaded with ideas you can improvise upon. But isn't it liberating just knowing you don't need to run out for specific ingredients, or do everything a recipe indicates?

If you disregard the complicated, time-consuming directions and the misconceptions you've heard, you'll discover that making an original pizza is as easy as making a mud pie, not as messy, and lots more fun!

KILLER PIZZA

Nothing calls people to the table faster than a homemade pizza pie hot from the oven. You don't need tons of time, or a special stone, pan, or a brick-lined oven to make it. The thought of lining an oven with bricks would convince the most dedicated cook to pick up the phone and order out! Fortunately, to make pizza you don't need a special type of yeast, flour, or special toppings, either.

All you need is a flat board or tabletop, a spatula or fork, a bowl, a metal or foil pan, and a pizza wheel or sharp knife to cut through the crust without messing up the goodies on top.

Wolfgang Puck became famous showing the world, including Hollywood movie stars, that lox, caviar, shrimp, lobster, goat cheese, and other opulent ingredients go beautifully on pizza. He became a world-renowned restaurateur by allowing his mind to run wild! Fantasy provides the raw material for creativity.

Now take a minute to daydream, because that's how creative ideas originate. The psychoanalyst Rollo May explained in his book *The Courage To Create* that the answers to problems come when the mind is at rest. I call it the "Lost Glasses Theory": You lose your glasses, keys, or anything, and only find them after you quit searching. To find something, create, or remember, you must focus and then let go! Creative people do that more easily. They get something to eat, or distract themselves in some way, knowing the answer to the problem they're working on will come.

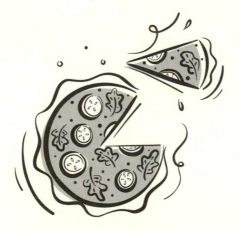

Albert Einstein discovered his theory of relativity while daydreaming. It's important to take the time to fantasize. So lie back, relax, and think of the toppings you'd enjoy most on your pizza.

Who knows, maybe the pizza you create will taste so good, you'll open a restaurant and become world-famous like Wolfgang. At the very least, you'll discover that pizza is a delectable, wholesome food, easily incorporated into a healthful diet.

Make Pizza Part of Your Diet

Pizza can be a greasy mess, or as nutritious as you'd like. It can offer protein, vitamins, and carbohydrates, all in one fairly low-fat, low-calorie package. Or, it can contain 450 calories per slice.

To make a delicious, low-fat pizza, omit the oil in the dough, use a combination of part-skimmed mozzarella and fat-free cheese, or leave the cheese off completely. I'd rather have no cheese than only use fat free, which is much too rubbery for my taste. But if you decide to grace your pizza with your favorite ingredients instead, you won't miss the cheese!

You'll find pizza can be tailored to a vegetarian diet, too, if you use a great-tasting sauce, omit the meat, and substitute veggies and other healthful toppings instead. It's easy to adapt pizza to your individual tastes and dietary needs, no matter what they are!

PIZZA GAME PLAN

Since the urge to eat pizza can strike at any moment, it's a good idea to have flour, dry yeast, olive oil, and your favorite toppings on hand at all times.

Shop the Specials for Ingredients

I mentioned (in chapter 2, on page 60), that in my pantry, I usually stock marinated artichoke hearts (or bottoms), packed in water, hearts of palm, mushrooms, Italian red pepper, onions, and oregano because I never tire of those items on pizza.

In the fridge I keep fat-free and part-skimmed mozzarella cheese, a jar of sun-dried tomatoes, Greek kalamata olives, minced garlic, onions, and fresh basil. If there's grilled chicken, shrimp, or lean hamburger left over, I might add one of those to my pizza, as well.

To save money at the market, I purchase every item I can on sale, and suggest you do the same. To keep my pantry and fridge well stocked, I need to follow a shopping list, but when I have staples on hand, I can concentrate on purchasing appealing items that aren't overpriced. I definitely prefer shopping without a list, because it's easier to discover new items that way!

CULINARY SECRET #3: Be imaginative! Although there's an art to making pizza, it's one of the easiest foods to ad-lib. Do whatever you feel like doing and enjoy yourself, instead of trying to impress others by making an exotic pizza. Simply use ingredients you like and you'll end up with a pizza you and your guests will want to devour immediately, hot from the oven.

Great Pizza Starts With the Dough

The dough is the trickiest part of making pizza. Not because it's difficult to make, but because it needs a few measurements and some forethought. With pizza, it's not a good idea to begin cooking when your guests arrive, the way you can with other dishes. My dear friend Paula tried it, and it was a disaster.

PAULA'S PIZZA PARTY

I was originally deterred from making pizza from scratch while watching Paula make it one day for her daughter's Girl Scout troop. Paula left school early to shop and make the dough, but the girls arrived just as she was beginning. The entire pizza-making process took three hours, much too long for the girls. So to tide them over, Paula began giving them anything and everything she could put her hands on to eat. By the time the pizzas were finally baked, the girls were asking for dessert. Paula asked me to stick a giant orange in her mouth the next time she volunteered her services in the kitchen.

Personally, I love homemade pizza too much to turn it into a forgotten art. And, knowing I can make it quickly, deliciously and healthfully—turns me on. I've shown Paula the easy technique that follows, and even she makes pizza successfully now!

THE BASIC PIZZA-ART FORMULA

This basic formula makes enough dough for one large pizza, or two small ones. I like to make two large pizzas at a time, bake them both, and if I'm lucky have leftovers the next day.

In a large bowl, dissolve a package of active dry-powdered yeast in one third cup plus three tablespoons of warm water. Yeast is a tiny plant that's alive and is activated when it hits the water, so immediately add a large pinch of sugar to the water to feed the culture. After stirring, add 1½ cups flour, a pinch of salt, and a quick swig of olive oil. If you prefer making fat-free pizza, replace the oil with cool water.

COOK'S TIP

If you're wondering if rapid rise, or a cake of refrigerated compressed yeast can be substituted, the answer is YES, all types of yeast are interchangeable.

Suggested Variations for the Dough:

- Replace one cup of the all-purpose flour with one cup whole wheat flour.
- Replace one half cup all-purpose flour with one half cup cornmeal.
- Add a few pinches of dry herbs or spices to the dough.

Now mix together the ingredients you've decided to use and place the ball of dough (it forms practically by itself) on a heavily floured board or table. Knead, or massage, like crazy! The more often you make pizza, the easier it becomes to go by feel and know whether to add more flour or water. The dough should stay together, spring back when poked, and feel pliable without being sticky.

When you're finished kneading the dough, place it on a heavily floured board or table and roll it out, as thin or thick as you like. Pull it, toss it in the air (if you can), and patch when necessary. I tried the tossing method once; it spun and landed on my white German shepherd's head! I suggest you avoid that particular method, but do whatever is necessary to stretch the dough to fit the pan.

KITCHEN TIP

Don't worry if you don't have a 12" or 14" pizza pan. Why not bake your pie in a round layer-cake tin, aluminum-foil pan, or skillet? If you're planning to make pizza often, I suggest you invest in a Silver Stone nonstick pizza crisper, or any other nonstick pizza pan.

Use olive oil, or cooking spray to lightly oil a pizza pan, cookie sheet, Pyrex dish, or whatever you're going to bake on. Sprinkle it with cornmeal if you'd like your pizza to have more texture. Place the dough on the pan, and allow it to rest there for at least ten minutes. The more time, the thicker the crust becomes. You can use this time to create or "doctor" a sauce, before getting the goodies ready to go on top.

SAUCES

If you're feeling adventuresome and in the mood for something unique, spice up your pizza with something other than the same old tomato sauce. Why not use barbecue, pesto, salsa, spaghetti, marinara, or hoisin sauce on pizza? You'll discover all types of innovative combinations by experimenting with various sauces. Remember to read the labels and make sure that none of the sauces you purchase contain cottonseed, palm kernel, or coconut oils. In addition, avoid sauces containing *hydrogenated or partially hydrogenated oils,* because they can clog your arteries. Instead purchase oil-free sauces or those containing moderate amounts of the healthful oils, such as canola, olive, soy, sunflower, or safflower. Better still, make a homemade sauce.

Create Your Own Sauce

To make a scrumptious homemade tomato sauce, begin by draining, coring, seeding, and straining canned tomatoes. This is a hands-on process. Hold each tomato, one-by-one, allowing the juice and seeds to fall into a dish or the kitchen sink, as you tug out the core from the top and loosen the seeds with your fingers. Place the flesh that remains in a bowl, and then put it through a mesh strainer. Add a little sugar, garlic, fresh or dried oregano, basil, and pepper flakes, according to what your taste buds dictate.

Sauce Alternative

At other times, I like to *sauté* (quick cook or sizzle in a small amount of oil) about six fresh chopped garlic cloves in a little olive oil. I drain the oil and add a can of Contadina tomato sauce, some fresh, sweet basil, salt, cayenne pepper, and sugar to taste. *Reduce,* or simmer, the sauce, until some of the liquid evaporates and it's the consistency you like for spreading on pizza. (See chapter 5, Page 125, because this also makes a fabulous pasta sauce.)

Ready-Made Pizza Sauce

When you want to cut down on the time you spend in the kitchen, healthful varieties of pizza sauce containing the better oils and very few calories are available in most markets and health-food stores today.

HEALTHFUL RECOMMENDATIONS

Brand	Type of Oil Added
Contadina	Oil-free
Healthy Choice	Oil-free
Progresso Pizza Sauce	Olive and Canola Oil
Ragú Pizza Quick	Soybean Oil

COOK'S TIP

Ready-Made pasta sauce can easily be substituted for the ready-made pizza sauces; the ingredients are practically the same. There are plenty of sauces made from organic ingredients in markets and health-food stores, too. (See the list of healthful pasta sauces, in chapter 5 on page 129.)

ASSEMBLING THE PIZZA

Once the dough has had a chance to rest, you're ready to place a rack on the bottom rung of your oven and preheat the oven to 500 degrees.

Take time to visualize the pizza you want to eat, and place the toppings you're considering on your counter. Pretend you're painting a picture using foods instead of paints, making each slice the one you'd like on your palate.

Pizza Possibilities

What if you were in a restaurant and Wolfgang Puck was going to cook for you? If he had every cheese, sauce, and topping imaginable, what would you like this famous chef to put on your pizza?

See the picture clearly. Is the cheese on top, or under the sauce? Some cooks like to follow the sauce with the cheese and goodies. Others prefer covering the cheese with the sauce so the cheese doesn't burn. Both ways work, there's no right or wrong!

Cheese

There's no limit to the types of cheese you can use on pizza. Fortunately, freshly grated Parmesan and Romano are available in most markets today, so we're no longer solely dependent on the cheese in the cylindrical cardboard containers.

Alone or combined, traditional mozzarella, or less conventional cheddar, Jack, Swiss, Muenster, blue, fontina, feta, brie, goat, Romano, or Parmesan are delicious. Use all cheeses moderately, however, because of their high fat content. Your taste buds and the calorie content of the cheese will dictate which ones to use.

CHEESE CHART

Cheese	Description	Calories/Oz.
Asiago	Sheep's milk cheese	110
Blue	Cows' milk; sharp, tangy flavor	103
Brie	Soft, cows' milk, creamy, fruity	70
Cheddar	Cows' milk; mild to very sharp	115
Di Capra	Goat Cheese	76
Emmenthal	Swiss cheese	110

CHEESE CHART (cont'd)

Cheese	Description	Calories/Oz.
Feta	Goats' or sheep's milk; sharp, and salty	75
Fontina	Danish; semisoft	120
Gorgonzola	Rich and creamy, Italian origin	92
Gruyère	Italians call it *groviera*	90
Jack Cheese	Cows' milk; bland, smooth	110
Mascarpone	Cheese from the cream of cows' milk	121
Mozzarella	Cows' milk; soft, moist	76
Muenster	French; soft cheese	104
Parmesan-Reggiano	Best *grana,* grated	130
Pecorino	Sheep's milk cheese	120
Provolone	Cows' milk cheese	135
Ricotta	Like cottage cheese, low in salt. Made from the condensed milk from sheep and cows	110
Swiss	Cows' milk; sweet, nutty	105

The Goodies

Besides the variety of cheeses and sauces that can be used to make your pizza, an infinite number of other delicious toppings can be added, as well.

INGREDIENTS TO PLAY WITH

Avocado	Artichoke	Hearts of	Shrimp
Black olives	hearts	palm	Crab
Green olives	Mushrooms	Onions	Lox
Greek olives	Jalapeños	Anchovies	Caviar

INGREDIENTS TO PLAY WITH (cont'd)

Salmon	Grilled	Grilled	Pears
Ground	broccoli	eggplant	Nuts
beef	Zucchini	Spinach	Pesto
Barbecued	Yellow	Tomatoes	Cilantro
chicken	squash	Garlic	Basil
Ground	Carrots	Apples	Oregano
turkey	Bell peppers	Pineapple	Tarragon

Add any other ingredient you enjoy, and let me know what I should add to my list.

ALLOW YOUR INSTINCTS TO SOAR

Now you're the famous chef. So go ahead and make your pizza exactly the way you'd like to eat it. Make it up! Remember, you have all the leeway in the world. If you allow your creative instincts to fly, you'll end up with the best-tasting pizza you've ever had. One that's loaded with lots of good nutrition, inspires others creatively, and looks like a beautiful work of art.

On Valentine's Day last year, my husband decorated a heart-shaped pizza for me. As Laura Esquivel says in *Like Water for Chocolate,* "A lot of love is the secret to preparing the perfect dish."

But you may still be wondering how can anyone create anything without becoming a nervous wreck? My only caution is not to add so many items that they become hidden and unidentifiable. When each flavor complements rather than smothers the other flavors, less is more!

With pizza, for example, you want to distinguish the flavor of the dough from the sauce and toppings. For that reason, it's best to save some of your available ingredients for another dish, or another day.

With experience, you learn what to leave out depending on shifts in your mood. One time your pizza may turn out bold, vibrant, and colorful, while another time mild and subtle, with only one or two flavors defining the dish.

COMBINATIONS THAT WORK

You may want to play around with a few of the following combinations:

Try This

A Southwestern pizza is easily created by adding cornmeal to the dough, and using salsa for the sauce. Cheddar cheese, grilled chicken, avocado, red and yellow bell peppers, green chilies, chili powder, minced garlic, cilantro, and red pepper flakes give pizazz to this pizza.

BAKING PIZZA

Make sure your oven is at 500 degrees. Place the pizza on the bottom rack and bake for twenty minutes, or until bubbly and golden brown. Then slice with a pizza wheel, so the goodies stay intact!

Try This

Too busy to eat healthy? My all-time favorite pizza begins with nonfat dough. After adding homemade tomato sauce, fat-free and part-skim milk mozzarella cheese, I place pitted Greek olives, fresh tomatoes, fresh basil, fresh mushrooms, artichoke hearts, roasted garlic cloves, and red pepper flakes in a decorative design. Then, immediately upon taking this pizza out of the oven, I sprinkle it with Parmesan cheese, sit down, and savor every morsel.

Try This

Pizza made with barbecue sauce, grilled chicken, fat-free cheese, and water-packed pineapple is always a hit. (I like Masterpiece Barbecue Sauce.)

QUICK TIP

Any type of pizza is delicious when cooked on the barbecue. Don't worry, the dough is firm enough, it won't slip through! Spray the grill with Pam first, throw some basil into the charcoal if you want to flavor the crust, and watch the pizza carefully. It can burn quickly, so don't walk away!

Make Vegetarian Pizza

What could be more special than homemade vegetarian pizza? Use organic veggies whenever possible. They're more flavorful, and taste delicious whether raw, steamed, blanched, or grilled.

Assemble the pizza by using homemade tomato sauce topped with Jack cheese, broccoli, eggplant, Maui onions, mushrooms, and tomatoes, fresh basil, oregano, and garlic.

While your pizza is still bubbling, sprinkle it with a little salt and red pepper flakes, just before serving.

Chelsea's Favorite

My daughter has been making homemade pizza from scratch since she was nine. When she wants to make her favorite, she uses ready-made pizza sauce, mozzarella cheese, lots of artichoke hearts, and pitted black olives. It has become one of my favorites, too.

Try This

A more traditional Italian pizza is created when you add garlic to the dough before baking. Top with pesto sauce, grated mozzarella and fontina cheeses, grilled chicken, sun-dried tomatoes, artichoke hearts, and mushrooms.

INTERESTING TIP

For a milder garlic flavor, use the larger "elephant" variety.

Make a Chinese Pizza

Hoisin sauce, shrimp, pea pods, bean sprouts, and mushrooms create a Chinese pizza celebration. (The sauce is available in the Asian section of the market.)

Try This

A feel-good, delicious pizza is made using whole-wheat dough, spaghetti sauce, fresh tomatoes, mushrooms, garlic, basil, and lean ground hamburger meat that's already been sautéed. Add grated Parmesan before serving.

Greek Pizza

This Greek surprise with double tomatoes is unsurpassed. To your dough, add Roma and sun-dried tomatoes, mozzarella and feta cheese, kalamata olives, green peppers, basil, and oregano.

Try This

Make a Pacific Rim pizza with sesame oil and soy sauce, mozzarella and fontina cheese, prawns, sun-dried tomatoes, red onion, fresh garlic and basil.

Make a Calzone

Place your choice of cooked fillings on half a pizza dough. Fold it down the center, then fold it over the goodies. Crimp, or scrunch, the edges together with a fork. Brush the top with beaten egg whites, and bake as you would a pizza, until golden brown.

LABOR-SAVING OPTIONS

With the exception of Boboli (the pizza pastry), I don't recommend frozen pizzas or ready-made pizza dough, because most of the time I can't distinguish their crust from the cardboard packaging they come in.

Bread Machines

To save time, make your pizza dough in a bread machine. Follow your user's guide.

Food-Processor Method

With a food processor, it's possible to make homemade pizza in less time than one can be ordered and delivered, especially if you use rapid-rise yeast. A food processor mixes and kneads dough in approximately two minutes. More time is saved with rapid-rise yeast, because dough needs only to rest awhile on the pan before baking. The entire pizza-making process, with this quick method, takes less than forty minutes. Check your user's guide for specific instructions regarding your particular machine.

Freezer Tips

If you want to make pizza dough to use in the future, it works best when it's frozen before rising. To freeze, form the dough into a ball, flatten into a disk, and place it into a zipper-lock freezer bag. Pizza dough freezes well for up to one month.

When ready to use, defrost eight to sixteen hours in the refrigerator, or four to nine hours at room temperature. Roll out on a pizza pan, allow to rise for ten minutes or more, and enjoy. Remember, the longer it rises, the thicker the crust becomes.

Cheese pizzas also freeze well, so you can freeze an entire cheese pizza, defrost and add other toppings before baking.

And since pizza is such a hit at parties, try making and freezing mini pizzas to serve as party appetizers. A cookie cutter, or the edge of a drinking glass, work well to shape the dough into small two-bite rounds. (See chapter 6, page 154.)

Quick Pizza Dishes

It's fun to whip up an exciting snack that's fun to eat using leftovers and healthful convenience items. Occasionally, after school, Chelsea and her friends toast English muffins, sprinkle them with cheese, spoon pizza sauce on top, add marinated artichoke hearts or olives, and toast them again until the cheese melts. Chelsea says that for the crust, Boboli, pita bread, and Eurobread work equally as well as English muffins.

PIZZA WITHOUT RECIPES

Homemade pizza is not only fun to eat, it's also fun to make. After making it once, I bet you'll find yourself wanting to make it often. Your pizza-tooth will crave homemade pizza, you'll yearn to get into the kitchen, and you'll wonder why you ever felt insecure about making it.

I love what Henry Miller wrote in his wonderful book *On Turning Eighty*. "One of the important things I learned in making watercolors was not to worry, not to care too much. I think it was Picasso who said, 'Not every picture has to be a masterpiece.' Precisely. To paint is the thing. To paint each day. Not to turn out masterpieces. Even the Creator, in making the world, had to learn this lesson. Certainly, when He created man He must have realized that He was in for a prolonged headache."

It's the same way with cooking: It's the process, not the product, that matters most. If making pizza ever feels like work to you, quit striving for perfection. Remember, perfectionism is the oppressor, so allow yourself to switch gears and feel ridiculous for a moment, and I promise you'll feel playful again.

Artists, writers, sports figures, musicians, and cooks produce their best work when they feel they're losing themselves in their activity, or playing. Cooking is about combining work and play together, or, put another way, designing and creating. Time flies by when you're in the flow. Warren Beatty has said, "A measure of success is when you don't know whether you're working or playing!"

With cooking, the experience of the art, the game, the process takes over, suspending the conscious mind. Isn't it refreshing when your censor takes a rest? Judgments and concerns don't have to monitor your every move. Without giving it a thought, you'll soon know which ingredients to put on your pizza. Almost everything you like goes well together, so once you're in touch with what you feel like eating, cooking creatively truly is as easy as pie!

The only way to fail at making homemade pizza, or at doing anything else for that matter, is to give up. So, why not give it a try? Don't give up till you're happy with the results, and you'll be a success. Then, invite an eclectic mix of people over for an innovative pizza party to celebrate! After all, it's the guests who make a party happen.

Pizza Meal Extraordinaire!

One night, pizza turned into the night's entertainment when I asked my guests to decorate their own. I used my Norman Rockwell eyes to envision this party. If you enjoy Norman Rockwell paintings, as I do, you know he never intended to make everything perfect. Instead, he put everyday items together in a unique way. His special flair was the result of attending to every detail and placing a surprise in every scene.

For my party I followed Rockwell's lead, providing toppings that aren't generally used on pizza. To make sure no one had to work too hard, I made the dough, rolled it out, and prepared a table with various cheeses, sauces, and the toppings before anyone arrived.

At dinnertime each person decorated his or her own personal pizza. One man decided to fold his pizza, and pinched the ends to make a calzone, or pizza pocket. So we'd all be able to eat at the same time, we put a few pizzas and the calzone in the oven to bake, and others on the barbecue to grill.

My husband tossed and served a giant green salad and brought out a selection of imported wines and beers. When it came time for dessert, I had planned to make nonfat yogurt sundaes, but now our guests were in a creative mood; they wanted to decorate their own.

When planning your pizza party, listen to your subconscious mind. Do what you envision, follow your fantasy, and you'll create a party that's perfect for your particular guests. I guarantee, no matter how you cut it, pizza is always a crowd pleaser!

Most kids would love to have a "create your own pizza" party. They might surprise you with peanut butter and jelly, potato chip, or funny-face pizzas. If you decide to give a pizza party for children, make sure to cheer these young cooks on by viewing their works of art with gentle eyes. Everyone becomes more creative when they're encouraged to follow through with their beliefs.

In his book *Zen in the Art of Writing,* Ray Bradbury reveals, "So again and again my stories, my plays teach me, remind me, that I must never doubt myself, my gut, my ganglion, or my Ouija subconscious again."

Now let's see what unique and gorgeous salad ideas *your* subconscious can conjure up in the chapter that follows.

CHAPTER 4

◆

Toss the Salad Recipes

"People need to care a lot more about where their food comes from—the farms, the animals, the farmers. That's the missing link between us and what we eat."

—Alice Waters

There's a restaurant in my neighborhood called *Souplanta-tion,* probably similar to one where you live, that's like a giant do-it-yourself salad bar. The other day, as people pranced onto the patio with their trays, an artist stood nearby sketching, and music was playing in the background. Being the incurable "foodie" I am, I sat there noticing that no two salads turned out the same. And I thought about the similarities between art, music, and food.

Artists blend soft and bright colors together, musicians contrast *fortissimo* and *pianissimo* (very loud and soft notes), and cooks blend, mix, and contrast colors, textures, and flavors to create dishes that complement or make up a meal.

Robert Crumb, the famous "Keep on Truckin' " cartoonist, says, "Creativity comes from following your stream of consciousness and letting go of *fixed* ideas." Since everyone likes varying amounts of different ingredients, salad recipes are unnecessary. In fact, when it comes to measurements, quantities speak for themselves!

If you're serving salad to four people, for example, you need approximately eight cups of ingredients. It's no more complicated or difficult than that! All fruits and vegetables go together, so whether you're concocting a main dish, the meal's sidekick, or a salad to conclude the meal—make it up as you go along.

ANTIQUATED SALADS

Lettuce in a bowl with a cherry tomato plopped on the top is hardly considered a salad anymore. For the most part, a large wedge of iceberg lettuce topped with Thousand Island (a mixture of mayonnaise, catsup and sweet pickle) is no longer popular, either. The regular, high-caloric salad dressings that were popular in the 1970s—blue cheese, Green Goddess, and creamy ranch—have been replaced with lite, lower calorie, more healthful varieties, or, best of all, with your own simple mixture.

Two tablespoons of regular French dressing contains 170 calories. The same amount of blue cheese contains 150 calories, and ranch contains 160. On the average salad, two tablespoons of these creamy dressings doesn't go very far. A ladle, or six tablespoons of one of these dressings, contains approximately 450 calories and more fat than a person on a 1,500-calorie diet should eat all day!

I remember ordering a chef's salad, when I was in my twenties, because I wanted to drop a few pounds, and being utterly amazed to learn that this traditional salad is more caloric than a four-course meal. The Thousand Island dressing alone contained 250 calories. Finally I knew why I was putting unwanted pounds *on* instead of taking them *off!*

Realizing that salads, and virtually every other dish, can be ordered healthful or unhealthful, eventually led to a book I wrote titled, *Not "Just a Salad" How to Eat Well and Stay Healthy When Dining Out* (Pharos Books). I'm sure you'll agree that food is more interesting when you don't order straight off the menu, or cook by the book.

A CARROT A DAY

Salads are exciting, they're visually appealing, and they're nutritious. Just switching from iceberg to romaine, spinach, and other dark, leafy greens will increase the beta-carotene in your diet. Beta-carotene, when eaten in foods, is one of the antioxidants that have a protective effect against cancer and other chronic diseases. It "soaks up" stray oxygen molecules called free radicals that cause cellular damage. That's quite a trick, and the beta-carotene in carrots, broccoli, and other yellow and orange fruits and veggies can do it, too. Sprinkle your salad with a little oil and you'll obtain vitamins A and E. In addition, crunchy salads are fun to eat.

Judy Collins once said in an interview, "I've discovered, that all you really need to make life really pleasant, at some moments anyway, is some onions, some mushrooms, some olive oil, a little garlic, and a short memory."

SALAD GAME PLAN

When you're concocting a salad, think about the other dishes you're serving. If the rest of the meal is spicy and hot, the salad should be cool. If the meal is on the simple side, make a salad that's crunchy, sweet, or tart. But, most important, the salad should surprise!

It's helpful to have an idea about how you're going to make a dish and approximately how many people you're serving. But there's no need to decide ahead of time *exactly* how your salad is going to turn out. A mistake in the kitchen often turns into a dish better than the one you were attempting. Classic Caesar salad was always the same until a New Orleans chef dropped barbecued chicken on top and realized how good it tasted. Consequently, Chicken Caesar is becoming a classic in homes and restaurants today.

To make a flavorful salad containing varying textures and rich colors, combine your three favorite fruits and/or vegetables.

Add your favorite fruit for sweetness, croutons or nuts for crunchiness. And, to turn your dish into a complete meal, add some low-fat protein—cheese, beans, or other complex carbohydrate ingredients. All that's left is selecting a sweet, tart, or creamy dressing made from flavored vinegars, healthful oils, and an endless variety of fresh herbs.

I once topped a superb lentil, tomato, and onion salad with goat cheese: The tartness of the vine-ripened tomatoes contrasted with the sweetness of the onions, and the softness of the goat cheese played off the texture of the lentils. It was the colors, textures, and contrasting tastes that made this dish wonderful.

When purchasing ingredients for your creation, avoid greens that show obvious signs of spoilage. Before making your salad, the dark, leafy greens should be given a good soaking in cold water and then shaken in a Turkish towel, or spun dry in a salad spinner to remove the excess moisture.

TWO TYPES OF SALADS

I've heard people explain that they don't prepare salads, or order them in restaurants, because there are so many choices and they don't know which one to choose. It's not necessary to choose just one, however, because you can have them all, on different days!

James Beard, on the other hand, simplified salad. He wrote in *James Beard's Simple Foods:* "There are two types of salad, of which the most familiar is the tossed salad, the kind that is vigorously tossed and turned until all the different ingredients are blended together with the dressing. The other salad *composé,* or composed salad, is composed in two senses of the word: composed of a variety of ingredients, and allowed to compose, or rest itself, rather than being agitated like a tossed salad." Beard's philosophy definitely makes salad-making simple. You either toss your favorite ingredients together in a bowl, or spread them out. It doesn't matter which type of salad you prefer, because variations of both are delicious.

Sometimes I think of a classic salad: taco, Caesar, or Chinese Chicken, and then because of my tastes, or what's fresh in the marketplace, change some of the traditional ingredients. The salad often turns out more to my liking, yet I've still cooked from a traditional point of view.

So, mix and match, rinse, cut or tear, but—whatever you do—don't worry about what to name your salad until after you've made it; otherwise you may feel confined by what has been done previously.

TOSSED SALAD COMBINATIONS THAT WORK

Mediterranean Mixed-Garden

Rinse and tear a few handfuls of dark greens per person. Add sliced tomatoes, carrots, red or yellow peppers, fresh parsley, basil, cilantro, sprouts, and mushrooms, or whatever else you like. You're creative, so make it up as you go along!

If you'd like, top your salad with crabmeat, flaked tuna, chickpeas, kidney beans, feta cheese, and croutons. Toss this salad with your favorite dressing (see ideas on page 103 of this chapter), and serve it with warm, quartered pita bread and a good bottle of wine.

WAISTLINE TIP

To cut calories from any ready-made salad dressing, mix it with additional vinegar or lemon juice.

Do As the Italians Do

Any salad, but especially one with dark, leafy greens that's served after the meal, as they do in Italy, tastes delicious tossed right at the table with salt, vinegar, and olive oil.

- First, toss the leaves with a few shakes of salt; this bruises the leaves slightly and smooths out the sharp taste of the vinegar.
- Next, add a few shakes of raspberry, blackberry, balsamic, pepper, or red-wine vinegar to moisten the leaves, and toss again.
- Finally, sprinkle the salad with extra-virgin olive oil, approximately one teaspoon per person. Toss until the leaves glisten. Add a touch of freshly ground black pepper. What better way to conclude the meal, and begin a romantic evening, with a fresh taste in your mouth?

Fresh Spinach Salad

This can be your whole meal. Wash spinach well, cut off the stems, and cut the leaves into a salad bowl. Add sliced red onion, mushrooms, watercress, crumbled feta or blue cheese, and homemade croutons. (Some ideas for making croutons follow.) You may want to add grilled chicken slices. Red Wine Vinaigrette (Lawry's Oriental, or any homemade version) tastes great on this salad.

The Mighty Caesar

Caesar is one of the most delicious and easiest salads to make. Rinse, dry, and chill the inner crunchy leaves of two heads of romaine lettuce. Cut lettuce immediately before serving. Top with homemade croutons (ideas for making them begin on page 93).

For the dressing, blend together approximately one eighth cup natural rice vinegar, one eighth cup water, two to four cloves of fresh garlic, a splash of lemon juice, a dash of Worcestershire sauce, four to five anchovy fillets, salt, and pepper to taste. Now slowly emulsify, or add approximately one eighth cup of olive oil, and blend again. (The dressing will thicken.) Taste and adjust the seasonings, making sure there's enough salt to balance the garlic. You may want to add grated Parmesan cheese to the dressing, or you may prefer the salad topped—as I do—with large shavings of Parmesan cheese. For a creamier dressing, add one quarter cup nonfat mayonnaise to the mixture.

Instead of making dressing from scratch, use Lawry's Caesar dressing when you're in a hurry; it's delicious. If you don't want to pour the dressing directly from the bottle—in front of guests—whip a little anchovy paste or fillets into the ready-made (in the blender this only takes a couple of seconds). Pour the dressing into a jar, measuring cup, or bowl, refrigerate, and toss before serving. Everyone will think it's homemade.

Doctoring? No big deal, I do it all the time, and don't say a thing! If you've opened a box and put the contents into boiling water, you've cooked. It's no different with dressing. (Avoid Lawry's Creamy Caesar, however, because unfortunately they've added *partially hydrogenated* soybean oil and they haven't taken the monosodium glutamate (MSG) out, yet.)

SAFETY TIP

There's a risk of salmonella poisoning from eggs, so *do not* add raw egg to Caesar dressing, or anything else you consume such as protein drinks, eggnog, ice cream, puddings, or mayonnaise. The best advice is always to cook eggs thoroughly!

CROUTON BASICS

- Use bread that's stale, or more than a day old; it makes delicious croutons. Sourdough, sprouted wheat, molasses, or corn bread work particularly well for this.
- If the bread isn't stale, freeze it, and thaw it long enough so a sharp knife (not a serrated one) can cut through.
- Remove the crust or—if you'd prefer—leave it on the partially frozen bread, and cut the bread into cubes. (It's impossible to cut fresh bread evenly.)

Low-Fat Croutons

- Warm some oil, because warmed oil distributes more evenly. For expedience, heat it in the microwave for a few seconds. Or, you could infuse garlic in the olive oil, which means heating some oil in a skillet with whole garlic cloves. Discard the cloves and proceed.
- Brush the oil on the cubes, or toss gently.
- Flavor the croutons by tossing them in Parmesan cheese, minced garlic, shallots, black or red pepper, or your favorite selection of dried herbs.
- Spread on a baking sheet. Bake, turning occasionally until brown.

Fat-free Croutons

Whip a mixture of one half cup water, one egg white, a teaspoon or more of garlic, two teaspoons or more of any herbs you like. On croutons, I enjoy the savory ones (oregano, sage, and thyme).

Brush this mixture on cubes of stale bread and bake at 300 to 350 degrees for eight to ten minutes, turning occasionally, until crisp.

MY FIRST CREATIVE SALAD

In the preface of this book, I told you about my first creative experience in the kitchen. If you recall, it occurred one night when I felt like eating a salad but didn't want to go to the market for lettuce. I diced cantaloupe, tomato, and avocado into a salad bowl, sprinkled the ingredients with a little salt and pepper, and tossed them together.

This combination took little effort, and got big applause! Now take a risk and try something *you've* never done before.

Something New (Pea Salad)

This works well as a salad and vegetable side dish combined. Rinse and cut watercress into a bowl. Add a bag of frozen peas, they'll defrost as you add a couple of handfuls of raw, shelled sunflower seeds, and small cubes of cheese (Jack's my favorite, but I also like Muenster, and Swiss). Toss well with your favorite dressing.

Another No-Lettuce Salad

Combine chopped tomatoes (they toss better than sliced), cubes of mozzarella cheese, pitted Greek olives, cubed bell pepper, fresh basil leaves, cilantro, watercress, balsamic vinegar, kosher salt and freshly ground pepper to taste. Let stand in the refrigerator for about half an hour. Before serving add flavored croutons and toss.

Taco Salad

Break up regular and/or black corn tortilla chips. Add some dark-green lettuce leaves, kidney beans, pitted black olives (sliced or chopped), cilantro, shredded cheddar cheese, avocado—some people add corn and grilled chicken, too.

The proportions don't matter. Just add these items and others in quantities equal to how much you enjoy them until the salad is large enough to satisfy the number of people you're serving.

You don't need a lot of dressing. Salsa, low-calorie ranch, or vinaigrette are equally delicious; vary it depending upon your taste buds at the time. Tossing these fresh ingredients well is the secret to making this salad a success!

Great Greek Salad

Into a serving bowl, dice fresh vine-ripened tomato and peeled cucumber. Add pitted Greek olives, bell pepper, onion if you like, and top with cubed or crumbled feta cheese.

This salad is heavenly when tossed with your favorite olive oil vinaigrette and served with pita bread and a chilled glass of wine.

Tomato and Sweet Onion Salad

If you're an onion lover, you'll have fun making and eating this one! Slice your two favorite types of onions thinly (I like Maui and red; Vidalia onions are great if you can get them). Add cherry tomatoes (red, and yellow—if you can find them) and drained, pitted black olives. Toss with a Caesar-type dressing, or a mixture consisting of a little olive oil, anchovy paste, and red-wine vinegar.

Create a pretty picture by covering individual plates with butter lettuce (or any other kind), add a big scoop of this salad, crumbled feta or goat cheese, and then sprinkle fresh basil leaves on top.

Cuisinart-Chopped Cobb Salad

Using a food processor is equivalent to having a *garde manger,* or chef, chopping and cutting vegetables right in your home.

Using the metal blade in your Cuisinart, or a sharp knife, chop the following ingredients (omitting what you don't like). Four or five leaves of romaine lettuce, a handful of parsley, watercress, yellow, green and red bell pepper, several carrots, and a few mushrooms. If you'd like, add diced tomato, avocado and grilled chicken or turkey. Toss lightly with your favorite Italian dressing.

Chopped Vegetable Salad

Take every raw vegetable you like, chop evenly, and mix together. Toss with your favorite dressing. (Unlike the Cuisinart concept above, this salad contains no lettuce.)

Chinese Chicken Salad

Marinate boneless, skinless chicken breasts in tamari (natural soy sauce, available in health-food stores). Then, broil or barbecue the chicken until it's done.

Meanwhile, little by little, drop rice sticks (available in the Asian section of the market) into a wok or skillet containing several cups of hot oil (soy, safflower, or corn oil work well). If the oil is hot enough, the white threads will puff up almost instantly. To make sure they cook completely, use enough oil; otherwise, the rice sticks will be as hard as rocks and impossible to chew. You must watch these puffed noodles carefully and remove them from the wok quickly, or they will burn and lose their pure white color. To drain the excess oil from these noodles, place them on a plate that you've covered with paper towels.

When the chicken is cool, shred it into strips with your hands. It tastes better when it isn't cut. Now add some shredded lettuce. Most people use iceberg, but I prefer romaine. Add finely chopped cilantro, and a tablespoon of diced preserved pimento. I like to add slivered almonds, or toasted sesame seeds. You could add diced red and green bell pepper, too.

Make a dressing consisting of approximately two tablespoons tamari or soy sauce, one quarter cup red-wine vinegar, one quarter cup rice vinegar, one quarter cup canola or sesame oil, one teaspoon sugar, one teaspoon red, hot pepper oil, shredded ginger, and chopped scallions. Otherwise, buy your favorite vinaigrette, and doctor with a little tamari, ginger, and sesame oil. (For an optional Oriental-Style Dressing, see page 105.)

Toss the chicken and vegetables in a large bowl, add the

dressing, and toss again. Now, add the rice sticks and toss once more. This salad is worth the effort!

Paula's Crunchy Salad

My friend Paula and her husband, Bill, made a delicious salad, except the rice noodles weren't completely cooked. Crunchy noodles were hanging out of my husband's mouth; Paula covered her mouth with her hands because she couldn't chew; Bill excused himself to dump his salad into the sink; and I was choking so hard I couldn't even talk. Everyone started drinking water and then, just looking at one another, we couldn't stop laughing.

Don't get discouraged. Paula made sure the noodles were cooked the next time she made this, and it was one of the best salads I've ever tasted! Paula said the key is not to scrimp on the amount of oil you put into your skillet or wok before cooking them.

Crunchy Salad with Peanut Dressing

Add anything you like that's crunchy, for this one. I usually julienne (cut into fine strips about the same size as a match stick) carrots, cabbage, shredded lettuce, mung bean sprouts, snap peas, cilantro, sunflower sprouts, and add some rice noodles. (See the Chinese chicken salad for an explanation.) Then add half-inch squares of firm tofu, usually available in the refrigerated deli section of the market.

For the dressing, thin a few tablespoons of peanut butter with rice vinegar and tamari (or soy sauce) to taste. Add grated ginger, a dash of sesame oil, and chili powder. Sweeten to taste with honey or maple syrup if it's too tangy. This dressing can be made in the blender or by hand. Toss well, and prepare to give your jaw a workout!

Grilled Vegetable Salad

This concept is a nice contrast from most crunchy salads, and there's nothing easier—or healthier—than a salad of grilled vegetables dressed simply with a splash of flavored vinegar, salt, and pepper.

If you lightly oil the vegetables before grilling, to keep them from sticking or drying out, it isn't necessary to add oil to the dressing. (Peppers can be roasted on a fork over a gas flame until blackened. They peel more easily if you place them in a brown paper bag for a few minutes while they're still hot—this steams the pepper and loosens the skin. Wait to peel them until they're cool enough to handle.) Toss and serve this salad, to each person individually, on a plate covered with a big, beautiful lettuce leaf. Top with feta cheese and shredded basil.

Shiitake Mushroom and Cucumber Salad

Here's an unusual combination. Soak dried shiitake mushrooms in warm water for at least a half hour. Rinse them, and slice thinly. Peel a cucumber, slice it lengthwise, remove the seeds, and cut it into slices—half-moons.

Sauté the mushrooms in a combination of equal parts soy sauce and Mirin (Japanese seasoning), until tender.

Toss the mushrooms and cucumbers together, with a little rice-wine vinegar, and more of the soy Mirin sauce if needed. Chill in the fridge. Top this delicious salad with toasted sesame seeds and cilantro before serving. It's the smoky flavor and firm texture of these mushrooms that makes this salad so good.

INTERESTING TIP

Chef Martin Yan writes in his *A Simple Guide to Chinese Ingredients*, "Rice wine is the product of fermented glutinous rice and millet. The resulting amber liquid is aged 10 to 100 years to achieve its rich full-bodied flavor."

Three-Bean Salad

Drain and combine (large or small) cans of cut green beans, garbanzo beans, and red kidney beans. (Stay open-minded about using certain canned items; they can be healthful and delicious!)

For the dressing, mix three quarter cup red-wine vinegar, one half cup canola oil, one chopped red onion, garlic, and some granulated sugar to taste. Toss and serve. Great with sandwiches at the beach.

THE ART OF CREATIVE GARNISHING

Some people get into the habit of cutting up the same salad ingredients in the same way, day after day. After a while it becomes boring to make salad and boring to eat it. Vary the sizes, shapes, and ingredients. You may want to add some of the items that follow:

Fruits and Vegetables. Dried fruits (raisins, dried apricots, and figs), sun-dried tomatoes, and all seasonal fruits and veggies.

Lettuce and Herbs. Arugula, butter, oak leaf, Belgian endive, escarole, radicchio, mizuna, lola, romaine, red romaine, red-leaf, salad bowl, sorrel, spinach.

Fresh Herbs. Basil, mint, cilantro, parsley, dill watercress—they're all delicious.

Bell Peppers. Red, yellow, orange, or green.

Onions. Maui, purple, and green; Vidalia; pearl; scallions.

Tomatoes. All colors and varieties.

Beans. Lentils, kidney beans, or chickpeas.

Cheese. Goat, feta, low-fat mozzarella, low-fat Jack, cheddar.

Olives. Chopped, sliced, or pitted; black or green.

Sprouts. Sunflower, radish, or alfalfa.

Meats and Seafood. Chicken, turkey, tuna, salmon, shrimp, scallops; leftover steak, sliced thinly.

Miscellaneous Items. Celery, carrots, cucumber, daikon radish, marinated artichokes, avocado, fresh or canned beets, mushrooms, toasted pine nuts, sesame and sunflower seeds.

VALUABLE TIP

Chop your favorite fresh herbs into your salad; they're so flavorful, you can use less dressing. A tablespoon of any type of oil contains 120 calories, so use it sparingly.

THE COMPOSED SALAD

Imagine a salad of artistically cut red, green, and yellow vegetables, olives, and meats arranged beautifully. This is an Italian antipasto, and a perfect example of a *composed salad*. The ingredients can be diced, cubed, julienned; raw, roasted, grilled, steamed, jarred, or even canned, if they are of contrasting colors and textures.

Use your sense of balance and composition as you artistically place items you like: meats, fish, cheese, veggies (artichokes, beets, string beans, potatoes) on a lovely platter.

If you don't have an attractive plate, cover a plain one with curly endive, chicory, escarole, or some other greens, and then carefully place the salad ingredients on top. Julia Child, writing about nouvelle cuisine, said, "When it's so beautifully arranged on the plate, you know someone's fingers have been all over it." Salads are particularly appealing, because of the way they look.

Fresh Mozzarella and Tomato Salad

With your creative fingers, place thick slices of juicy, vine-ripened, red tomato between slices of fresh Buffalo Mozzarella cheese. Drizzle with virgin olive oil, and decorate the plate with leaves of fresh basil. All this crowd pleaser needs is some crusty French bread on the side.

KITCHEN TIP

Buffalo Mozzarella cheese is usually available in the deli section of the market. Left-overs should be rinsed and stored in fresh water! If you continue to replace the water every few days, the cheese keeps well in the fridge for about a week.

Fennel and Hearts of Palm Salad

Arrange slices of canned hearts of palm, sliced fresh fennel bulb, chopped roasted red peppers, pine nuts, sliced olives, grapefruit sections (without the membrane), and avocado slices on torn butter lettuce. Your salad will look as if it came out of a magazine. Drizzle a light vinaigrette over this unusual salad, and serve.

Salad Niçoise

With this salad, the French have tastefully combined the composed and tossed salad. The classic Niçoise contains no cooked vegetables, or lettuce, and never tuna and anchovies together, but I prefer it this way:

Tear romaine lettuce and arrange on a chilled platter, or on individual plates. On top of the lettuce, place olive-oil or water-packed tuna, olives, quartered tomatoes, boiled new potatoes, hard-boiled eggs, asparagus, steamed green beans, anchovy fillets, and slices of sweet red onion. Drizzle with vinaigrette or ranch dressing, serve as is or toss at the table before serving.

NOW FOR THE DRESSING

It's surprising the way we take perfectly delicious, healthful salads and load them up with lots of salty, fatty dressing. Remember, a simple salad can become as highly caloric as a four-course meal. And you might enjoy a four-course meal more than a salad drenched in dressing.

Fortunately, there's a revolution taking place in the way we dress salad. We're realizing there's no point in ruining delicious greens, so we're making and buying more healthful varieties of dressings, and using less of them.

Make Your Own: The Basic Formula

The dressing is such an intricate part of the salad that you may want to make your own, and save ready-made dressings for dishes that take longer to prepare.

There's really no mystery to making your own great-tasting vinaigrette from ingredients you probably already stock in your kitchen. Homemade versions are lower in salt and oil than the store-bought varieties, and less costly, too. (I don't like fat-free dressings, so I always add at least a little oil because I enjoy their nutty flavors.)

To make up a basic dressing, add equal parts olive oil and vinegar (or lemon juice), in a bottle. Add salt and pepper to taste, and shake. This simple yet delicious crowning glory, with or without variations, enhances any salad beautifully. The chart that follows will help you decide what type of vinegar to use but, depending upon the flavor you prefer, they're interchangeable.

VINEGAR CHART

Vinegar	Flavor
Balsamic vinegar	Rich, sharp, almost sweet flavor
White distilled vinegar	Sharp and strong
Cider vinegar	Strong and tart
Wine vinegar	Mild and less acidic
Sherry vinegar	Full-bodied flavor
Fruit or herb vinegar	Mild flavor, low acidity
Rice-wine vinegar	Mild and sweet

When I'm in the mood, I omit the vinegar and merely sprinkle a little virgin olive oil and kosher salt on organic greens. Eating a simple salad like that leaves a fresh, clean taste in my mouth.

All dressings can be mixed by hand or emulsified (mixed, in a food processor or blender, so the oil is equally distributed throughout). To do this, add all the ingredients and, lastly, while the blade is twirling slowly, add the oil.

Low-Fat Variation

To cut down on calories, dilute one half cup of vinegar with an equal amount of water or juice. Add your favorite herbs, a dash of lemon juice, and, for more flavor, a tablespoon of olive oil.

Adding a tablespoon of Dijon mustard—named after the region in which it was created—further spikes up the flavor and provides variety. Bottled in the refrigerator, dressing keeps well for two weeks.

KITCHEN TIP

If you firmly roll a piece of citrus fruit back and forth on your counter, with the palm of your hand, it softens the fruit and it becomes much easier to juice.

Try This

When you're in the mood for a creamy ranch dressing, mix equal parts of nonfat sour cream, buttermilk, and mayonnaise. This is a base to which you can add your favorite dried seasonings: oregano, basil, marjoram, white pepper, salt, fresh minced garlic, and onion. To make this even more flavorful, I add a little crumbled goat, feta, or blue cheese, and a few drops of RedHot Cayenne, or Tabasco sauce.

QUICK TIP

When I was a kid, after adding a vinaigrette, my mom almost always tossed our salad with a tablespoon or two of sour cream. Now I do the same with a nonfat variety and still enjoy the creamy texture it creates.

Contemporary Roquefort or Blue Cheese Vinaigrette

This is marvelous on Mediterranean or spinach salad. Mix a little olive oil with lemon juice and vinegar. Add some crumbled Roquefort or blue cheese, kosher salt and ground pepper to taste.

Oriental-Style Dressing

To make a dressing with an Asian flair, mix approximately one quarter cup red-wine vinegar with a little sesame oil. Add soy sauce, freshly grated ginger, minced garlic, pepper, and toasted sesame seeds. For variety, you can use a bit of plum sauce instead of the sesame oil, and rice vinegar instead of the red wine. Add some chili powder and, with a flick of your wrist, you've turned it into a Thai dressing.

HERBS AND SPICES

Add to any dressing one or more of the following season-ings to taste. The herbs can be fresh or dried: basil, chives, dill, fennel, garlic, lemon juice, pepper, salt, shallots, or whatever you have on hand that would please you.

Fresh herbs can easily be dried in the microwave. Place the herbs on a paper towel and zap them for a minute on high. Turn the herbs over and repeat the process until they're dry. Herbs store well in a cool dark place for several months, or for as long as they maintain their fragrance.

READY-MADE DRESSINGS

Many consumers stay loyal to a particular dressing, without thinking about the ingredients it contains. As with other com-mercially made products, make certain the dressings you buy contain no monosodium glutamate *(MSG)*, an additive that makes some people sick. And, avoid all varieties of salad dress-ings containing the *hydrogenated* and *tropical oils* (coconut, palm, or cottonseed oils), because they can clog your arteries. Most oils such as soy, safflower, canola, corn, sunflower seed, are healthful if they're not hydrogenated. In salad dressings, however, I prefer the rich taste of olive or sesame, but that's strictly a matter of taste. (See chapter 5, page 126 for more in-formation about oils.)

NUTRITION TIP

Beware of oil-free dressings. They usually contain an abundance of salt, sugar, or artificial sweeteners to make up for their lack of flavor. (Personally, I haven't found one that has a good taste.)

I've looked at a lot of labels and tasted a lot of dressings. The following chart lists a variety of healthful brands of salad dressings, and the Best Tasting Bets, rated in my order of preference: (***, **, *), three stars being best. Consider these recommendations, or select others.

DRESSING RECOMMENDATIONS

Brand	Product	Oil Used
Brianna's	French Vinaigrette	Canola Oil
	Honey Mustard	Canola Oil
	Italian	Canola Oil
	Poppy Seed	Canola Oil
Joey D's***	Chinese Chicken Salad	Sesame Oil
Kraft	Creamy Italian	No Oil
Lawry's**	Italian With Parmesan	Soybean Oil
Matheney's*	Honey Mustard	No Oil
Newman's Own	Vinaigrette	Olive or Soybean Oil
Pritikin	Herb Vinaigrette	No Oil
	Sweet And Spicy	No Oil
	Italian	No Oil
	French Style	No Oil
Trader Joe's	Italian Dressing	No Oil
Wishbone	Thousand Island	No Oil
	Creamy Roasted Garlic	No Oil

QUICK TIP

Most supermarket managers are happy to order these products for a customer if they are out of stock or have not previously carried them. Just let them know.

How To Cut Fat from Ready-Made Dressings

- Dilute an oil-based dressing with a little water or lemon juice.
- Try mixing an oil-based dressing with a ready-made "no-oil dressing."

- To coat your salad with less dressing, evenly, use a few squirts of dressing from a spray bottle, instead of pouring.
- Dilute creamy dressings with buttermilk, plain nonfat yogurt, or a little skim milk.
- Dress your salad with a flavored vinegar, such as raspberry, balsamic, or rice wine.

CULINARY SECRET #4: Never overdress your dishes. Use a modest amount of dressing on your salads, and serve some sauces on the side, so you can dip instead of eating foods that are dripping wet.

FRUIT SALADS

Summer and Winter Cold Fruit Salads

Dice your favorite *seasonal* summer fruits, and you'll end up with a totally different salad than when you combine your favorite winter fruits.

Leave these delicious salads plain, or dress with your favorite ready-made raspberry vinaigrette. Fruit salads are also delicious sprinkled with a touch of fresh lemon, lime, or orange juice.

Hot Fruit Salad

Open and drain a large can of chunked pineapple. Place the fruit in a glass baking dish. Add cans of your favorite halved fruits—peaches, pears, apricots—all drained.

Layer with cinnamon, nutmeg, ground ginger, and one half cup brandy.

Now, add a can of cherry-pie filling on top, and bake for about an hour at 350 degrees. Serve hot or cold.

This fruit salad also makes a lovely side dish when served with grains, poultry or meat, or a scrumptious topping over nonfat frozen yogurt or low-fat ice cream.

Berry Delicious

This dish makes a pretty salad. Layer a quarter cup each of your favorite berries in a goblet or glass. (I prefer blueberries, raspberries, and strawberries.) Make one for each guest. Sprinkle in a few tablespoons of pineapple juice, and top with your favorite type of chopped nuts. This also makes a refreshing dessert.

THE QUICKEST SALADS

Cooking, unfortunately, is becoming an endangered art, since most adults work outside the home and don't have much time or energy to cook. When you've worked all day, arrived home at 7:00 P.M., and bedtime for the kids is later and later, who wants to spend time in the kitchen?

Here are tricks for preparing foods quickly so you and your family and friends can sit down around the dining room table more often for a delicious, home-cooked meal. Restaurant meals are available to everyone, but since home cooking comes from love, it's always cherished more.

Salad-in-a-Bag

If you don't have time to wash, dry, and tear lettuce, yet you still want a delicious salad, look for bagged lettuces available in most supermarkets today.

Clearly, salad-in-a-bag is healthy fast food! An extravagance, well worth every extra dime, since this convenience food provides variety and saves time. However, only purchase refrigerated packages containing "use-by" dates that provide enough time for you to make use of the product.

Salads are boring when only one type of lettuce and carrots are added. So in addition to a variety of prewashed veggies, purchase bags of spinach, cabbage, radicchio, arugula, and combinations of baby field greens, but make sure your store-bought salad isn't discolored or wilted.

To avoid fat, don't purchase bagged varieties containing croutons and dressing. They usually contain unhealthful oils, unwanted calories, and a hefty price tag.

Make Your Own Salad-in-a-Bag

Why not make your *own* salad-in-a-bag? It doesn't take much more time to make a large salad than a small one, so when you have a little extra time, wash it, spin it, or air dry it, and you'll have the freshest, tastiest prewashed salad for times when you're in a rush!

Lettuce can be stored in lettuce spinners, or packed in a breathable plastic bag, poked with a few holes. To absorb extra water, tuck some folded paper towels in the bottom of the bag. Refrigerate it, without dressing, and the salad will stay crisp for at least a week.

OUR FOURTH ANNUAL BLOCK PARTY

One of my favorite summertime activities is our annual neighborhood block party. On a designated night, my neighbors and I rope off a nearby cul-de-sac and create a giant salad bar. Families volunteer to set up long tables, and bring utensils, salad ingredients, dressings, ready-made salads, freshly baked breads, roasted garlic, beer, wine, and soft drinks. Then the fun begins!

Last year I didn't have enough time to prepare the huge salad I promised to bring, but I made salad for twenty-five people in practically no time, because I found bagged organic salad ingredients in the market.

I'm convinced that this event makes all the neighbors more friendly and helpful toward one another throughout the entire year. Lately, when I walk my dog, everyone waves and says hello, so the party has made living in the neighborhood more fun. If you want to organize a block party, read on. Why not consider creating a pasta party for your neighbors?

CHAPTER 5

◆

Perfect Pasta without Recipes

"Everything you see, I owe to spaghetti."
—Sophia Loren

On the bottom of the menu at Eddies, my favorite casual restaurant in Telluride, Colorado, it says *"Eata pasta and skia fasta."* There aren't many foods I enjoy more than a steaming bowl of hot pasta. I've finally realized that nothing—not even pasta—will ever make me a downhill racer. But I still enjoy a plate of fettuccine at any altitude, whenever I can.

I could eat pasta every day, it's so satisfying. And remember, coaches advise their athletes to eat this delicious food several hours before competition, since it's a rich source of complex carbohydrates and provides energy!

Pasta isn't fattening if you don't add cream sauces, butter, and fatty cheeses. A four-ounce serving—two cups cooked—of any pasta without sauce contains only 400 calories, no cholesterol, no sodium, protein, fiber, and very little fat.

NUTRITIONAL DIFFERENCES

Fettuccine Alfredo, traditionally made with cream, butter, and parmigiana cheese, and served with fettuccine noodles, is always avoided by health-conscious people because of its high-fat content. But don't fret too much. If you follow the cooking techniques in this chapter, creamy-white, neon-green pesto, or rich tomato-based sauces, can be poured over your pasta any time you like . . . without guilt!

MAKE PASTA PART OF YOUR DIET

On the U.S. Department of Agriculture's Food Guide Pyramid—which recommends what Americans should be eating—pasta and noodles are listed along with bread, cereal, and rice. Easy to prepare, pasta is one of the most diverse foods made from flour.

Rocky, one of my friends, a middle-weight boxer who had a three-win and two-loss record, began winning all his fights after including pasta in his diet regularly. He attributes his increased endurance and perfect record to eating more pasta. Unfortunately I can't promise that pasta will turn you into another Rocky Balboa, but it's so delicious that I can guarantee you'll enjoy every bite!

FORGET TRADITIONAL PASTA RECIPES

Traditional pasta recipes are more intricate than necessary. In fact, they can be downright intimidating. Why should the mere idea of having a few people over, even for a simple pasta dinner, conjure up images of intensive planning, list making, sauce up to your elbows, and doing things for guests that take hours of execution?

To make great-tasting pasta, you don't need a ton of ingredients, fancy equipment, or the IQ of a scientist. All you need is a little slot of time, a pot, some water, any type of pasta, and a few of your favorite ingredients. Pasta is one of the easiest foods to improvise, and, it's delicious tossed with nothing more than a little olive oil and Parmesan cheese.

PASTA GAME PLAN

Stock Up On Ingredients

You'll find all the delicious items you need to make healthful dishes at your local market and health-food store, because as more health-conscious consumers are demanding more healthful foods, manufacturers are offering better products.

As I mentioned in chapter 2, on Page 60, in addition to various dried pastas, you'll find in my cupboard: canned peeled tomatoes, tomato puree, prepared sauces, dressings, and a variety of dried and canned beans. These foods are healthful and keep well, so I can purchase them safely in larger quantities, and I suggest you do the same. Other ingredients such as cheese, vegetables, and leftovers may already be in your fridge.

Improvise Recipes

To create delicious, free-style pasta dishes, think about Italian dishes you've enjoyed at other people's homes, in restaurants, and those you've previously made yourself. If you get into the habit of asking waiters and chefs about the preparation of restaurant dishes you enjoy, you'll learn a tremendous amount about cooking. You'll also be able to distinguish every ingredient in each dish, so re-creating it or making it more to your liking becomes easy. In other words, you can make any dish taste more delicious than the original, because your cooking IQ increases.

While waiting in the grocery-store checkout line, or when you're cooking, decide how you'd like to improvise your favorite dish. Then, simply do whatever you feel like doing. If you don't know how to get started, simply think about incorporating a variety of shapes, colors, and textures into the dish, and you'll have an *idea,* or at least a direction. Don't feel intimidated. Remember, everything has been done by someone else before. There's no such thing as a totally *original dish,* because creativity simply comes from re-creating what you like, but with a fresh approach. What should you do, you ask, if you're stuck and have absolutely no idea of what to cook? Use a little deductive reasoning. It works like the following algebraic equation.

CULINARY SECRET #5: If ingredient A goes with B, and C goes with B, A will probably go well with C. For example, since chicken goes with tomatoes, and pasta goes with tomatoes, too, then chicken and pasta will most likely make a delicious combination. With this inferential cooking equation in mind, you'll find that foods you thought would clash make the perfect match.

The next chance I get, I'll make a dish that combines a healthy version of *pasta del mare* (pasta with seafood) and *pasta primavera* (pasta with fresh vegetables). If you think that's a good idea, try it, too!

The Best Pasta for the Job

Select from the 600 available shapes and colors of pasta. Although all pasta dough is similar, certain shapes work better with certain sauces. For example, the surface space on fettuccine, linguini, and spaghetti allows the sauce to stick on the strands. The corkscrew shape of fusilli accommodates beans and cut-up vegetables beautifully. Tubular penne, hollowed-out rigatoni, shells, and orecchiette ("little ears") are ready pockets for pastas containing thicker sauces, small bits of meat, or vegetables cut into strips. For even distribution of sauce and pasta, try to match the size of the pasta with the other ingredients you're using. The following chart shows some of the more popular shapes from which you may choose.

PASTA CHART

Popular Pasta Shapes	Descriptions
Agnolotti	Round ravioli filled with meat
Angel hair	The thinnest pasta
Cannelloni	Flat squares of pasta rolled around a stuffing
Cappelletti	"Little Hats," flat or round squares with filling
Conchiglie	Giant pasta shells, delicious hot or cold, stuffed with seafood, meat or vegetables
Elbow macaroni	Curved shapes often used to make macaroni and cheese
Farfalle	Butterfly, ribbon bows
Fettuccine	Flat noodles, 1/4-inch wide, delicious fresh
Fiochetti	Bows—kids love this shape
Fusilli	Corkscrew shaped
Gnocchi	Pasta rounds made with potato, flour, and usually egg
Lasagna	A wide, flat pasta used in baked dishes
Macaroni	Hollow pastas; there are more than twenty sizes
Mostaccioli rigati	Diagonally cut tube-shaped pasta
Orecchiette	"Little Ears"; round pasta easily fills with sauce
Orzo	Pasta as small as rice
Penne	Short tubular pasta
Ravioli	Filled pasta squares
Rigatoni	Large, tubular pasta, three inches in length
Rotini	Wheels
Shells	Shell-shaped pasta
Spaghetti	Dried, thin, long strands of pasta
Spinach fettuccine	Green, flat noodles flavored with spinach
Tagliatelle	Long, thin noodles, good in soup

PASTA CHART (cont'd)

Popular Pasta Shapes	Descriptions
Tortiglioni	Spirals curved to capture sauces, the multicolored ones are good for making colorful salads
Tortellini	Small, stuffed twists
Vermicelli	Very thin spaghetti, sold in clusters or long boxes, the perfect pasta for light sauces

---

KITCHEN TIP

Fresh pasta is perishable, but will keep for a week in the refrigerator, or for up to two months in the freezer. Dried pasta keeps almost indefinitely, but to minimize the loss of riboflavin, purchase pasta in opaque packages, when you can, and store it in your cupboard.

Egg Pasta

Egg pasta or noodles contain more protein, vitamins, minerals, cholesterol, and calories than egg-free varieties. They tend to be sweeter, softer, and stickier so they're delicious in casseroles. Thin egg noodles are common in chicken noodle soup, and the wider varieties work well in sweet dishes such as Kugel.

To provide the benefits of egg noodles without the added cholesterol, manufacturers are making egg noodles using only the egg white.

Just thinking about the various types and shapes of pasta will inspire your creativity. How easy it would be to sauté chopped fresh tomatoes, chopped ripe olives, and minced garlic in a little chicken broth. Top spaghetti with this mixture, and sprinkle the dish with Parmesan cheese. Simple ideas are endless.

When I saw fiochetti (bow ties) on the supermarket shelf the other day, I was inspired to make mushroom pasta. Bow ties will complement mushrooms nicely because both items are delicate. At home, I sautéed sliced porcini and shiitake mushrooms in some homemade vegetable broth, allowed it to *reduce down* (evaporate a little), and poured the sauce over the pasta. (Refer to chapter 7, page 176 to learn how to make vegetable stock, or broth.) The pasta and mushrooms were delicious tossed with a touch of sesame oil, some snow peas, cilantro, and Parmesan cheese. Caramelized onion would be good in that dish, too.

Servings

Plan on cooking at least the entire contents of a box of pasta at a time. Sixteen ounces of dry pasta yields between eight and nine cups of cooked pasta. It varies, because certain shapes absorb more water and expand more than others, but that doesn't matter. Just make enough to enjoy a hearty main dish the day you cook, and hopefully you'll have leftovers for emergency snacks and meals. Plain leftover pasta can also be added to minestrone soup and pasta salads.

You'll want to serve more pasta to each person than the suggested two ounce serving suggested on the box, however. Two ounces only makes one cup of cooked pasta. And everyone, I guarantee—including you—will want second portions of the delicious, nutritious pasta dishes you make.

Water

Most pasta recipes tell you that sixteen ounces of pasta needs six quarts of water, but fortunately you don't need to lug that much to the stove.

Choose the appropriate-size pot, and add enough water to cover the approximate amount of pasta you're going to use. There's no need to measure. Turn the heat on high, and when the water is boiling *rapidly,* add the pasta, turn the heat down, stir once or twice—and you've begun!

Oil

You don't need to add the recommended oil to the water. Oil adds unnecessary calories; one tablespoon contains 120 calories, and pasta won't stick together if you simply give it that quick stir.

Salt

Most recipes say to add salt to the water, but excessive sodium has been linked to high blood pressure, so why add it when it doesn't improve the flavor? I know, some people say that salt keeps the water from boiling over, but it actually increases the boiling point. What it actually does is make the water boil more quickly.

So, unless you can't wait for the water to boil, I advise adding the salt to the sauce, instead of the water; you'll use less and taste it more. Better yet, omit it completely, since we only need one teaspoon of salt per day and most people get more than they need!

Reduced-salt pasta is delicious if you season with zesty ingredients, like onion, garlic, peppers, and herbs instead of salt. Unless you're vigorously exercising in extremely hot weather, you'll get enough salt in your foods by only adding it to dishes when it's needed.

Cooking Time

Without taking a single recipe book off the shelf, it's possible to make a hearty and delicious pasta dish in the time it takes pasta to cook. Most recipes say it takes twelve minutes to cook pasta, but that depends upon how thin or thick the noodles are. Generally speaking, pasta is ready when it looks more translucent than opaque and tastes firm, not pasty or overdone. Angel hair, the thinnest pasta, cooks in a mere one to two minutes. How you like your pasta also affects the cooking time. Some people enjoy their pasta al dente (firm to the bite, or with a little spring and life), because overcooked pasta tends to clump and get sticky. Others like their pasta softer.

There are other variables, too. Pasta cooks slower or more rapidly at different altitudes and in different types of pots. The cooking time also depends upon whether you use whole-grain, durum wheat, spinach, artichoke, enriched white flour, or other varieties of pasta. As you can see, recipes, box directions, and cookbook authors can only approximate how long it's going to take to cook pasta in your pot, on your stove, and to your liking.

I'll always remember Harvey, a man I dated before my marriage, who invited me over for a *gourmet* pasta dinner. I was impressed until he began throwing the noodles against the wall to see if they were too tough, too mushy, or done. I had never heard of that method before, so I politely sat at the kitchen table hoping the gourmet part of the meal would kick in soon! It took twelve throws before one noodle stuck.

To my utter amazement, Harvey never picked up the noodles off the floor, and as I looked around I saw marks all over the walls from his previous pasta dinners. Our relationship, needless to say, didn't last long.

However you test pasta, I don't recommend throwing it against the wall to see if it's done. Taste a small piece and you'll know!

Removing Pasta from the Water

When pasta is cooked to your liking, there are various ways of removing it from the water. You can use a slotted spoon, pour the pasta into a colander and drain, or simply spill the water into the sink, while holding the pasta in the pot with a big spoon.

Don't Rinse Pasta

Unless you're trying to cool a dish down quickly, don't rinse pasta. It stays hotter when you don't run water over it as the box directions suggest. Pasta is supposed to be both hot and starchy.

VALUABLE TIP

When you want to cook pasta ahead of time, and don't want to add sauce or oil to prevent it from sticking, submerge cooked pasta into ice water for a few minutes, drain, and refrigerate. If you do that, it won't turn to cement!

NOW FOR THE SAUCES

It's easy to make delicious low-calorie pasta sauces if you don't add cream, butter, sausage, fatty meats, or unhealthful oil. If you don't purchase items containing more than two grams of fat per serving, you won't need to "fat-bust" your kitchen, because it will already be done!

When serving pasta, use only enough sauce to coat; if you add too much, the pasta becomes rich and soupy. Try various serving styles. Place some sauce in a bowl and top with pasta; mix the pasta with sauce before you serve it; or, if you prefer, top plain pasta with sauce and cheese.

Create Your Own Sauces

There's absolutely no need to simmer pasta sauce on the stove all day, the way we've heard. A delicious green, white, or red sauce can be made in the same amount of time it takes pasta to cook.

PESTO SAUCE

When you're in the mood for something besides a tomato-based sauce here's a clever, exciting way to get dinner on the table in minutes. My husband asks me to make pasta with pesto when he wants to drop a few pounds, and still enjoy a satisfying meal. As far as Robert's concerned, there's nothing better than homemade pesto.

Pesto is not a specific dish, but the name for a paste-style sauce traditionally made by processing herbs, nuts, oil, and Parmesan cheese. Originally pesto was made in a mortar and crushed with a pestle, hence the name *pesto* which means "mashed" or "crushed."

The store-bought pestos taste good, but they contain too much oil and cheese, and therefore more fat than anyone needs. I prefer the clean, low-fat taste of homemade pesto and its brighter, neon-green color. Cooking delicious, healthful food is a precious gift you give yourself and the people you love. (And they'll love this one!)

HOMEMADE PESTO BASICS

Boil some pasta. Then, in a blender, combine virgin olive oil with a small handful of nuts. (Sunflower seeds, almonds, peanuts, macadamia, pine nuts all work well.) Extra-virgin olive oil is so flavorful, it's easy to use a light hand with both the oil and the nuts. Add a little minced garlic, Parmesan cheese, and fill the remainder of the blender with one or two leafy green vegetables—Italian parsley, watercress, cilantro, arugula (a peppery salad green), spinach, or basil. Pulse-blend rapidly again. The mixture should turn into a paste, rather than a liquid. If you can't get the blender going, add a tiny amount of hot water left over from cooking the pasta, instead of adding more oil.

After your chosen pasta shape is cooked to the consistency you like, pour most of the water from the pot, leaving a few tablespoons. Then, add enough pesto to flavor the pasta and provide color. Sprinkle each dish with grated Parmesan cheese, and serve.

One afternoon, a few friends stopped over unexpectedly. They wanted to go out to eat, but since I had lots of organic basil and arugula growing in my garden (my two favorite greens), and boxes of fettuccine in the pantry, I invited them into the kitchen to talk while I made pesto. The only problem, I discovered, was that I didn't have any nuts, and only enough Parmesan cheese to sprinkle on top of each person's plate. It didn't matter. The dish was lower in calories, and everyone thought the results were absolutely scrumptious! Sometimes it's easier and more fun to entertain unexpected guests, because you don't have time to get nervous!

KITCHEN TIP

Parmesan is a full-fat cheese, but a little goes a long way. One tablespoon of grated Parmesan has just fifty calories. There are fat-free varieties available, too. But, if you're freezing pesto, omit the cheese, and if desired fold it in before serving. Pesto stores well in the freezer for up to a year, and in the fridge for up to a month.

Make extra pesto. You might want to brush a thin layer on grilled meats and fish, or stuff chicken with pesto. Pesto is scrumptious on pizza, instead of tomato sauce, especially when you add artichoke hearts. String beans, potatoes, and other cooked vegetables taste delicious when tossed with pesto. Add sliced potatoes to your pesto pasta, or cooked chicken cut into bite-size pieces. Use pesto as a sandwich spread, or hamburger topping. I promise, your friends and family will enjoy anything, and everything, made with pesto. It's incredibly delicious!

One night I came home late from work, and had no idea of what to make. I ended up putting about three tablespoons of store-bought pesto into the blender with a large bag of frozen spinach. When I tasted how good my pesto presto turned out, I even surprised myself!

Try This Guilt-Free, Creamy, White Sauce

To make this creamy sauce, you begin by making a roux. A roux is a thickening agent that can be used to thicken anything that's too liquid, such as gravies, or sauces.

In classical French cooking, a roux is made with equal parts butter and flour.

NUTRITION TIP

Butter and stick margarine contain saturated fat that can clog your arteries. I recommend eliminating them from your diet.

A HEALTHY ROUX

To make a healthful roux, mix equal parts flour and olive oil together. A quarter cup of each works, because a little goes a long way. Use a whisk (a wire beater) to prevent lumps. If you don't have one, a fork works, too.

To flavor this creamy, white sauce, make an onion clouté. An onion clouté is half an onion that's peeled and stuck with whatever seasonings you want to use. I generally use cloves as thumbtacks to hold a couple of bay leaves and fresh herbs in place.

Next, pour skim milk or 1% buttermilk into a saucepan. The amount of sauce you make is determined by the amount of milk you add. Put the onion clouté into the milk and bring it to a gentle boil. Reduce this mixture to a simmer, and remove the onion.

Now, gradually add the roux, a teaspoon at a time, until this delicious sauce reaches the thickness you prefer. Add low-fat ricotta cheese, fat-free Parmesan cheese, spices and herbs—garlic, white pepper, a pinch or two of nutmeg to taste, or whatever you prefer.

> **CREATIVE TIP**
> Baked potatoes, chicken, fish, turkey, or vegetables are also delicious when topped with this low-fat, creamy, white sauce.

A Colorful Idea

To make deliciously flavored, beautifully colored pastas, stir a few tablespoons of curry powder, chili powder, cumin, or turmeric right into the boiling cooking water. These spices smell marvelous while cooking. Turmeric and curry provide a bright golden-yellow pasta; chili and cumin turn the pasta golden brown. Flavored pastas go best with any tomato-free sauce, or even just a little garlic and olive oil topped with Parmesan cheese.

BUILDING A BASIC RED SAUCE

With the exception of my "Guilt-Free, Creamy, White," red tomato-based sauces are less caloric and fatty than the white ones. If a red sauce is too thick, water it down with a bit of wine, the water you used to cook the pasta, or a can of mushrooms with a little of the liquid.

Made in the ways that follow, red pasta sauces are definitely nutritious, delicious, and low in calories.

Try This

To make a delicious, chunky-vegetarian sauce, begin by opening a can of pureed tomatoes. Add a can of cored, peeled tomatoes, and your favorite cut-up vegetables.

You may want to add: chopped onions, bell peppers, sliced mushrooms, garlic (minced, crushed, or sliced), fresh or dried basil and oregano, carrots, zucchini, eggplant, fresh tomatoes, and sliced mushrooms. (It's amazing what you can do with left-over salad ingredients.) Cut the ingredients uniformly, because visually appealing food (made with love) always tastes best! The proportions are unimportant. Just put in larger quantities of the items you enjoy most. Simmer the sauce as long as you want. Then, for zest, spike it with a couple of tablespoons of wine vinegar.

This sauce freezes well and is delicious over just about every food: fish, chicken, eggs, baked potatoes, rice, and of course—pasta.

Pasta Sauce That's Sensational!

To make a smoother tomato-based sauce, sauté about eight cloves of chopped garlic in a small amount of olive oil. Add Contadina tomato sauce (my favorite brand), sliced fresh basil, salt, cayenne pepper, and a little sugar to taste. (See chapter 3, because this sauce is also wonderful on pizza.)

QUICK TIP

For variety, add lean sautéed ground turkey, chicken, or beef to any tomato sauce. Ground turkey should say "all meat" on the label, or the skin may have been added. "The Turkey Store" is a brand I recommend and it's available in most supermarkets, coast to coast. The same low-fat meats can be used to form "meatballs." Season and sauté them in a skillet coated with Pam before adding them to the sauce.

NUTRITION TIP

To purchase beef that's lowest in fat, ask the butcher to grind stewing beef. The fat is trimmed, so it's leaner and less costly than the leanest prepackaged varieties. If your meat department doesn't carry prepackaged turkey or chicken, ask the butcher to grind it for you.

My Favorite Standby

This dish is incredibly easy, yet one of the most delicious. Sauté minced, crushed, or sliced garlic in a little olive oil. Add salt, black pepper, and red pepper. (I keep a ready-made mixture of these Italian seasonings on hand, because I use it often.) Add peeled, or unpeeled, cut-up, fresh tomatoes, a dash of any type of wine or sherry, and if necessary a little water left over from cooking the pasta. (Taste as you go, and always remember to think of water as an ingredient to cook with.)

Eat a portion of this dish the day you make it, refrigerate the rest, and add more fresh or frozen vegetables the next time you eat it to vary the texture and taste.

KITCHEN TIP

It's always optional, but when you want to peel fresh tomatoes effortlessly, plunge them first into boiling water, and then into cold water. The skins will crack and remove easily.

Tomatoes should always be kept on the kitchen counter, because if they're refrigerated they'll lose their flavor.

FATS ARE NOT CREATED EQUAL

Oils are 100 percent fat, but they don't fall into neat *saturated, monounsaturated,* and *polyunsaturated* fat categories. Fats are combinations of these fatty acids, each producing different effects in your body. The least-saturated oils are the more healthful ones, because they don't clog your arteries the way the highly saturated ones do. But remember, all oils are high in calories (one tablespoon contains 120 calories), and a high-fat diet is linked to certain forms of cancer. Although for optimal health, we need oil in our diets (I prefer mine sprinkled over a salad), all oils should be used in moderation!

Whenever you purchase products containing oil, or cooking oils, make sure they are high in *monounsaturated* fat and contain less than 18% *saturated* (unhealthful) fat. That translates into avoiding the less expensive, tropical varieties: cottonseed, palm kernel, and coconut oil.

THE BREAKDOWN ON VEGETABLE OILS

Oils	% Polyunsaturated	% Monounsaturated	% Saturated
Canola	32%	62%	6%
Safflower	75%	12%	9%
Corn	59%	24%	13%
Soybean	59%	23%	13%
Olive Oil	9%	72%	14%
Peanut	32%	46%	17%
Sesame	40%	40%	18%

THE TROPICAL OILS

Oils	% Polyunsaturated	% Monounsaturated	% Saturated
Cottonseed	52%	18%	26%
Palm Kernel	2%	10%	80%
Coconut	2%	6%	87%

The percentages do not add up to 100% because the oils contain other fatlike substances.

In addition, always avoid products that contain *hydrogenated, partially hydrogenated,* or *"one of the following"* oils. (If a product contains a healthful oil, doesn't it make sense that the manufacturer would name it?) Hydrogenation should definitely be avoided. That process solidifies oils, resulting in *trans fatty acids* which increase saturation, and therefore clogs your arteries. In other words, hydrogenated or saturated fats act like cholesterol in the body, so avoid them!

Stick butter and stick margarine are hydrogenated, the tub types are partially hydrogenated, and the liquid varieties are *not* hydrogenated, so they're the least saturated, and therefore the best ones to use. I mentioned, however, that I avoid all types of margarine. In my cooking, I don't need butter or margarine; I prefer the taste of healthful oils. From looking at the previous chart, you'll see that canola, safflower, corn, and soybean are the better choices, so always look for them in the pasta sauces and other products you buy.

Try This

Keep a fifty-fifty mixture of olive and canola oil available in your refrigerator. Olive oil provides the flavor that tastes good with pasta, and canola oil lowers the amount of saturation you're adding to your dishes. Store all cooking oils in the refrigerator, and they'll stay fresh longer.

Nutritionally speaking, extra-virgin, virgin, fine, and ungraded olive oils—produced in France, Italy, Spain, Greece, and California—are no different. These terms relate to the first, second, and third pressings. Extra-virgin olive oil, the most expensive, is minimally processed because it's from the first pressing. Virgin olive oil is the next pressing, and *pommes* (pure or ungraded) olive oil is the last. There are so many grades, because Italians feel the same way about their olive oil as their wine.

When deciding which one to purchase, let your taste and pocketbook be your guide. And, once you become acquainted with various grades of olive oil, you may want to keep more than one in your fridge.

READY-MADE SAUCES

When you're in a rush, you may decide to use a delicious, ready-made, healthful pasta sauce instead of making your own. Hundreds of convenient, ready-made, tomato-based sauces prepared without sugar, salt, and even oil are available. You'll find them on the shelves and refrigerated in the dairy section of your local market, varying in cost from reasonable to pricey.

They're packaged in jars, bottles, microwavable pouches, plastic bags or containers. Whatever your preference, with or without mushrooms, vegetables, or meat, the options are unending.

Manufacturers must list the most prevalent item in a product first, the next most dominant second, and so on. To avoid fat, don't buy products when the first three items listed are cheese, cream, or oil. Remember, cottonseed, palm kernel, and coconut oils cost less, so manufacturers prefer them. If we all boycott products containing hydrogenated or partially hydrogenated vegetable oils, manufacturers will eventually change their ways.

The tomato-based brands I've listed below are all healthful and good tasting, but since some taste better than others, I've indicated {***, **, *} for "Best Tasting Bets." Three stars indicate the best of the best on the chart that follows:

SAUCE RECOMMENDATIONS

Brand	Product	Variations
Cí Bella		No salt, no oil
Classico	Spaghetti Sauce Spicy	Red Pepper, Four Cheeses, Mushrooms, Olives
	Di Napoli	Tomato and Basil
Conca D'oro***	Marinara	Salt added
	Napoletana	No added salt, olives & capers (they contain salt)
	Puttanesca	No added salt, garlic, red chili peppers, capers, anchovy paste
Contadina	Tomato Sauce	No oil
Enrico's	Pasta Sauce	Olive oil
Healthy Choice		No Oil
Hunts Old Country	Spaghetti Sauce With Mushrooms	Soybean & olive oil Soybean & olive oil

SAUCE RECOMMENDATIONS (cont'd)

Brand	Product	Variations
James Darren		Olive oil
Mama Rizzos**	Regular Flavor	Pepper, Mushrooms, Onion
Millina's Finest Organic	Fat Free	No oil
Miur Glen Organic	Low Fat	Canola & olive oil
Miur Glen Organic	Fat Free	No oil, minimum salt
Paul Newman	Marinara	Soybean & olive oil
	Mushroom	Soybean & olive oil
Pritikin Original	Spaghetti Sauce	No oil
Ragú*	Spaghetti Sauce	Olive oil
	Homestyle	Corn oil & mushrooms
	Today's Recipe	Corn oil
	Garden Harvest	Corn oil and salt
	Chunky Mushroom	Corn oil and salt
	Tomato Herb	Corn oil and salt
Trader Joes	Sauce with Mushrooms & Green Peppers	Olive oil
	Sauce Alla Trader Giotto	No Oil

Read the Labels

If you're interested in purchasing a sauce that isn't on the chart, carefully read the label of the brand you're considering to discover the type and amount of oil used.

The amount of salt and sugar is also important, if you have hypertension, diabetes, or if you're trying to lose weight. That's what's great about cooking without recipes; you can adapt any dish to your needs.

For the average healthy person, a safe and adequate amount of salt is 1,100 to 3,300 milligrams per day (2,000 milligrams of salt equals 1 teaspoon).

Improvise Your Favorite Pasta Dish

About once a month I used to go out of my way to stop by a little restaurant in Westwood Village, California, to eat my favorite pasta, shrimp, and scallop dish. Then, one day, I peeked into their kitchen and saw how much salt and oil the chef added. Since the dish is made fresh, I asked him to leave out the oil, and reduce the salt in the preparation of my food. Most chefs will accommodate a patron's needs.

I enjoyed this dish so much, I decided to make a healthier version at home. By cooking the seafood in ready-made, fat-free spaghetti sauce, adding baked eggplant—a favorite ingredient of mine—and lots of garlic and sweet basil to make up for the loss of flavor from taking out the fat, I created a more delicious dish than the restaurant version I had loved. I felt lighter getting up from the table, too.

MORE INGREDIENTS TO HAVE FUN WITH

Sun-Dried Tomatoes

If you have an abundance of red ripe tomatoes, and some time, it's fun to make your own sun-dried tomatoes. Roma tomatoes are best, but all varieties—except cherry tomatoes—work well.

Thinly slice fresh tomatoes, remove the seeds, and roast them in a 200-degree oven for about four hours, or until dry. Store them in olive oil, and refrigerate them. The tomatoes and the oil are extremely flavorful, and since the store-bought varieties are pricey, making your own saves money.

Garlic

Numerous studies indicate that garlic may protect against heart disease and stroke. There are also reports of its antibiotic powers, ability to lower blood pressure, and its anticancer activity.

To bake one or more whole bulbs of garlic, remove the outer layers of skin, and cut the pointed end off each bulb. Pour a few drops of olive oil into the cut end, and sprinkle it with a little kosher salt, pureed basil (available in jars in the market) or whatever seasonings you prefer. Wrap each garlic head in foil and place them in the oven on a baking sheet, for about forty minutes at 350 degrees.

When baked, liberally spread the garlic on a thick slice of warm bakery bread. It's also delicious in hot or cold pasta dishes, and "to die for" mixed into mashed potatoes. If you place leftover roasted garlic in plastic bags and seal them, they'll keep in the refrigerator for a week.

To save energy, bake garlic when you're lighting the oven to make something else. Sometimes I put an eggplant in the oven, at the same time as garlic, to serve over pasta with marinara sauce later that week.

Blanched garlic also tastes great in pasta. Place peeled cloves into boiling water for two to three minutes, remove, and slice. Prepared this way, garlic is very strong, so use it moderately— especially if you have a date that night!

Ethnic Noodles

You don't have to travel overseas for exotic items if you peruse the Asian section of the market for unusual items. Boiled rice noodles are delicious with shrimp, and tossed with a little sesame oil and curry. Chinese lo mein (soft noodles) are wonderful pan fried in very little oil, plain or topped with oyster sauce. (Some say that this Chinese noodle topped with a meat mixture was the first spaghetti.) Flat little squares of pasta can be made into *Potstickers* (dumplings) when filled with any meat mixture. To secure the filling, fold all four corners toward the center, like a baby's diaper. Then sauté quickly, or steam. (See chapter 6, page 155 for details.)

The Japanese often make spaghetti with various types of noodles, curry sauce, shredded beef, mushrooms, and bell peppers when they want a quick bite. *Soba* are handmade buckwheat noodles, *udon* are thick, round wheat noodles, and, my personal favorite, *somen* are thin wheat noodles. You may enjoy *somen* hot or cold, topped with sliced red cabbage and tahini-miso-peanut sauce. To make the sauce, simply blend equal amounts of tahini and miso with peanut butter, add a touch of water, a little lemon juice, soy sauce, grated fresh ginger, and scallions to taste.

Herbs and Spices

Don't season the dishes you make with only salt and pepper. Try a variety of herbs and spices, and if you don't know their names, don't worry. If an herb smells as though it would enhance a dish, rub it between your fingers, into the palm of your hand, or shred it with a knife, and add it into a portion of the dish. Sometimes I add a seasoning directly into the pot, but when I'm unsure, I put a few spoonfuls of whatever I'm making into a cup, add the seasoning in question, and taste the dish. If the seasoning fights the flavors I'm using, I put it aside. If it enhances them, I add more to the batch. Remember, what you leave out is always as important as what you put in!

When I'm surfing the TV channels, I stop immediately when I catch the late Bob Ross, a cable-TV artist, whose credo was, "Artists don't make mistakes, they just make happy accidents." He created gorgeous landscapes by tapping dark colors against light and playing with textures. "In your world," he advised, "it's up to you to decide where the trees belong."

As I watched Bob's thirty-minute programs, as he changed the flavor of his painting with shades of colors using a two-inch brush, I'm always convinced I can paint. And the very next day I am an artist discovering whether or not oils and acrylics work together harmoniously on my painting.

Cooking is no different. Just as artists mix paints on their palettes, to see which colors their paintings need, cooks use their noses and palates when deciding which herbs and spices to use. Playing with seasonings is the same as painting with colors because both allow you to explore new frontiers. Look at herbs and spices as you would crayons when drawing a picture. Choose your flavors. Select various textures and colors. Mix, match, and combine them. Ask yourself, what does this dish need? Artists, musicians, and creative cooks are inquisitive, ingenious, and inventive.

When cooking, you're merely creating your interpretation of a particular dish, not reinventing the wheel, so don't hesitate to mix and match herbs and spices from various cuisines. If you add basil to pasta, why not add curry or cilantro, too? I didn't warm up to cilantro for a long time, but now I crave its flavor and, as you'll see throughout this book, I think it enhances food beautifully.

PURCHASE HERBS IN SMALL QUANTITIES

Even if you keep your dried herbs in a dark place and cover them tightly, they can get stale and lose their flavor after six to twelve months on the shelf. You'll know when to replace them; if they're stale, they won't smell potent.

Except for curry, garlic, onion, turmeric, and cumin powder, I use fresh herbs almost exclusively. They're more flavorful, more fun to use, and less costly in the long run.

An excellent cook I know thought herbs needed to *stew,* or cook for a long time, to bring out their flavor. Then he realized he enjoyed the taste of a dish more when he tasted it at the *beginning* of the cooking process instead of at the end. He began adding the herbs toward the end of the cooking time, and his food began tasting more flavorful. I suggest you do the same!

TO STORE HERBS

Wrap any leftover fresh herbs in a damp paper towel and keep them in the refrigerator to preserve their freshness as long as possible. Fresh herbs should be used within five days, or they'll lose their potency and wilt. If you have fresh herbs on hand you're not ready to use, rinse, dry, and place them in airtight plastic bags, and then freeze them for future use. (See chapter 4, page 106, to learn how to dry herbs in the microwave.)

Herbs and other condiments can change the complexion of a dish completely. Have fun, you can't go wrong!

Put the following herbs on your artist's palette, mix and match them, and you'll find they're delicious in any pasta dish:

capers	Italian parsley	peppercorns
cayenne pepper	marjoram	pepper flakes
cilantro	onion	shallots
garlic	oregano	thyme

Torn basil and thyme sprinkled over a pile of pasta adorns every dish beautifully, but, to be honest, the seasonings I decide to use mainly depend upon what's available in my garden, or fridge. Seriously consider growing your own fresh herbs. (See chapter 7, page 217, for details.)

QUICK TIP

Basil is best when the leaves are dark green and the stems aren't black at the ends.

Great Gifts

It's simple to flavor all types of vinegar, so there's no need to purchase "designer" vinegars. Create mild, peppery, or sweet flavors by dropping garlic, tarragon, rosemary, shallots, leeks, onions, peppers, peppercorns, or any other flavorful ingredient into a bottle of vinegar. Simply refrigerate a few days before using, and shake well. If you're giving this as a gift, be certain to use a pretty bottle.

SAFETY TIP

Do not bottle flavored oils, because they can carry botulism. To infuse oil with flavor, heat garlic and herbs in oil, strain, and use immediately. Discard whatever you don't use!

PAULA HATES CLEANUP

My friend Paula, the one who loves to eat but doesn't enjoy cooking, also hates cleanup! She'll do anything to get out of cleaning pots and pans.

Paula was trying to save time, and since she's ecologically minded, she took my suggestion and baked a whole eggplant in an oven-safe dish while she was roasting six large baking potatoes. She had everything right, except one small detail: She forgot to prick the potato and eggplant skins with a fork. You can imagine what happened. It took her two hours to clean up the explosion. (Too bad her dog, Beau, doesn't like eggplant!)

Paula had to order takeout that night for the family, but promised not to retire from cooking just yet. The next day she baked an eggplant again, and you can bet she remembered to prick the skin before putting it in the oven. After it cooled, she peeled it, added it to a ready-made spaghetti sauce, and poured the combination over hot pasta for a delicious dish without much cleanup.

FEARLESS DISHES IN ONE POT

If you hate washing dishes, and like to cook quickly, too, "one-pot pasta" is the answer for you.

Easy Cleanup

Boil water, and add a few chicken breasts to the pot. It doesn't matter if the ribs are attached, or not.

While the chicken is cooking, cut up three or four of your favorite vegetables. (I like zucchini, carrots, snow peas, and mushrooms.) Cut on the diagonal; carrots and zucchini look more appealing that way. When the chicken turns white, or opaque, remove it from the pot with a slotted spoon and allow it to cool in a bowl. Shred it into a serving bowl, or cut it into bite-sized pieces, removing the skin and bones.

Place the vegetables, one variety at a time, in a strainer and cook them to your liking in the same pot of boiling water. (When the colors become brighter, the vegetables are cooked al dente, but you may prefer them softer.) Add the vegetables to the bowl.

Cook the shape of pasta you prefer in the same hot water in the pot and when cooked, add it to the chicken and vegetables in the bowl. A ready-made ginger and soy sauce-based dressing accompanies this dish beautifully. This dish is delicious when served at room temperature or cold.

PASTA-SALAD POSSIBILITIES

Sometimes the hardest thing to decide is whether to eat your pasta hot or cold, it's so delicious both ways. But when I'm in the mood for cold food I always think of pasta salads, because they're the easiest dishes to improvise.

When you're served a delicious pasta salad at your friends' house, a restaurant, or if you see a good-looking one in the deli case somewhere, examine it. Ask for a taste, and then when you're in the mood, experiment incorporating your tastes and style. Just by cutting the vegetables differently—chunky or thin, straight or on the diagonal—changes the complexion of a pasta salad completely. Make any pasta salad you admire more delicious, freestyle!

Ingredients from Your Kitchen

Now take a look at the ingredients in your refrigerator, freezer, and cupboard, and think about what type of pasta you're in the mood to eat. You may see these items: grated Parmesan cheese, mozzarella cheese, cooked chicken, seafood, cooked lean ground beef, leftover turkey, marinated mushrooms, artichoke hearts or bottoms, capers, broccoli, carrots, steamed zucchini or eggplant (cut julienne or matchstick style), fresh basil, onions, shallots, every-color bell pepper (red, green, yellow, or purple), and every type of olive—Italian, Greek (green, or black).

Quiet your mind, and you'll soon begin seeing food in the same way a chef does. Remember, there's no need to measure, or worry about proportions. Just add ingredients you think will complement your pasta salad. These ingredients are foolproof, so add them in the quantity and combination you prefer. The more often you cook creatively, the easier it becomes. In no time at all, you'll be making mouthwatering pasta salads, without ever opening a cookbook.

String beans, sautéed eggplant, pine nuts—or any variety of nut for that matter—will add flavor and color to your dishes. Just thinking about penne (my second-favorite pasta shape), beans, olives, artichoke hearts, and basil makes me want to go into the kitchen and whip up something for lunch. Thank goodness I cook with healthful ingredients and use the techniques I've been telling you about, because I've never missed a meal while writing this book!

Combinations That Work

Try This

Toss cooked pasta with a little olive oil and rice-wine vinegar. To make a delicious pasta salad, add cut-up pieces of skim-milk mozzarella cheese, and a can of your favorite beans (drained garbanzo or kidney beans work well). Add olives, artichokes, hearts of palm, some cut-up fresh tomato, and basil. Or, substitute any ingredient you like. I try to keep a supply of this dish in the fridge, because my daughter, Chelsea, and her friends thoroughly enjoy it as an after-school snack.

Try This

I like to ask famous chefs what they concoct when they get hungry while relaxing at home. Gray Clauson, the executive chef at the Bel Air Hotel in California, tosses pasta with leftover pesto, salmon pieces, garlic, olive oil, Parmesan cheese, and lots of fresh cilantro. He says he enjoys this dish hot or cold.

Try This

In a bowl, mix two teaspoons of olive oil with two teaspoons of red-wine vinegar. Add chopped fresh basil leaves, a teaspoon of Dijon mustard, toss with hot pasta, and add kosher salt and freshly ground pepper to taste. Then, depending upon your mood and what's in the house, add any or all of the following ingredients: bell pepper, chopped sun-dried tomatoes, fresh tomatoes, pitted Greek olives, Parmesan cheese, feta cheese, capers, artichokes, chopped green onions.

I'm sure you can come up with additional ingredients I've never thought of.

Try This

Toss pasta, goat cheese, pine nuts, and sun-dried tomatoes in a ready-made Italian vinaigrette dressing for an Italian salad.

Try This

Fusilli (corkscrew-shaped pasta), feta cheese, and kalamata olives taste great with your favorite Caesar dressing.

Try This

Pasta (any shape), roasted eggplant, tomatoes, fresh mozzarella, basil, capers, and olives tossed with French vinaigrette dressing for a Middle Eastern pasta dish.

PASTA-SALAD DRESSINGS

Any dressings you make or "doctor" for a tossed or composed salad will also taste good on pasta salads. (Turn to chapter 4, page 103, for more tips and ideas.)

Don't hesitate about using one of the many ready-made healthful varieties of salad dressings on your favorite pasta salad. Your personal preference determines which dressing to use on which dish. Vinaigrettes or ginger and soy sauce-based dressings taste great with every type of pasta.

Try This

To make a light dressing that goes well on any pasta salad, mix a little olive oil, rice wine, balsamic, and red-wine vinegar with some minced garlic, salt, and pepper to taste.

FROZEN ASSETS

When used to its utmost advantage, the freezer is one of the best time-saving, labor-saving devices available. It gives you time away from the kitchen with more energy for whatever brings you pleasure. Freezer meals take no additional shopping, and only a little more chopping.

If you haven't thought ahead, use the microwave to defrost food before cooking. When baking food that's still partially frozen, allow extra time in the oven.

- Freeze single portions of leftover pasta for times when you don't want to cook.
- Freeze pasta with sauce, and add different vegetables before reheating. Frozen vegetables are no less nutritious than fresh ones that have been transported. Locally grown produce, in season, is still the best choice, so whenever possible, purchase produce at your local farmer's market. It's amazing how much better organic produce tastes!
- Freeze little packages of cooked, lean meats. Serve a vegetarian-style pasta meal one night, and add turkey, chicken, or beef to the dish the next day.
- Freeze homemade vegetable and chicken broth in ice-cube trays. Pop a cube into your skillet whenever you want to sauté without butter.
- Herbs and spices stay potent longer if stored in the freezer.
- Whenever you cook dishes that freeze well, prepare duplicates in freezer-to-oven dishes. It's just as easy to prepare two or three lasagnas, for example, as one. Lasagna freezes best after being cooked first.
- When you're in the mood for a home-cooked meal but don't feel like cooking, take a ready-made dish out of the freezer in the morning and stick it in the refrigerator. It will thaw and be ready to heat that night. Don't thaw foods on the kitchen counter, however, or unwanted organisms may grow.

QUICK PASTA DISHES

When you feel like a pasta meal, it's possible to eat almost immediately without doing anything fancy. I consider it fast food.

Try This

Here's another oil-free pasta dish that only takes ten minutes to make. And you don't have to open any cans. Sauté six to eight peeled, diced tomatoes in a little homemade or store-bought defatted chicken or vegetable broth. It's not necessary to peel the tomatoes, but I like them that way. Add fresh or store-bought minced garlic, shredded fresh basil and/or oregano to taste. Simmer, and spike the sauce with a little red-wine vinegar and red-pepper flakes to taste.

Try This

To prepare a delicious lasagna casserole quickly, use corrugated noodles; they don't need precooking. To begin, oil a casserole and, in any order, layer the dry noodles, marinara or meat sauce, drained cored canned tomatoes, olives, vegetables, and cheese.

Low-fat mozzarella, ricotta, and Parmesan-Reggiano complement lasagna beautifully. For a creamy effect, try mixing a couple of tablespoons of the healthful Alfredo sauce (discussed earlier in this chapter, on page 123), or plain low-fat ricotta cheese mixed with a red sauce.

Make sure you add enough liquid to this dish to steam the noodles thoroughly. Cover the casserole with aluminum foil, and bake for about forty-five minutes.

Easy Manicotti

To make this delicious dish, stuff the largest raw noodles you can find with a mixture of the following ingredients: low-fat ricotta cheese, firm tofu, plain nonfat yogurt, grated part-skim mozzarella, snipped parsley, Italian herbs, red-pepper flakes, and fresh basil to taste.

Lightly oil a casserole dish, pour a layer of your favorite ready-made pasta sauce on the bottom. Place the stuffed manicotti on top. Add more sauce, cover with foil, poke a few holes in the foil, and bake for about fifty minutes at 350 degrees, or until the noodles are soft.

Pasta and Broccoli

To put these perfect partners together, cook your favorite type of pasta. Meanwhile, in a skillet, simmer several fresh cloves of garlic in olive oil and steam broccoli *flowerets* to desired tenderness. Pour the oil and garlic over the pasta, add fresh lemon juice to taste. Stir in the broccoli, and toss.

For a Different Taste

To make an unusual pasta dish, place a little olive oil, capers, tomatoes, onion, and boneless sardines in the bottom of an ovenproof baking dish, and bake. Top with cooked pasta, and toss. Robert Morley says, "No man is lonely while eating spaghetti." I think he's right!

Try This

If you don't feel like assembling food at the last minute, toss some cooked pasta with a little olive oil or ready-made spaghetti sauce while it's still hot, and refrigerate. When you're ready to eat, merely sauté some scallops and shrimp, and most of the work is already done. Microwave the pasta, top with the sautéed shellfish, and sprinkle a little Parmesan cheese on top.

NUTRITION TIP

Shrimp is high in cholesterol, 150 milligrams in a 3½-ounce serving, but it's still a good food. Shrimp is low in calories, and the same serving only contains 0.3 grams of saturated fat.

The American Heart Association recommends keeping your cholesterol intake under 300 milligrams a day.

This is Fast and Delicious

Cut bread into one-inch squares, toss them into warm olive oil that has been infused with fresh garlic cloves. Mix the bread cubes with pasta and diced red-ripe tomatoes. You could add diced red onion, capers, chopped parsley, cilantro, peeled and diced cucumber, kosher salt, freshly ground black pepper, red wine or balsamic vinegar. Make it as simple or complex as you like; either way you can't go wrong.

Try This

My husband makes kugel (a noodle dish, traditionally made with eggs and cheese), but his version is healthful. He adds a mixture of five egg whites, two cups of nonfat milk, nonfat cottage cheese (or a little low-fat ricotta), to cooked egg fettuccine, linguini, or whichever pasta shape we have on hand. He always adds yellow raisins (or black), and cinnamon. When he wants a crunchier texture, he adds nuts as well. I like this dish hot after it has been baked for forty-five minutes at 350 degrees and lightly browned on top. It's also delicious served cold the next day!

PASTA MEAL EXTRAORDINAIRE!

Have you ever seen a plant that was colored wrong, or a tree, flower, or fern in a forest that looked as though it didn't belong? I had the privilege of walking through a rain forest in Australia once, where one tree was growing out of another, every plant was colored beautifully and placed exactly where it should be. Nothing seemed out of place, because with nature everything goes together. The same theory applies to cooking. It's easy to combine ingredients together tastefully, because all food comes from nature.

When making a pasta meal, strive for integrity rather than perfection, and nothing much can go wrong! I guess you could overcook the pasta, but you won't if you taste it periodically. If it overcooks, because you forgot it on the stove, save it for the dog, and cook some more.

I suppose you could add a dressing you don't like, but you won't if you taste it first. You could drown the pasta in dressing, but that won't matter, either. Knowing you, you'll use your noodle, and add more pasta to cut the amount of dressing down.

When you want to turn a simple pasta dish into a special meal, begin by serving a *bruschetta*-type (peasant bread) appetizer. To make this extra-special treat, purchase a crusty Italian or French baguette from your local specialty bakery and cut it into slices on the diagonal. Make an olive oil, garlic, fresh tomato, basil combination, and brush it on the little slices. Place them on a cookie sheet, and broil them for about eight minutes, or until hot.

Then, light a candle and offer your friends some *San Pelegrino* (Italian mineral water), beer, or wine. Are those ideas too simple? Serve some rapini (Italian broccoli) steamed and then sautéed in a little olive oil and garlic. Your guests will say, *"Brava!"*

In Italy, before dessert, a salad usually concludes the meal. Serve a fresh mozzarella and tomato salad, or tossed green. (See chapter 4, page 91, for ideas.) You'll learn how to make an incredibly refreshing, Italian-style dressing.

I recommend a light dessert of fruit and cheese, or serve lemon ice in a cantaloupe's scooped-out rind, along with a few chocolate-dipped *biscotti* (Italian biscuit cookies) and a cup of freshly brewed, Italian coffee. (See chapter 11, for more dessert ideas.) That's all it takes to make an incredibly delicious pasta meal extraordinaire. And, who knows, maybe before you entertain next time, you'll make one or two unique "go-withs" for your guests after reviewing the next chapter.

CHAPTER 6

◆

"Go-Withs": Unique Extras Make the Difference

"Cooking is like love. It should be entered into with abandon or not at all."

—Harriet Van Horne

Have you ever had a dining experience where every dish was "ho-hum" except one? And then that unique "go-with," or side dish, with its bang-up flavor, interesting texture, and colorful appearance turned the entire meal into a celebration?

I was at a Greek restaurant for a business meeting, and just after we sat down, the waiter placed eggplant, sweet potato, and hummus spreads on our table. Although the entire meal was well prepared, everyone agreed that the appetizers "broke the ice," made the process of ordering more relaxing, and that made the meal more special.

If I were a restaurateur, I'd place signature spreads, dips, finger foods, sauces, stuffing, or unique little extras on every customer's table free of charge. I'd use marinades to make the flavor of the dishes I served stand out. These extra touches wouldn't be expensive, but they would surprise! Aren't you elated when a waiter surprises you with a little "taste" of something unique to begin or end a meal—even when you didn't order it? (We all want to believe unsolicited calories don't count!)

EXPERIMENT: "YOU CANNOT LEARN LESS"

Serving unique extras at home creates that same comfortable feeling, so I began putting together some "go-withs." I improvised the spreads I had tasted, and created different "go-withs" after analyzing ingredients and considering whether or not the perceived results were worth the time, effort, and expense I'd incur. It was a bit tricky at first, but the more I experimented, the easier it became.

I listened to the intuition that spoke inside me while I purchased ingredients at the market, and cooked at home. Sometimes that voice, or my subconscious mind, with its ideas and inspiration, came from my head; other times it emanated from my heart. Once in a while, my stomach growled fiercely and told me exactly what to do!

The key is figuring out what will taste good without using up your calorie allotment for the day, or too much of your precious time and energy. Some experiments will work out, and others won't, but you'll learn more either way.

I like to think of what Buckminster Fuller, the inventor who became famous for designing geodesic domes, once said: "There are a number of very important irreversibles to be discovered in our universe. One of them is that every time you make an experiment you learn more quite literally, *you cannot learn less.*"

SPREADS

In addition to enjoying cooking for the creative process, spreads and other dishes always turn out more to your liking when you follow concepts, or strategies, instead of recipes. You may love garlic, olives, or cilantro and put a lot of them into your dish. Or you may not like garlic, or some other ingredient, and decide to leave it out completely.

"Go-withs" spark up any meal, because mixing traditional with unique makes every occasion more eclectic. Now put on your creative hat, *spread* your wings, and improvise little extras to surprise your family and friends. Use the ideas that follow for inspiration.

Eggplant Spread

Grandma-ma Sultana made this dish for me when I was only eight, and I remember liking it. I guess I've always had a taste for the unusual!

Wash an eggplant, prick it several times with a fork, and bake it for about forty-five minutes—as you would a potato. Allow it to cool, mash it with a potato masher or fork, add some minced garlic and onion, a little virgin olive oil, a dash of lemon juice, salt and pepper to taste. Place this spread in a bowl or platter. Decorate it with olives, green onion, and cilantro or parsley, and serve with dark bread. (My daughter looked at this dish and said she'd never eat it. Then she tasted it and could barely stop.)

Sweet-Potato Spread

To make your meal more sensual and exciting, blend together the following ingredients: baked sweet potato, fresh ginger, onion powder, garlic powder, a few drops of water, and a little sesame oil. Serve in a little pot or dish alongside your favorite crackers.

Hummus Spread

You don't need measurements to make hummus. Drain a can of garbanzo beans and puree with a little of the liquid. Add some miso, a little olive oil, cumin, salt, and garlic (I like a lot). Add red or yellow bell pepper for color and variation. Garnish with a little paprika, chopped parsley, cilantro, or Greek olives.

This spread is great on pita wedges, sliced veggies, or add a little more liquid and it becomes a great dip with chips.

On Halloween, blend in some grilled red pepper or sun-dried tomatoes and the dip turns orange. Add a few drops of red food coloring and it will turn red for Valentine's Day. Add some green food coloring for St. Patrick's Day. Or, why not place one dish of hummus sprinkled with cilantro and another with paprika side by side on Christmas?

Make Babaganoush

Try mixing the eggplant spread with the plain hummus for *babaganoush,* a famous Mediterranean spread.

Olive Tapenade

If you like olives, this *tapenade* or pungent olive spread is for you. In a food processor fitted with a metal blade, combine drained, sliced, ripe black pitted olives, capers, and a little olive oil. You could also add green olives, anchovies, sun-dried tomatoes, and basil! Process until finely chopped, serve at room temperature and spread on your favorite crackers or crunchy bread.

Try This

I tried this one day when I was thinking about how I like anchovies blended in Caesar dressing a lot more than when they're sitting on top of the salad, whole. (I think about things like that.) I blended anchovies, a little lemon juice, Parmesan cheese, and black olives. Spread this paste on baguettes—sliced on the bias—top with a piece of Buffalo Mozzarella cheese, a small slice of tomato, and a beautiful fresh basil leaf. (See chapter 4, page 102 for more information about this cheese.) Sometimes it's interesting where the inspiration for a dish comes from!

DIPS

A dip adds flavor to food by coating it, and, just as the name implies, you *dip* or dunk your food into dips. Dips are more fluid, and have less body than spreads.

Artichoke Dip

This dip is perfect for large parties. Drain water-packed artichoke hearts and cut them into big chunks. Add equal parts of fat-free mayonnaise and freshly grated Parmesan cheese. Pour this mixture into an oiled baking dish, and bake at 350 degrees for about thirty minutes, or until hot and bubbly. Sprinkle olive slices, or cilantro on top, and serve hot alongside slices of baguette, fresh vegetable slices, or tortilla chips. (If you have a fondue dish, dig it out to keep the dip hot!)

Try This

Place a tall glass overflowing with fresh bell pepper, carrot, celery sticks, and jicama on the table alongside a little dish containing about two to three tablespoons of balsamic vinegar, virgin olive oil, and seasonings such as thyme, basil, oregano, salt and pepper to taste.

INTERESTING TIP

Jicama is a slightly sweet, white, crunchy root vegetable that takes on the flavor of the dip or dressing it accompanies.

Use Dip to Make Cheese Bread

I brush a mixture of balsamic vinegar, olive oil, and seasonings (or any balsamic-based salad dressing), on French bread, cut lengthwise, place slices of cheese on top, and broil it until bubbly. It makes every meal more interesting.

Layered Mexican-Style Dip

To make a layered dip, oil a glass bowl or baking dish and spread a layer of refried pinto or black beans. Add a layer of nonfat sour cream, a layer of guacamole, spicy salsa, chopped cilantro, basil, or olives. A layer of Mexican rice somewhere along the way might be nice. Add chopped onion, grated cheddar, feta, Jack, or goat cheese, too. Layer however you like, the options are endless! (See chapter 10, pages 258 and 274 for more information about refried beans and guacamole.)

You can serve this dip at room temperature, or heat it in a 350-degree oven for about ten minutes, or until the cheese starts to melt. Either way, serve this dip alongside a big bowl of tortilla chips.

FINGER FOODS

Why do we like finger foods so much? Perhaps it's the tactile, toddlerlike experience of eating with our hands. Wouldn't it be interesting to serve an entire dinner that required no silverware? Some of the foods might be folded like little packages, they'd be easy to pick up and bite-sized so you could pop them into your mouth. On the other hand, if the finger foods are meant merely to whet your guests' appetites and alert them to what's coming, serve only enough to pique their interest!

Banana-Chicken Appetizers

This will stimulate your guests' appetites. Purchase boned and skinned chicken strips—the type available for fajitas. Marinate the chicken in any Italian or oriental salad dressing for an hour or more. Wrap each piece around a chunk of banana, insert a wooden skewer, and broil or barbecue. These will disappear quickly, and everyone will ask for more!

Try This

Pour a jar of dry-roasted, salted nuts on a cookie sheet, sprinkle them with a little water and then a combination of onion, garlic, and red chili powders. Just about every powdered spice would work to season these nuts.

If you want more spice, add cayenne pepper. Shake the pan, so the nuts roll around, and roast them on a low heat, about 250 degrees for ten to fifteen minutes or so. They'll become soft, and then crunchy again as soon as they cool. Serve them with your favorite beer or sodas.

Snack on Soybeans from the Pod

Soybeans in the pod are a little hard to find. Because they haven't become popular in the United States, I buy them whenever I see them. They look just like pea pods, but taste better. All you have to do is rinse and boil them in salted water for about fifteen minutes, or until slightly tender. Eat as you go, removing them from the pod, like peanuts.

Roasted Soybeans

Rinse some soybeans, remove them from the pod, and spread them out in a shallow pan. Turn the oven on high, about 425 degrees, and allow the beans to roast about fifteen to twenty minutes, or until brown. (Watch them carefully, because they can burn quickly.) Sprinkle with salt—plain or seasoned—and start snacking!

NUTRITION TIP

Soybeans are exceptional in several ways. Approximately 34% of their calories come from protein, and they are rich in a unique group of cancer fighters called phyto-chemicals, found in plant foods.

Italian Olives

To start, purchase a jar of pitted green olives, and pour out most of the juice. Add a mixture of olive oil, minced garlic, and your favorite herbs to the jar—thyme, oregano, and rosemary—it's your call. Allow the olives to marinate at least three hours. These marinated olives taste good alone, on pasta, antipasto salads, or mini-pizzas.

Mini-Pizzas for Unexpected Guests

Every once in a while you need an instant fancy appetizer— a real crowd pleaser. Friends drop in unexpectedly, they don't leave, everyone gets hungry, and you ask them to stay. Now what? If you keep foods stockpiled in the pantry and freezer, you have a trick up your sleeve that makes spontaneous entertaining easier, and more fun.

From now on, whenever you make homemade pizza (see page 72), make extra dough for appetizer-sized pizzas. You can use a round cookie cutter to cut the dough, or, if you don't have one, the top of a drinking glass is fine. Brush a little sauce on top (don't add anything else), and "underbake" the baby piz-zas slightly, before freezing them. They'll stay good for up to six months.

When you're ready to serve, place the mini-pizzas on a cookie sheet, brush them with pizza sauce again, add cheese, peppers, olives, anything you like, and bake them for about five minutes, or until they're hot and fully cooked. Everyone will be impressed!

Stuffed Mushrooms

Have you noticed how the "stuff" that gets stuffed into food can make or break a meal? It's like opening a Christmas present from a handsome man you've been dating for a year and a half. It's a disappointment to get a kitchen utensil, even if you love to cook, if you were hoping for an engagement ring.

To make mushrooms that don't disappoint, purchase about four large button mushrooms for each person you're serving, plus six extra mushrooms. Wipe them with a damp cloth, remove and chop the stems.

Heat a skillet, add some olive oil, sauté some chopped onion, mint, and the chopped mushroom. Cool this mixture, add bread crumbs, some Parmesan cheese, if you like that taste, chopped cilantro or parsley, a little chicken broth, salt and pepper to taste.

Stuff the mushroom caps with this mixture, bake till hot, and serve directly from the oven.

Beyond the Button

This is extremely easy, yet makes a spectacular side dish with a rich earthy flavor and meaty texture. Brush portobello mushrooms with olive oil, maybe a little garlic and salt, and grill them until tender.

"Potstickers": Pan-Fried Steamed-Dumpling Surprise

These little packages are usually eaten as appetizers, but with salad, or rice on the side, my family makes them a meal.

Make the filling by mixing ground chicken or turkey with finely chopped onion, garlic, and julienned cabbage, bell pepper, carrots, mushrooms, and chilies. Add soy sauce, a little sesame oil, and cilantro—if you have it on hand (substitute parsley when you don't).

Wrappers specifically made for potstickers are available in most supermarkets and Chinese specialty shops. They're called won ton or *Nasoya* egg-roll wrappers. Any brand is good.

Moisten the edge of each wrapper, one at a time, place a teaspoon of the raw filling in the center, and firmly press the edges together.

To cook these little packages, heat a skillet, add oil, and begin browning them. Turn, and stack them around the outer edge of the pot. Now, add a little water in the center of the pot, a few teaspoons at a time. Cover and steam until the potstickers are fully cooked. Remove them carefully so that these potstickers won't *stick to the pot*! Provide each person with a little bowl containing the dipping sauce, suggested below.

SAUCES

When making a sauce, think of it as an accompaniment. It should act as a companion that complements, but it should never overbear. Fool around with the ideas that follow.

Potsticker Dipping Sauce

Blend soy sauce, water, miso, fresh ginger, and garlic. Add cilantro and a little sesame oil, too, if you'd like. (I enjoy this dipping sauce on fish and rice, as well!)

For another taste, put out some Chinese mustard with the sauce. My daughter likes dipping her potstickers into plain rice-wine vinegar.

Paula's Barbecue Sauce

Paula taught me how to make this easy, versatile barbecue sauce after she basted her Thanksgiving turkey with it last year. She combined soy sauce with a little sugar, added some ketchup, chopped garlic, a little balsamic vinegar, and pepper to taste.

The turkey was incredibly delicious basted with this sauce, and I guess her dog Beau liked it, *too*. After dinner, as we were eating dessert outside, we looked up and saw him running across the yard with the entire carcass hanging from his mouth.

Paula and her family were looking forward to leftovers, so she cooked another turkey the next day. This time she added A.1. and Worcestershire sauce to the above combination and said it was even better. (Beau couldn't reach it!)

Basting Sauces

Thin your favorite flavor of jam or jelly with your favorite flavor of juice (I like apricot with orange), and brush it on meat during the last five minutes of cooking. This is a great idea for anything grilled.

Two More Quick, Easy, and Delicious Ideas

Baste poultry with apricot jam mixed with crushed pineapple and French dressing, or your favorite barbecue sauce mixed with crushed pineapple.

Impress Your Guests with Papaya/Mango Salsa

Make this papaya/mango salsa for your guests, and they'll always remember your dinner party. This sauce is wonderful on or alongside beans and corn tortillas, grilled chicken, or

Cajun fish. (I use Chef Paul Prudhomme's seasoning for blackened redfish, but always substitute olive oil for the butter he
suggests on the box.)

Even if you don't have papaya and mango at the same time,
you can make this salsa by combining the following: diced papaya and/or mango, peeled cucumber, tomato, white vinegar,
a little sugar, cilantro, and your favorite herbs and spices. Use
your fertile imagination, and you may even surprise yourself.

My Honey's Cranberry Sauce

Over the years, my husband has made this "go-with" differently each time, and it has always been good. To start, heat a
pot of water on the stove, and wash fresh cranberries. Add the
cranberries to the pot, stir, and they will begin popping. (Robert
says that process will make the skins softer.) At this point, he
adds seeded oranges or tangerines, with their juice, some water,
and white or brown sugar to taste. Add lemon juice, chunks of
fresh or canned pineapple, raisins or currants, if you like, or
perhaps a peeled apple cut into small cubes.

Allow your mixture to simmer covered, (or uncovered if it's
too thin) for about fifteen minutes, and serve hot or cold.

MARINADES

The word "marinade" originally evolved from the Latin word
"mare," which means the sea, because it was originally used
to steep food in salt water to flavor and preserve it.

Today a marinade is considered a hot or cold, wet or dry seasoning used to tenderize and improve the flavor of chicken,
turkey, fish, beef, fruit, tofu, or vegetables. Marinating is one
of the best ways to add unique flavor to food without adding
fat. (See chapter 9, page 236, for ideas regarding marinating
tofu.)

SAFETY TIP

Never use a marinade that you're using on raw meat as a sauce, because it may be contaminated. If you want to make a sauce from the marinade, double the recipe and refrigerate half. Then you can use the portion that has not been in contact with the raw meat as a sauce after the meat is cooked.

Wet Marinades

Wet marinades are usually made up of an acid, an oil, and an *aromatic*—a sweet, spicy, savory, or fragrant flavoring—and each of these components has an important function.

The *acid* makes the meat tender. So use more and stronger acids for tougher meats. If possible, marinate or steep foods in a glass dish, because the acid can affect an aluminum pan adversely.

The tenderizing effect of marinades is subtle, however, so it's also important to match the right cut of meat with the proper cooking technique. (If you're not sure what type of meat to purchase, most butchers are extremely helpful.)

The *oil* in a marinade prevents the meat from drying out and sticking to the grill. If you want to avoid adding the oil to the marinade, however, you can spray the cooking surface with oil instead. And as for the *aromatics,* you have probably already guessed: they add flavor.

Remember always to refrigerate food while it's marinating, to turn it occasionally, and never to leave it at room temperature, as bacteria may form.

Tougher, thicker meats require more time soaking (several hours or overnight); chicken parts need approximately four hours; and seafood, thin cuts of poultry or meat, and nonmeat foods such as fruits, veggies, and tofu need only an hour or so in the bath.

If you want meats to brown, it's best after marinating to paper towel-dry meats before cooking. Once the food is cooked, always place it on a clean platter rather than the plate that held the raw food, which can be a source of harmful bacteria.

With the abundance of aromatics nature provides, there are no limits to the number of possible marinades. The only boundaries are the cook's imagination!

Think of the exotic flavors from your background, your roots, your birthplace or favorite country, and select one, two, or three acids, several aromatics, and only add oil when you feel it will add to the flavor of the dish. Use more of an ingredient for a stronger flavor, less when you want it milder, and voilà you've made an original marinade!

MARINADE CHART

Acids
lemon, lime, orange, grapefruit, pomegranate, tomato juice, tomato sauce, salsa, mirin, red and/or white wine, mustards, vinegars, pureed fresh fruit.

Oils/Fats
sesame, olive, canola, walnut oils; yogurt, buttermilk, chicken and beef stocks and broths

Aromatics
celery, carrot, onion, scallions, garlic, salt, peppercorns; black, white, cayenne, chili peppers; paprika, allspice, ginger, clove, cinnamon sticks, cumin, star anise, coriander, cardamom; basil, rosemary, thyme, dill; white and brown sugar, maple syrup.

Here are some combinations of seasonings you may want to dabble around with. Life truly is a matter of choices!

ASIAN

Beef, turkey, fish, and tofu will taste juicier after bathing in this Asian marinade. Blend approximately two parts soy sauce, one part water, fresh ginger, sugar, and mirin wine. Sometimes I also add a little sesame oil, minced garlic, diced scallions, seeded jalapeño—or any other hot peppers—white wine, or a little maple syrup or sugar to taste.

INTERESTING TIP

Mirin is a low-alcohol, sweet, golden wine made from glutinous rice, also referred to as *rice wine*. It adds sweetness and flavor to marinades, sauces, and dressings. It's available in the Japanese or gourmet section of most supermarkets.

SCANDINAVIAN

All types of seafood are tastier after being marinated in lemon, oil, dill and other fresh herbs. And, most types of fish taste good with a little lemon and orange juice, ginger, garlic, and lemon-pepper.

ITALIAN

Fruits, veggies, tofu, and all nonmeat foods can be marinated for an hour or overnight in vinaigrette with additional garlic and basil. If you prefer making your own marinade, mix a little olive oil with lemon juice, garlic, basil, and other fresh herbs.

These foods can be drained and served as they are, broiled, baked, or grilled. Eat them alone or combine them with other foods.

MEXICAN

Barbecued chicken has more of a flair after soaking up the flavors from salsa, cilantro, onion, and lemon or lime juice.

INDIAN

For variety, cumin, ground coriander, oregano, and minced or crushed ginger and garlic and shredded ginger are also great on broiled, baked, or barbecued chicken. Yogurt, dill, and garlic is another winning combination on chicken.

Dry Marinades, or Rubs

In my cupboard, I keep a mixture of paprika, a little chili powder, kosher salt, and freshly ground pepper. This easy dry marinade is perfect for barbecuing, broiling, and roasting chicken.

After washing the bird, I spray or rub it with olive or canola oil, and then massage or rub the dry marinade into it so it will adhere. This isn't an exact science; adding any or all of your favorite dry herbs will only make this mixture better.

Ready-Made Rubs

When I don't want to make my own marinade, Chef Emeril Lagasse's essence makes wonderful seasonings for vegetables, poultry, meat, and fish. Seasonings are used to enhance the flavor of food or as Emeril says, "Take it up a notch without significantly changing it."

On the TV Food Network, Chef Emeril sprinkles his seasonings on dishes right before serving—like confetti—to decorate the food. Every dish looks appealing! You can watch Mario, who believes in cooking with the freshest ingredients, and all the other talented chefs on the TV Food Network, as they create incredible dishes by adding a bit of this and a bit of that. All the creative chefs today are suggesting you add, and leave out, what you want! Study Martin Yan ("Yan Can Cook"), Graham Kerr, and the Frugal Gourmet on their cooking shows to examine their innovative ways. Imagine what you'd like to do, and then, as soon as you can, get in the kitchen and do it!

QUICK TIP

If you add a product *before* cooking, it becomes a dry marinade; if you use it *during* the cooking process, that distinguishes it as a seasoning. Buds, fruits, flowers, bark, seeds, and roots from aromatic plants are called *spices;* a blend of spices is called a *seasoning,* or blend.

There are many wonderful ready-made blends that can be used as marinades or seasonings. I often use Chef Paul Prudhomme's Magic Seasoning Blends as marinades, seasonings, or like confetti with tremendous success!

JELL-O MOLDS

Have you ever noticed how Jell-O brings out the dabbler in most cooks? That's why Jell-O molds make perfect "go-withs."

Jell-O was brought out in 1897 by Kraft General Foods, and it hasn't changed much over the years. Jell-O molds were extremely popular in the 1950s but they became passé during the 1960s and 1970s, probably because consumers felt it took too long to set. The speed-set method was developed, and since Jell-O is a comfort food, it's making a comeback that goes hand in hand with the rebirth of home entertaining.

Follow the directions on a package of your favorite flavor of Jell-O: add water, stir, and refrigerate. Or *speed set,* replacing ice cubes for some of the water so you won't have to wait so long. Or, if you prefer, replace the water with fruit-flavored soda or fruit juice. Here are a few ten-minute ideas to tickle your fancy. Take a look and, as always, allow your imagination to fly far and wide!

Recapturing the Fifties with Strawberries

I like strawberry or banana-strawberry Jell-O best, so to a six-ounce package, I add water, one large *can* of crushed pineapple, two to three mashed bananas, and a container of frozen strawberries with the juice.

Pour the fruit and liquid into an oiled mold that's deep enough to hold two batches of this concoction, and refrigerate the first layer until firm. When it's set, add a layer of lite sour cream, or sliced fruit, and create another layer of fruit and Jell-O by beginning the process all over again. (The second layer is poured on after the first layer is firm.) Your guests' lips will start smacking just from looking at this mold.

INTERESTING TIP

You should not put *fresh* pineapple into Jell-O because the acids will eat through the protein in the gelatin. Canned pineapple works fine, because the canning process alters the level of acidity.

Frothy Jell-O

Here's another idea that's easy to improvise. To begin, dissolve strawberry, lemon, blueberry, or any flavor of Jell-O in one cup of boiling water, and allow it to cool. Meanwhile, in a mixer, blend a small carton of the same flavor of yogurt, add the Jell-O, and whip until frothy. Add fresh fruit at this point if you want.

Set the Jell-O in an *oiled* cake tin. (I like the round ones with the hole in the center, but you may prefer another shape.) It can also be layered in a bowl or Pyrex-type dish. Refrigerate for about two hours, or until set. Then, an extra layer can be added (as in the previous suggestion above).

> **QUICK TIP**
>
> To remove Jell-O from its mold, allow the Jell-O to sit at room temperature for a few minutes, run a sharp knife around the edges, place a flat plate across the top, and turn the whole thing over until it loosens. If the mold is stubborn, and won't come out, help it along by placing a warm wet towel along the sides and edges of the container.

Unique Carrot Mold

I remember my mom making variations of this mold for holiday dinners, and they always got lots of attention. She'd peel and grate carrots, and add them to orange, lemon, or lime Jell-O dissolved in about half the amount of water called for on the package directions. (The Jell-O has to be thicker, because the carrots are heavy and contain a lot of water.) She'd pour this mixture into a star, heart, or circular-shaped mold, refrigerate, place the mold on a plate, and serve it immediately. Or, if we weren't ready to eat, she'd refrigerate it again. I'm going to ask Susan, my mother, to make it again!

POTLUCK THANKSGIVING

In November 1993, my family, friends, and I decided to get some of our "go-withs" together and do a potluck Thanksgiving dinner. The meal was so tantalizing that we've made potluck Thanksgiving a tradition at my house.

The term potluck was originally used to show hospitality when a salesman invited a heavy-buying customer home for whatever food happened to be in the pot at that time.

Today, however, potlucks have turned into parties where everyone brings a dish. I've been to potlucks where nothing much (or *nothing*) was specified, and a beautiful balance of food resulted.

Other hostesses rely on luck in a different way. They devise menus by writing appetizers, salads, entrées, and desserts on slips of paper, and what you are asked to bring in your pot is the luck of the draw.

Potluck Game Plan

My family decided upon a *potluck etiquette* after our first event. I'll explain our way of orchestrating our dinners, which have been successful.

POTLUCK ETIQUETTE

- We make food that is easy to transport, and doesn't require a lot of last-minute preparation.
- We present the food we make in an attractive dish, and bring along the appropriate utensils. (That way, no one feels flustered at the last minute.)
- We write our name on masking tape, and stick it to the bottom of our dish.
- We leave leftovers for the host unless they're offered to us.
- We wash and dry the dishes we bring, and remember to take them home.
- If you host a potluck party, invite your guests to put together a sampling of the leftover dishes to take home—except, perhaps, for the one or two you may want to keep for yourself!
- The family who hosts the Thanksgiving dinner makes the turkey and stuffing, so it stays hot and doesn't have to be transported. (I'm always thrilled to do it, especially when I don't have to do everything else.)
- We eat around three o'clock in the afternoon, knowing that by the end of the meal we're going to be stuffed.
- Dessert is served several hours later, so we can relax and digest our food first. The kids play, and the adults socialize.

Superwoman

I remember Thanksgivings in the 1970s, and feeling I wasn't doing a good job unless I served at least six dishes made from scratch. Although I entertained a lot, and everything always had to be perfect, I didn't enjoy it much. I was in the kitchen while everyone else was socializing and having a good time.

We've all had unpleasant experiences entertaining like superwoman, and then discovering the bottom line: It's not worth it! You work on a meal for days that takes less than an hour to eat. It's difficult to relate to your guests, because you're geared up, rushing around making sure everything is done, while everyone else is geared down for a relaxing time.

I never asked for help, until I became more savvy about entertaining. I didn't accept help when it was offered, and after our guests left, my husband and I always cleaned up by ourselves.

Superhuman

I'm a mother now; time seems to gallop by at a quicker pace. I no longer have a need to do everything myself. It was difficult at first, but ultimately I enjoyed saying good-bye to the superwoman inside me! Instead of being superwoman, I'm a wiser superhuman, and definitely superproud when my three grown stepkids and the other family members bring over their lovely creations on Thanksgiving. No one has cooked all day, no one is tired, and everyone is able to have a good time.

CULINARY SECRET #6: Find the easiest way possible to get the people you care about together, and remember that everyone needs assistance!

My Gratitude Stuffing

Whether you call it stuffing or dressing, I make this dish from scratch on most holiday occasions. It's quick to prepare, and one of the most satisfying, delectable, and memorable dishes to eat. (Prepackaged stuffings contain hydrogenated oils.)

I also make stuffing whenever I'm feeling particularly grateful about something going on in the world, or in my heart. Then, as I hear my guests say, "Pass the dressing again, *please,*" I feel even warmer inside.

Depending upon the number of people you're serving, and the size of the bird you're stuffing, slice one or two loaves of two- to four-day-old bread into large bite-sized cubes. I prefer using a combination of sourdough and olive, herb, or whole-grain bread, and I usually purchase it at a specialty bakery, so it's especially good. If by the time you're ready to make the dressing the bread isn't stale, toast it in the oven with a low heat before cutting it. If you don't want to stuff the bird, because that slows down the cooking process, dressing can also be baked in an oiled oven-safe dish.

To make memorable stuffing, heat some olive or canola oil in a skillet and sauté chopped onion, celery, and garlic. (Make sure the fire is hot enough that everything sizzles.) You could also add some thinly sliced fennel and/or anise. I can hear the hissing sound, just describing this dish, and I can smell how good it's going to taste!

After the veggies are soft, toss in fresh or dried chanterelle, morel, Italian brown, button, or oyster mushrooms; they're all wonderful and add rich, smoky, woodsy flavors to stuffing. You can even add a packaged combination of fresh or dried mushrooms, available at most markets today, but be sure to soak dried mushrooms in chicken broth, first. In addition to the mushrooms, add fresh herbs—basil, sage, cilantro, (or bottled poultry seasoning).

Next, add some homemade chicken stock (see chapter 7, page 176) or defatted canned broth. To make this dish vegetarian, simply use vegetable stock instead.

Depending upon the size of your bird, here are some basic stuffing suggestions regarding quantities of various ingredients:

STUFFING CHART

Poultry Weight	**6 lbs.**	**10 lbs.**	**12 lbs.**	**20 lbs.**
Bread Squares	10 cups	15 cups	18 cups	30 cups
Chopped Onion	1 cup	1¼ cups	1⅓ cups	2 cups
Chopped Celery	1 cup	1¼cups	1⅓ cups	2 cups
Chopped Garlic	1 clove	2 cloves	3 cloves	4 cloves
Fresh Mushrooms	1 cup	1¼ cups	1⅓ cups	2 cups
Dried Mushrooms	½ cup	¾ cup	1⅙ cups	1 cup
Fresh Herbs	¼ cup	½ cup	¾ cup	1 cup
Stock	1 cup	2 cups	3 cups	5 cups

These guidelines are generous and they're only meant as recommendations. It's more important to mix, look, feel, and smell the food you're making. Is it too moist, too dry, or just right? If it's too dry, add more stock, or if it's too wet, add more of the dry ingredients. The consistency can be a little drier if you're stuffing it into a turkey, chicken, or Cornish hen, since it will acquire more moisture while it cooks.

Other ingredients people traditionally add to stuffing include: apples, raisins, prunes, dried apricots and cranberries, nuts, and sautéed turkey liver, onions, and celery.

To prevent the growth of bacteria, stuff your bird at the last minute, and not too tightly. All of the stuffing probably will not fit into the bird (especially if it's a Cornish hen). With turkey, you can add a little dressing to the neck cavity, too, and if you loosen the skin around the breast area carefully, by moving your fingers around underneath, you can bake some dressing underneath that'll taste incredibly delicious! (Invite me over if you do!) And, if there's still extra dressing, remember you can bake it separately in an oven-safe dish.

People who cook without recipes realize that as long as you use your common sense you can throw ingredients in willy-nilly. This impromptu way of cooking has been popular for so

long that there's a name for it in Yiddish, *shitaron*. Throw in a
bit of this and a bit of that while cooking and you'll discover
that the only rules in cooking have to do with safety. Otherwise, none of it makes much of a difference!

SAFETY TIP

A turkey must be cooked in a 350-degree oven, and the stuffing needs to reach
165 degrees. An unstuffed bird may cook faster, but the oven should still be set at
350 degrees. (For roasting times for stuffed and unstuffed birds, see chapter 1,
page 34.)

THE PARTY OF THE YEAR

Thanksgiving is my favorite holiday because it's centered
around food. Last year, my oldest stepdaughter, Lisa, brought
over her Jell-O cassis. My middle stepkid, Laura, brought per-
simmon pudding and whipping cream. Steven, my stepson,
made his yam casserole specialty. (He pureed several baked
yams and a little brown sugar together, and attractively fanned
slices of baked apples on top before baking it.) My husband
organized the tables and made his famous cranberries, while
my daughter, Chelsea, decorated the tables. She stood a bunch
of asparagus on end (tied together with streamers), and strewed
fresh cranberries, kumquats, avocados, persimmons, and whole
nuts across the tables in a decorative design. I set the table with
a variety of pastel-colored plates. My mom made pumpkin,
blueberry-cream, and apple-crumb pies. My in-laws brought
themselves to Los Angeles all the way from Chicago. And my
brother, Barry, brought our mom—with the pies—bread, beer,
wine, and his famous holiday punch:

Barry's Refreshing Punch

My brother mixes a bottle of apple and cranberry juice together, adds about two cups of strong herbal teas (cranberry,

lemon, apple-spice or a combination). He adds a few cinnamon sticks, whole cloves and orange peel; chills it, and serves this refreshing drink over ice.

Chef Kathy's Eggless Eggnog

Sometimes I make an eggless eggnog that chef Kathy Diamond, from Basalt, Colorado, invented and taught me to make. It's simple! Combine the following ingredients together in the blender until smooth: one block of soft silken tofu; they vary in size but it doesn't matter, about four cups of Vanilla Rice Dream, pure maple syrup, pure vanilla extract, and brandy, rum or Cointreau to taste. (Rice Dream is a dairy-free milklike liquid, made from brown rice, that is lactose-free, and 99% fat free. (It is available in most supermarkets, and the 6,600 natural-food stores throughout the United States.)

Kathy suggests you sprinkle nutmeg on top of this drink; taste it; add anything else it needs; and see how smooth, creamy, and delicious healthy eggnog can be.

Your friends may not want to change their eggnog, and don't expect everyone to immediately agree on having a potluck Thanksgiving next year. Brilliant ideas never start out being accepted! Especially if you've been doing Thanksgiving at your house, and preparing the dinner yourself. But, I guarantee, if you take the time to implement this new plan, you'll be glad by next November that you did.

Now that we have our creative juices flowing, let's continue and make some *stew*pendous *soup*rises.

CHAPTER 7

◆

Stewpendous Souprises

"A person who cannot make a good soup should not be allowed to marry."

—Morton Shand

Soup-making is as limitless as a cook's wildest imagination. Just as no two books on the same subject turn out the same, there are at least 1,001 ways to make vegetable soup. A cook or a writer begins with an idea, finds his or her special voice, and then gets out of the way so the creation may take on a life of its own.

Visualize the kind of soup you want to make. Build the dish by adding your favorite vegetables, stock, beans, grains, pasta, herbs, and other seasonings. Then let go of your vision and let the soup take on its own character.

Soup-making is also a lot like parenting. You pour everything that's good into your precious infant—time, love, energy—and if you do a good job, your baby becomes a child who becomes his or her own person. Hopefully a human being you admire, but probably unlike anyone you imagined!

I equate soup-making with writing and parenting, though not necessarily in that order since, for me, being Chelsea's mom is more delicious than eating the best soup while reading the juciest story!

Moviemaking is another creative art I have a passion for. So you can understand how excited I was, during a five-hour flight to Colorado, to sit next to Robert E. Wise, the man who directed both *West Side Story* and *The Sound of Music*. I remember as a young girl watching *West Side Story* repeatedly because of Natalie Wood. So, I gushed while telling Mr. Wise how talented he is, and asked to what he attributes his success.

"It's all in the casting," he replied modestly. "Jerome Robbins and I were viewing Warren Beatty on film, looking for Tony, when Natalie came on the screen. We forgot about Tony and yelled, 'We've found Maria.' Start with great actors, and a great product results."

During that conversation I was taking a break from writing this chapter about soup, so naturally I thought, "Start with great ingredients, and a stupendous soup practically makes itself!"

SOUP'S HISTORY

Soup-making took on a whole new meaning for me once I realized that people have been making impressive soups since the beginning of time, simply by putting their favorite ingredients together in a big pot filled with water. Adam and Eve probably hung in the sun a big kettle of water that contained everything they could get their hands on, which was edible.

As time went on, soup was cooked over open fires, but the basic process of putting ingredients into liquid didn't change very much. So, no two soups turned out exactly the same! Stoves were invented in 1795 by Count Rumford, but people continued to follow the same time-tested guidelines for making soup.

A particular soup, called *restaurant,* from the sixteenth century in France, was responsible for coining the term we use today for our public eating establishments. This popular soup was probably the first popularized "health food." And, little by little, the cooks who made this soup printed the word **r e s t a u r a n t** above the door of their eating houses, and

eventually their establishments became known as restaurants, originally pronounced, "re-sto-rant."

In the wartime 1800s, soups were canned to answer Napoleon's need for a safe and varied food supply for his men. During World War II, soups were dehydrated so they could be stored easily and prepared quickly in the field.

Sometime during the 1950s, commercially frozen soups had their heyday. And today, frozen, microwavable soups have become a healthful fast-food alternative. Frozen soups are more like homemade than canned, in texture, but still I'd rather forgo convenience and make my own. When you're in the mood, nothing substitutes for homemade soup!

HOMEMADE SOUP

Whether I'm serving soup as the meal, to start the meal, or to set the tone of a dinner party, homemade soup is one of the most versatile, comforting foods you can serve. Soup both brings back and creates memories, and it's economical!

Most of the time, to make great soup, you don't have to run out for special ingredients. Some of the best soups are nothing more than inventions created by the cook when the refrigerator is being cleaned out. Soup is also one of the most satisfying foods to prepare because of the creativity it permits the cook. There are no rules for making a "good" pot of homemade soup. How do you like your pea soup? The verdict is split! Some people like it chunky and spicy, while others prefer it smooth and creamy.

In addition, studies show that soup can play a significant role in a weight-loss program. It takes more time to eat than other foods, so people generally consume fewer calories when they start their meal off with a piping-hot bowl of low-fat soup. And, calorie for calorie, it's more nourishing and filling than most other foods. You feel full, and a message is sent to your brain signaling satiety, which curtails your appetite.

Soup's On

Soups can be appetizers, flavorful side dishes, hearty main dishes, and even desserts. Chowders, consommés, and stews all come under the classification of soup. But to keep soup-making simple, think of soups in three basic categories: *thick, clear,* and *pureed.*

A thick soup is created basically from dumping water, stock, and your favorite chunky ingredients into a pot. Strain what results and you end up with *broth,* or clear soup, a mere liquid in which something has been cooked. I don't know about you, but clear broths leave me as empty as a boring conversation.

For a more substantial, creamy dish, *pulse-blend* or quickly combine a thick soup in the blender. It becomes *pureed,* or smooth like baby food is, but full of flavor. A dish you'll want to savor.

But no matter what texture or flavor of soup you want to attain—thin or thick, light or rich—always remember the following culinary secret.

CULINARY SECRET #7: Start out with wholesome, good-quality ingredients, and a heavenly dish will result.

M. F. K. Fisher wrote in her wartime classic, *How to Cook a Wolf,* that making soup is virtually always the second skill a beginning cook acquires: "The natural progression from boiling water to boiling water with something in it can hardly be avoided and in most cases is heartily to be wished for."

Most homemade soups can be frozen and kept for months in airtight containers. Make large quantities, and put portions away for times when you want a wholesome meal, yet don't have the time to cook.

When I don't know what to make my family for dinner, I defrost a homemade soup I've deposited in the freezer for a rainy day, and stop at the deli for sandwich ingredients. I don't have to cook and we still have a satisfying meal. (It's also smart to have frozen, homemade soup on hand to defrost and heat for anyone who gets sick!)

The Stock Pot

So many delicious dishes, including stews and stir-fries, are based on a good stock, and so are marvelous homemade soups. A stock is basically the same as a clear soup or broth, except in its use. I use canned broth occasionally, for soup-making convenience, but I believe some soups require the rich essence of a homemade stock, and that has to be *made.*

Make stock when you're planning to be home for several hours and you have ripe veggies in the fridge. If you don't have stock ingredients on hand, it's worth purchasing them especially for that purpose. A stock containing meat takes a few hours to cook, but you can relax and go on with your life. After all, a watched pot, as you know, never boils.

To create a flavorful stock, begin by *sweating* or sautéing chopped onions, garlic, carrots, and celery in a big soup pot containing a little oil. Make sure the oil is hot enough that you hear the veggies sizzle when you put them in. (Cooking is not only about taste, it's about sound and smell.) Sweating the vegetables, before adding the water, is an important step since the caramelized bits that brown and stick to the soup pot create a richer stock with a deeper color. (Onions have more sugar than any other vegetable, so when they're sautéed or caramelized they become golden brown, sticky, and sweet.)

Add turkey, chicken, or meat and bones to the pot, whatever vegetables you have available, and enough water to cover. Parsnips, fennel, carrots, celery, onions, leeks, asparagus, and mushrooms all work well. It doesn't matter how the veggies are cut, or whether or not they're peeled, as long as they're scrubbed, since they'll be discarded later. Add herbs and seasonings depending upon the flavor you want to create such as basil, bay leaves, thyme, oregano, and cloves.

When I know I'm going to make a stock, sometimes I save the liquid that's left over from cooking other vegetables during the week, so I can add it to the pot. (It's an easy way of adding additional nutrients.) Finally I place a lid on top to partially cover the pot.

VALUABLE TIP

Thanksgiving is always a good time to start a stock pot with the leftover turkey carcass. For beef stock, ask the butcher to sell you shank bones with the meat attached. For chicken stock, purchase chicken parts (necks, wings, backs, legs) or save carcasses in the freezer until you have an opportunity to make stock.

Bring the mixture *slowly* to a boil. There are two secrets to making a good stock: First, after the initial boiling, don't allow it to boil again, or the fat will homogenize and become impossible to remove. Second, a scum rises as the soup cooks and must be skimmed away periodically with a shallow ladle or slotted spoon.

Simmer this brew for several hours, or until the solids have given up their essence to the liquid and therefore become worthless. Turn off the flame and discard the solids. Strain, when the liquid is cool, and you'll have a delicious stock.

QUICK TIP

For straining, use cheesecloth, a coarse cotton gauze available in most markets. The same method is used to turn your stock into a clear broth. Otherwise a colander, that perforated utensil often used to drain pasta, strains fine!

Once the stock is strained, pour it into clean containers and refrigerate. The fat will rise to the top, solidify, and act as a sealant until you're ready to remove it and freeze the stock in sealed containers. It's convenient to freeze some of the rich stock in ice-cube trays, and later place the cubes in freezer bags for longer storage. I like using the cubes of frozen stock whenever I want to sauté food without oil.

WAISTLINE TIP

To remove the fat from a soup, stew, or canned stock, refrigerate it and the fat will be easy to spoon out since it will congeal at the top. If you want to remove the fat from a pot of hot soup, float a paper towel on top.

VEGETARIAN STOCK

If you omit the chicken, meat, and bones, vegetarian stock is made using the same method above except that it only takes forty-five minutes to cook. There's no need to refrigerate vegetarian stock before using it, since there won't be any fat to skim.

For more flavorful vegetarian soups, try garnishing them with a little olive oil, nonfat yogurt, or nonfat sour cream in each person's bowl at the end.

SOUP GAME PLAN

There are just as many ways to start a soup as season a soup, but usually I begin by *sweating* or sautéing lots of cut-up onion, garlic, and sometimes a pinch or two of red pepper flakes in a small amount of oil. This sears the flavor into the onions and elevates that plain boiled flavor. In addition, sautéing the onions and garlic makes the house smell as homey as baked bread when it comes straight from the oven.

A realtor once told me to sauté onions just before our potential buyers walked in. Our house sold, so—who knows—maybe that's why. Whenever I sauté onions and garlic to make soup, everyone always comments on how great the house smells.

NUTRITION TIP

Garlic is one of the oldest foods, dating back to 3000 B.C. It's touted not only for its flavor-enhancing qualities but also its antioxidant and antibiotic effect. Slice or dice your own, or to save time buy crushed garlic at the market. And never, never worry about adding too much to a pot of soup—the flavor becomes mild from simmering it in the liquid. Garlic is good with so many foods.

Taste, smell, and look at your creation as you go along and ask yourself these questions:

- Does the soup smell delicious?
- Does the soup taste the way I like it?
- Do the color combinations complement one another?
- Are the vegetables cut attractively?
- Are the ingredients in bite-sized pieces?
- Is the soup complete, or is it asking for something else?

Thick Soups

Hearty homemade soups can be made even thicker by adding cheese, barley, potatoes, rice, bulgur, or peanut butter, but for good health, *never* add cream. Flour, arrowroot, or cornstarch—when thinned with a little hot liquid to prevent lumps—are good thickeners, too. Adding a roux, described on page 123, is another way to thicken soup.

If the soup becomes too thick, it can be thinned by adding more water, stock, tomato juice, or perhaps a little milk.

MEDITERRANEAN CHICKEN SOUP

I make variations of this soup often, since it's a favorite of mine, allowing one chicken breast and two cans of liquid per person.

For three servings, sauté diced onion, garlic, and celery in a little hot olive oil. After the onions become translucent, add three cans of defatted chicken broth and an equal amount of water. Add three skinless, diced chicken breasts, and boil approximately fifteen minutes, or until the chicken turns white. Add a can of whole, peeled Italian or diced tomatoes (with the puree). Season to taste with the three C's: cinnamon, cumin, and cayenne (I like a lot), plus salt and pepper. Add snipped fresh cilantro or mint, one half cup uncooked couscous, and three-quarter cup diced dried apricots. (The apricots taste a lot like carrots, only better.) Simmer this soup approximately twenty to thirty minutes, and enjoy!

HEARTY VEGETARIAN VEGETABLE SOUP

You can't make a bad vegetable soup if you use your six favorite veggies! It's important to limit the number of vegetables you use, because if you use too many the flavor becomes overwhelming. To speed up the soup-making process, clean and chop the vegetables that take longest to cook first and put them into the pot. Then clean, chop, and cook as you go along.

Vegetables from the onion family (leeks, shallots, garlic, and onions) give the soup a lovely flavor, so choose at least two and sauté them in a big soup pot containing a little oil. (Remember to make sure the oil is hot.) Add root vegetables such as carrots, parsnips, turnips, beets, and all types of potatoes. Yams, sweet potatoes, acorn and butternut squash give vegetable soup a sweeter, richer flavor and rustic color.

Next you need liquid. Add several cups of homemade vegetarian stock, water, tomato juice or a combination of all three.

You might also want to add A.1. steak sauce or Lea & Perrins Worcestershire sauce for flavor before simmering everything together in the pot. If you want a richer tomato flavor, add some tomato paste to thicken, cored stewed tomatoes, tomato sauce, or again—all three.

After the tougher, longer-to-cook root veggies have had a head start, add the vegetables you've selected that require less cooking time such as Chinese pea pods, tomatoes, mushrooms, broccoli, celery, or crookneck squash.

Add the leafy greens (spinach, kale, or mustard greens) last since they require the least time to cook. Adjust the seasonings and simmer until the veggies are cooked exactly the way you prefer them. And just before serving, for the best vegetable soup you've ever tasted, add a few drops of olive oil to each bowl!

TURKEY AND RICE SOUP

Sauté a diced onion, a few cloves of garlic, and perhaps sliced carrots in a little olive oil. Add raw ground turkey, and sauté it (like hamburger). Mix, and pour in approximately six cups of homemade chicken stock. (Canned chicken broth is okay in this soup if you make sure it's free of MSG, and you remove the fat that congeals at the top.)

Now add approximately one cup of white or brown rice that has been rinsed well. You may want to add mushrooms before the soup is completely cooked. Simmer until the rice is soft, or for about forty-five minutes to one hour. Add salt to taste just before serving. Make this for your family. It's simple yet incredibly soothing and delicious.

NUTRITION TIP

Since some packaged ground turkey is a combination of white meat, dark meat, and skin, it can be either a high-fat or lean food. Remember, it's best to purchase brands that are all-white meat. The brand "The Turkey Store" is available coast to coast, and it's all white meat without skin added.

BEEF, BARLEY, AND MUSHROOM SOUP

In a large soup pot, sauté one finely chopped onion. When it is translucent, sauté two pounds of lean ground beef. (Ask the butcher to grind "stewing beef.") Drain the fat from the cooked meat, if there is any.

Add approximately eight cups of stock. I prefer beef for this one, but chicken or vegetable also tastes good. (Canned broth can be substituted, but remember to remove the fat.) Rinse two cups of barley and add it to the pot along with bay leaves, celery, and carrots, if you like, and the seasonings you prefer. (I keep shakers in my kitchen containing a mixture of my favorite five herbs.) Add button or shiitake mushrooms, thinly sliced. Bring to a boil and simmer for an hour, or until the barley is fully cooked. (Remember to remove the bay leaves. If swallowed, they may damage someone's esophagus or stomach.)

COOK'S TIP

If you have a soup recipe that doesn't call for a grain, add one anyway. You can't go wrong with barley, rice, millet, or bulgur. Remember, though, they absorb liquid, so you may need to add more.

CABBAGE SOUP

Again, sauté a couple of onions in a little hot oil. (Onions truly are the base for so many dishes.) Add a head of green cabbage, which you've washed and thinly sliced, and a couple of cans of stewed tomatoes—with the juice. Remember to remove the core of the tomatoes. Pour in several cups of stock, whatever type you have on hand: Vegetable, chicken, or beef are all good. For sweetness, add raisins, maple syrup, or brown sugar—or a combination of all three—to taste.

You may want to add small pieces of meat to jazz up this soup. Lean beef (prepared for fajitas) or shank bone with meat work well.

MINESTRONE SOUP

One of the most satisfying foods is minestrone soup. Begin again by sautéing onions, garlic, and pepper flakes in a large pot containing a little oil. Add a few fresh tomatoes, a few cups of vegetable or chicken stock, and a can or two of stewed tomatoes with the juice. I like to add more diced onion, chickpeas, sliced zucchini, carrots, oregano, pasta, thyme, salt, black pepper, and a little maple syrup, because those are my favorite minestrone ingredients and seasonings. Top this soup with Parmesan cheese before serving. Isn't it fun to improvise?

ONION SOUP

This dish, practically the national dish of France, is so easy to make and good that it may amaze you. For each person you're serving, peel and slice one yellow, red, or Maui onion (or a combination of the three) and sauté in a little olive oil until translucent. Sprinkle with flour and stir. Add approximately two cups of beef or chicken stock for each onion you used. Bring everything to a boil, and then simmer for two to three minutes.

Meanwhile, sauté one slice of French bread per person in a mixture of olive oil and garlic, and toast them. Place one piece of this toasted bread at the bottom of each serving bowl, and fill with the cooked onions and broth. Top this soup with slices of Jack, provolone, Muenster, or Swiss cheese—my favorite—right before serving. Heat each bowl in the oven or microwave until the cheese melts and the soup is bubbling hot. Interestingly enough, this soup is refreshing in the summertime.

Try This

The next time the temperature gets above 100 degrees, begin your meal with a frosty bowl of gazpacho. Chilling the soup bowls ahead of time makes this dish refreshing.

Peel (if you prefer) and chop *finely* four large tomatoes, a cucumber, an onion, green pepper, garlic, cilantro, and a couple of stalks of celery after peeling off the porous strings.

Add a couple of cups of tomato juice (V-8 works well), a little red-wine vinegar, Worchestershire sauce, my favorite Frank's Original RedHot Sauce, a little salt, and pepper to taste. Stir the ingredients together, taste your creation, and adjust the seasonings.

Cover and chill several hours, allowing the ingredients in the soup to *marry,* or blend the flavors. As with most soups, the flavor improves with time. Serve in chilled bowls. Top with croutons, nonfat sour cream, diced avocado, or a combination of all three.

THE MAGIC OF SOUP

Since comfort is the essence of soup, it's no wonder a bowl of homemade soup often acts as a preventative or curative health measure. If I'm feeling out of sorts, run-down, cranky, generally irritable, or if someone in my family is sick, I'll make a pot of soup. (Cooking makes me feel better, and so does the soup!)

Most of us have been brought up with a family soup-tradition that promises to cure all ills. Here's my grandmother's. It's made with tofu which wasn't popular or readily available during her time, but she was way *ahead* of her time!

Grandma-ma's Cure-All Tonic Soup

This soup will make you feel better when you're sick, and tastes good even when you're well! As an old German proverb says, "A good cook is the best physician!"

Bring a couple of cups of chicken broth to a simmer. Add slices of fresh gingerroot, squares of firm tofu, and a tablespoon of miso paste that has been mixed with water. Serve with a few slices of green onion floating on top, and a bowl of steaming-hot white rice on the side.

NUTRITION TIP

Miso is a paste made from fermented soybeans. It has a rich flavor and a salty taste somewhat similar to tamari. It should be added toward the end of soup-making, and not boiled, because excessive heat destroys its beneficial enzymes.

THE ABC'S OF BEAN SOUP

(Bean Soups open up another whole world!)

A. Rinse beans in a colander, looking for foreign objects, such as pebbles, because beans come directly from the farm. There is no need to soak beans overnight, since this process does not eliminate the properties in beans that cause gas, and only cuts the cooking time down by approximately five minutes. (See chapter 10, page 256, for more information.)

B. If you're not ready to make the soup, once you've rinsed the beans, cover them with water again, and some plastic wrap, and place them in the fridge until you're ready to cook.

C. To make most types of soup, sauté a chopped onion or two, plus a few cloves of garlic in a little hot oil. Add pepper flakes or your favorite hot sauce when you want your soup to have more pizzazz. The options are endless from here!

VALUABLE TIP

Epazote (also spelled epizote and apasote) is magic for reducing the enzyme in beans that produces gas in many people. It also provides a wonderful flavor to every dish containing beans. It can be purchased in Hispanic specialty markets, in addition to some American supermarkets now. This dark, leafy-green plant is also available at most nurseries, so grow it in your garden, or in a little pot on your porch. You'll use it often. It's easy to grow, and does best in full sun and poor soil.

Anise and bay leaves reduce beans' gas-producing abilities, too, but remember bay leaves should never be swallowed!

LIMA BEAN SOUP

Begin by sautéing three small or two large onions in a soup pot with olive oil. Remember, caramelizing, browning, or cooking the onions really well gives the beans a sweet, flavorful essence. Meanwhile, wash a pound of lima beans, disposing of stones or any other foreign objects.

Now add the rinsed beans, epazote, and enough water to cover everything by about two inches. Add a small can of tomato paste to the beans and onions, and allow everything to cook thoroughly.

The trick of this soup is to simmer it a long time—a couple of hours or more—until the beans absorb most of the water and the soup becomes thick. Add salt and pepper to taste. (The only way you can ruin this dish is to leave it on a roaring flame until all the liquid evaporates, and everything burns.) For a hearty meal, all you need with this filling soup is crunchy salad and bread.

LENTIL SOUP

My friend Paula makes a simple lentil soup that's extremely comforting to eat. She calls it "Luscious Lentil." In a soup pot, sauté some chopped onion and garlic in olive oil. Add a few cups of homemade chicken broth, depending upon the number of people you're serving (canned chicken broth will do, fat removed). Toss in some bay leaves, thyme, fresh rosemary—left on the stem—pepper, chopped basil, and a splash of balsamic vinegar.

Add washed lentils and epazote and simmer about an hour, or until the beans are tender. Add salt and pepper to taste, and serve. Imagine eating this soup with crusty garlic-croutons floating on top.

For variety, Paula sometimes substitutes red wine for the vinegar, and adds sautéed celery and leek to the soup. Yellow squash and carrots are also interesting additions. For another effect, Paula says to try pureeing about a third of this soup and then putting it back into the pot.

Paula is definitely becoming a cook. She says it's the options that make this soup fun to make!

BLACK-BEAN SOUP

More black-bean soup is eaten in Guatemala than any place in the world. Their technique for making this soup is easy, and the results will make your mouth water.

Wash a pound of black beans, looking for stones, but make sure not to soak these beans overnight. You don't want to wash away their gorgeous purplish-black color.

Put the beans in a soup pot, add some epazote, and cover with water by about three inches. (For this soup, you don't need the added flavor from broth.) Bring the water to a gentle boil for about fifteen minutes, and simmer the beans for a half hour or so.

Add a diced onion, a few whole cloves of garlic, salt, and simmer this soup for another couple of hours, or until the beans are soft.

Sometimes I puree half the mixture with the onions, garlic chunks, and some of the liquid, depending upon the consistency I want. Then I add the mixture back to the pot. A little cumin brings out the bean flavor.

Heat and serve this soup with hot tortillas on the side, and a nonfat sour cream-plain yogurt combo drizzled on top.

COOK'S TIP

There are those who dollop, and those who squiggle. If you're a "squiggler," like me, keep a squeeze bottle containing fat-free yogurt and/or sour cream in the fridge for dressing up soups and other dishes.

PUREED SOUPS

A food processor at medium speed or a blender at low speed is used to puree soups in small batches. If a soup is hot, fill your blender only to the four-cup mark, remove the feed cap in the center of the blender cover, stand to the side of the blender, and don't put your hands near the opening while it is running.

Pureed soups are usually made with "starchy vegetables," because they're the easiest to blend. The consistency of this soup is coarser and healthier than a cream soup which—as you might guess—contains cream.

Sometimes I substitute 1% buttermilk to get the blade to move freely, or a few tablespoons of the cooking liquid, but I never use cream. To create a rich, full-flavored soup, make sure to sweat the veggies before adding them to the liquid. (See page 176 of this chapter for details.)

CARROT SOUP

Peel and steam two pounds of carrots. Add a little olive oil to a soup pot and sauté an onion or two, a large leek chopped finely, and a bulb of fennel (it looks like celery and smells like licorice, but don't confuse it with anise). Add about four cups of chicken or vegetable stock (canned broth won't do in this one), a little lemon juice, a tablespoon or so of orange juice, salt and white pepper to taste.

Reduce or simmer the liquid until half of it evaporates or becomes more flavorful from decreasing the volume. Puree everything in a blender, pour the soup back into the pot, and heat thoroughly. Drizzle nonfat yogurt or nonfat sour cream on top of the soup and sprinkle fresh chopped dill or fennel tops in a pretty design before serving. This soup is one of my favorites!

TOMATO SOUP

If you want to make soup, and have an abundance of red vine-ripened tomatoes available, begin by simmering a cut-up fennel bulb in enough water to cover for about three hours. (You can get a little R&R while it's reducing.)

Now, thinly slice another fennel bulb and sauté it in canola, olive, or any other healthful oil. Quickly pulse-blend together the fennel reduction (simmered fennel and remaining water), sautéed fennel, and tomatoes—about three per person (seeds and all)—and put the combo into the soup pot to heat. You want the tomatoes to remain a little chunky. Season with maple syrup, salt, and pepper, and heat.

I like to drizzle yogurt on this soup, and sprinkle black and white sesame seeds on top. You can either toast sesame seeds for a few minutes in a skillet and mix them with some that are raw, or sprinkle a prepared sesame seasoning on top.

QUICK TIP

Eden Organic Sesame Shake, a sesame and sea-vegetable seasoning, is delicious on soup, grain, and vegetable dishes. It's available in most health-food stores and some markets nationwide, so look for it on the shelf.

ZUCCHINI SOUP

Mix about four cups of water, a little at a time, with approximately four tablespoons of miso paste until there are no lumps. A whisk works great for this. I use light miso, but any type works fine.

Sauté, or sweat, onions, fresh basil, and about seven peeled or unpeeled, sliced zucchinis in olive oil. Puree it all, heat, and serve sprinkled with a little Eden Shake on top. (See tip above.) This technique also works well with any type of yellow squash. (See page 185 of this chapter for more about miso.)

EGGPLANT SOUP

Tell me an ingredient you like, eggplant for example, and I'll tell you fifty things you can do with it. Here's the first!

Sauté some onions, garlic, and cilantro in oil. Add the meat, not skin, from a couple of eggplants you've roasted in the oven. Sauté and add a little salt, cumin, and black pepper to taste. Puree (thin with a little chicken broth), heat, mix in a couple of drops of sesame oil, and serve with minced parsley, cilantro, some other greens, or sesame seeds sprinkled on top. My family enjoys eating toasted pita bread with this soup, or with croutons floating on top.

Try This

Make something new every time you puree. Peel and chop a few potatoes, a couple of leeks, and a couple of yellow onions. Toss them into a soup pot—there's no need to cut them fancy. Add some spinach, kale, or whatever greens you prefer. Cover with chicken broth, and allow everything to simmer for an hour or so. Puree, add salt, and you have potato leek soup. Add watercress and you've made watercress soup. Stir in milk and you've made vichyssoise!

FRUIT SOUP

Fruit soups are decorative and refreshing starters for a brunch or warm-weather dinner.

CITRUS SOUPRISE

Instead of serving the same old fresh orange juice in a glass at your next brunch, pour it into pretty, chilled, individual soup bowls and use it as you would a good stock. Float melon balls, berries, sliced apples, bananas—your favorite fruit. Chill, serve, and eat it with a big spoon.

FRUIT SOUPRISE

Separately blend any two fruits that contrast in color, approximately four cups each. Peaches and strawberries, pineapple and mango, or cantaloupe and honeydew work well. Add a little *lemon juice* and sugar to taste to one of the fruits. To the other, add a little *lime juice* and sugar to taste. If the fruit is really ripe, there may be no need to add sugar, because the flavor will come from the fruit's natural sweetness.

To serve, pour equal amounts of the two fruit mixtures—at the same time—into chilled soup bowls. Drizzle plain yogurt on top and, before serving, add a sprig of fresh mint leaves.

(Depending upon the fruit, nutmeg, cinnamon, ginger, cumin, chili, or pumpkin spice may add a nice touch, too.)

QUICK TIP

If fruit smells sweet on the outside, it will probably taste sweet on the inside.

HAWAIIAN GAZPACHO

Pulse-blend, or use the food processor, for a few minutes to blend your favorite summer fruits together. I've used mango, papaya, pineapple, and a little ginger. Float a squiggle of yogurt and a sprig of watercress or mint on top. This soup tastes as good as a smoothie, but it's chunky instead of smooth.

NOW, FOR THE STEWS

The distinction between soups and stews used to be easy to make: If the cook added dumplings to her soup, the mix became a stew. Today, however, the distinction is not as clear. It's not uncommon to serve the flavorful ingredients from a soup as a stew, and the liquid from a stew as a soup.

Basically a stew is nothing more than a thick soup, without a hint of pretension, cooked in a single pot or kettle, and eaten with a spoon, knife, and fork. It has complex flavors, yet consists of nothing more than meat, fish, or poultry, mushrooms, onions, and vegetables with seasonings that *seethe* or gently "stew" in a sauced liquid. A heartier stew is achieved by flouring the meat or chicken before simmering.

Fortunately, the making of a good stew doesn't require a great deal of effort, and it doesn't require many other dishes on the menu. With a tossed salad and a good, crusty, fresh bread, stew makes a delicious meal. Or serve it over rice, cracked wheat, or pasta to soak up the rich sauce.

To balance this comfortable meal, I suggest serving something a little fancy for dessert. You can afford the calories once in a while!

The Heartiest Meal-in-a-Bowl

To make a soul-satisfying pot of stew, cut approximately one pound of beef into fairly large pieces, and trim the fat. (Or, better yet, ask the butcher to do it for you.) Contrary to popular belief, the coarser, more fibrous cuts of meat don't become tender from stewing, so purchase chuck, sirloin, or another good cut of lean meat.

Flour the cubes of meat and sear, or brown, them in a pot to seal in their juices. Transfer the meat onto a plate.

Brown lots of onion, adding a little oil if necessary. Put the meat back into the pot and add enough beef stock to cover, along with a couple of bay leaves, thyme, a few cloves of garlic, tomato sauce, plus peeled carrots (or butternut squash that has been browned under the broiler), and potatoes cut attractively. (Potatoes are cooked when it's easy to insert a fork inside.) Use whatever veggies you like as long as you end up with a total of at least five cups.

Add fresh mushrooms when you have them, or dried mushrooms that have been soaked in warm water. Use the revived mushrooms, along with the soaking liquid, to enhance the flavor of the stew, and add a little red wine for more flavor if you'd like. Bring this stew to a boil and simmer it for about an hour.

If you want to thicken this dish, mix a couple of teaspoons

of cornstarch in a little bowl with about a quarter of a cup of hot liquid from the stew. Add this thickening agent to the pot and simmer with the lid half off until the liquid is reduced, at which point this stew is cooked to perfection. (Don't forget to remove the bay leaves!)

CURRY VEGETABLE STEW

Begin by steaming potatoes and your favorite seasonal veggies such as carrots, and *broccoflower*—the genetically combined cauliflower-broccoli. Meanwhile, heat some canola oil in a skillet and add onions, garlic, jalapeño peppers, and cubed green apples, several teaspoons of curry powder, and an equal number of teaspoons of tomato paste. Mix together with vegetable broth, perhaps some apple cider, then gently add the veggies. Heat and serve this dish over noodles or rice.

SOUL-SATISFYING SEAFOOD SUPPER

My husband and I were entertaining our dear friends visiting from Spain. They are accustomed to eating late-night suppers, so we wanted something easy to make and simple to serve; something that would also provide a comfortable air of informality.

Bouillabaisse seemed like the perfect answer since I could make this souplike stew ahead of time, and then place the big kettle right on the table so my guests could ladle it out for themselves.

As soon as we started to eat, the conversation came to a halt. Everyone seemed to slow down for a while (maybe in part because they had to deal with taking the shells off the hot seafood).

To make bouillabaisse, sauté a chopped onion (garlic if you want) and bell pepper in a large soup pot containing a little hot olive oil. Add one large can of peeled tomatoes—remove the cores—a large can of tomato sauce (or crushed tomatoes) and a package of dry spaghetti-sauce mix. (I like Lawry's, because it doesn't contain MSG.)

Toss in fresh basil if you have it, salt, pepper, and about two cups of water. Simmer this mixture for about ten minutes before adding a cup of dry white wine—any type will do.

Now all you need is the fish, and that can be almost any type. Depending upon what's available, the number of people you're serving, and your budget at the time, shrimp, lobster tails, red snapper, rock cod, scallops, and clams all work well. Simmer for another ten to fifteen minutes. The clams are cooked when the shells open.

I served my bouillabaisse with chilled chardonnay, warmed crusty French bread, and a variation of the marinated broccoli (on page 213 of the fruit and veggie chapter that follows).

CHAPTER 8

◆

Fruit and Veggie Lovers Don't Need Recipes

"There's the idea that you either lead a sensual, rich life and die young, or you avoid life and eat boring food."

—Dean Ornish, M.D.

When my brother and I were kids, our parents promised us membership in the *clean-plate club* if we'd finish our vegetables. Mom would tell Barry, "Eat your broccoli, and you'll get dessert." If I'd eat my spinach, until the hand-painted cherries on the china were visible, Dad would tell me to close my eyes, and wish for anything I wanted. I'd ask for Bazooka bubble gum night after night, and I was always amazed when it magically appeared on the table. I was only three, but how could I be so stupid? Today I'd be more creative and probably ask for a Jeep Cherokee Limited Edition!

It's unfortunate that bribes are necessary to get kids to eat their veggies. But without rewards, why would anyone even think of eating creamed onions, buttered carrots, or succotash? And did anyone actually look forward to that infamous string-bean recipe from the 1970s? You know the one—canned green beans mixed with a can of mushroom soup, topped with canned onion rings, and then baked. *Yuk!*

195

FIVE A DAY

Specialists from the U.S. Department of Agriculture, the National Academy of Sciences, and the U.S. Department of Health and Human Services agree that we'd all be healthier if we included five servings of produce in our daily diets.

We've got the message, and we know that eating more foods from this category makes us feel full, so we eat less, and therefore don't have to meticulously count calories or worry about our weight. Fruits and veggies are Mother Nature's perfectly packaged, naturally delicious, fat-free foods. So, why don't we eat more of them?

It still amazes me, after years of counseling, that people watching their weight continuously eat packaged fat-free foods such as brownies, cookies, and muffins—loaded with salt, sugar, and calories—yet ignore the delicious *fat-free* fruits and vegetables available in every marketplace.

New clients often ask me *why* they're overweight. They want to know if it's because of their genes, an underactive thyroid, or some other medical condition. These factors are important considerations, which must be checked out, but weight is usually a direct result of what we eat, and how much of it, in addition to how much or little we exercise.

To prove that theory, play a little game with yourself next time you're at the market shopping. Notice various customers and, depending upon their weights, guess whether their carts are mainly loaded with produce, or with processed foods. You'll probably win the prize!

Although most people are trying to lose weight, statistics show that thirty-five million Americans between the ages of twenty-five and seventy-five are overweight, and unfortunately that's a record high! In addition, more children are obese than ever before. Kids today spend hours sitting in front of the computer and the TV snacking on processed foods. Everyone would be healthier and thinner, if they'd simply eat more foods that come from the trees, plants, and ground rather than processed foods from packages.

The Ten Percent Club

If you want to lose weight, become a member of *The Ten Percent Club* today—that special ten percent of the population who eat and enjoy five servings of fruits and vegetables daily. This includes select vine-ripened, hothouse, frozen, canned, dried, or freeze-dried produce prepared deliciously, simply, and as nature intended them! There's no initiation fee to join, and Mother Nature offers irresistible incentives.

For such little effort, you get strong teeth, healthy hair, and sensational-looking skin. Produce is naturally low in calories, fat, and sodium. It has no cholesterol, and provides fiber, which in turn promotes a healthy digestive tract.

Broccoli and other *cruciferous* vegetables (cauliflower, brussel sprouts and cabbage), often used in specialty dishes, contain the largest amounts of beneficial antioxidants, including beta-carotene.

Switching to dark leafy greens, and eating more yellow- and orange-colored vegetables rich in beta-carotene, such as carrots, squash, and yams, also doubles your calcium and folacin (an important B vitamin), and increases your vitamin C five times.

No less important, there are vitamins A, B, and C in veggies, plus minerals such as calcium, magnesium, zinc, iron, and selenium. In addition, there are indoles, which block carcinogens in plant foods and appear to protect us against heart disease and cancer of the colon, ovaries, stomach, breast, and lung. If that's not enough to convince you to eat your vegetables, you should know that eating dark leafy vegetables, such as spinach, collards, and kale, reduces the risk of *macular degeneration*— the leading cause of irreversible blindness among older Americans today.

PURCHASE THE FRESHEST PRODUCE
AVAILABLE

It's a lot more tempting to eat vegetables that taste delicious, so because of their superior taste I purchase organically grown produce whenever I can. Until recently, no one knew precisely what *organic* meant. Now we know that organically grown fruits and vegetables have been grown without the use of pesticides and other synthetic chemicals.

It was Alice Waters, owner of Chez Panisse restaurant in Berkeley, California, who, in 1971, began exploring the benefits of organic in this country. She was on a taste search for fruits and vegetables as delicious as those she'd eaten in France, and she found the answer. Her food, made with lots of fresh fruits and vegetables, was dubbed "California Cuisine," and that type of cooking is popular today throughout the nation. It's easier to find organic produce today since companies such as Albert's and Mission International are delivering to all major metropolitan areas in the country and shipping to most regions in the continental United States and Canada.

Fruit and veggie dishes can't help but taste delicious when you use good produce, fully vine-ripened fruits and vegetables, picked when they're at their peak, ready to eat.

CULINARY SECRET #8: Purchase and enjoy certified organically grown fruits and vegetables whenever you can.

"Certified organically grown" is produce grown in soil that is free of all chemicals (even added nitrogen) for three years, to make sure residual toxins are no longer in the ground. Farms in the process of becoming organic are called "transitional farms." To be certified organic, a farm cannot use any form of pesticide, herbicide, or fertilizer.

Perfect Produce Isn't Worth Pesticides

Organic produce sometimes appears better, bigger, brighter, and fresher. At other times it looks discolored, since there are no dyes used. Without the use of pesticides, the skins on various fruits and vegetables can be imperfect and have marks. And sometimes, without waxes and fungicides that seal in moisture and prevent mold, organic fruits and vegetables aren't as colorful or shiny. But let's take a lesson from the Europeans.

In Europe, where fewer pesticides are used, people judge produce on taste, not looks. (Perhaps that's why Europeans rely more on flavor than on recipes.) They purchase delicious produce even though it's smashed, scarred, and more expensive—which is a little hard to understand, considering the savings gained from not using chemicals.

Organic produce is more costly because organic farming is more labor intensive; weeds and pests must be removed by hand, which outweighs the savings farmers gain by avoiding chemicals. But, as more growers switch to organic farming, organic food costs are going down. When you purchase organic products, you're investing in a method of production that's environmentally sound!

Organic Farmers and Their Creative Ways

Organic farmers advocate techniques that promote a positive health-style, since the methods they use enhance the safety, nutrition, and taste of our food supply. To divert bugs without pesticide contamination, farmers plant alfalfa between their crops. Others place flat boards along the base of the plants, because slugs attach themselves to the dark underside. During the night, farmers turn the boards over and remove the slugs.

Also, ladybugs, and other "good" bugs, are brought onto the farm to destroy aphids and similar pests. One ladybug can consume several thousand aphids in its life span.

To scare gophers and blackbirds away, organic farmers place toy snakes on the ground and fly helium balloons in the sky. Scarecrows are also strategically placed to protect the goods. I, myself, have a plastic owl in my little garden, and sometimes I spray cayenne pepper in water on the leaves at night to deter those nasty pests. Paula has three mousers, cats that live primarily outside and chase away the birds, squirrels, moles, and mountain beavers that disturb her garden.

Tremendous advantages result from these farmers' efforts. Since organic produce doesn't require peeling to remove the wax coatings, fungicide residues, or pesticides from their skins, people who consume organic produce obtain more fiber in their diets.

Once you experience the fresh clean taste, you'll want all your produce to be grown organically. Tell your grocery-store manager you want organic produce. If it's not available in your local supermarket, or if the produce manager isn't willing to obtain at least some organic produce, don't shop there anymore; find another market. Natural-food stores always carry at least some organically grown foods, and there are 6,800 of them located throughout the nation today.

FARMER'S MARKETS

Whenever possible, shop at your local farmer's market. All around the world, farmers and their managers are organizing farmer's markets to give the local growers a chance to show off and sell their wares to the people that live in their neighborhood. Most of the produce is organic and freshly harvested.

The farmers are usually in town only one or two days a week, so it's not always convenient to get there. The produce, though, is usually much better tasting, less expensive, and there is more variety from which to choose.

There's a real sense of excitement among the people bustling through a farmer's market! If you stop at one of the grower's stands, and you don't recognize a vegetable, it's common to get a quick cooking tip. The growers want to talk to you. And it's easy to build a bond or friendship with the growers, because it's a symbiotic or mutually beneficial relationship.

The organic-food market, according to the Department of Agriculture, is growing rapidly. There are now approximately 2,410 farmer's markets across the country, and that number is increasing rapidly.

Where I shop, in Westwood, California, the growers always advise me about what's best to buy. And if I take something home and it's not good, it's not unusual for them to replace it the next week if I tell them about the problem. And have you ever noticed how healthy most of the organic farmers look? They have a special radiance.

Shopping at a farmer's market gives you a chance to eat local produce that's fresher, since it hasn't been shipped. Purchase the produce you like that looks bright in color and feels firm to the touch, but shop frequently because fruits and vegetables grown and shipped without chemicals spoil more quickly.

To find out where there's a farmer's market in your area, you can contact the U.S. Department of Agriculture, and request a free brochure. Or, the farmer's markets are listed, state by state, with information relative to each market, on the World Wide Web: (www.usda.gov/ams/states.htm)

U.S. Department of Agriculture AMS-FMD
P.O. Box 96456
Room 2642, South Building
Washington D.C., 20090-6456
Phone (202) 720-8317

Roadside stands, along rural roads, also make it possible to purchase directly from the farmers and break up the monotonous routine of shopping. So look for them, stop, and shop.

PURCHASE SEASONAL PRODUCE

I became a faithful lover of locally grown seasonal fruits and vegetables one carefree summer in Hawaii, too many years ago. I snacked on guavas that grow wild along Maui's roads, bananas and papaya directly from the trees in Kauai, and pineapples fresh from the fields in Lanai. I experienced how food should taste, and never forgot it.

Have you ever eaten a tomato that truly smells and tastes like a tomato should, or an ear of corn that tastes so delicious you prefer it plain? You won't settle for anything less once you've tasted mouthwatering seasonal produce. But purchasing it becomes confusing while standing in the supermarket and seeing corn, for example, in December. Before the advent of improved storage and transportation techniques, corn on the cob was a summer treat while its flavor was at its peak. But now, many fruits and vegetables are available year-round.

Purchasing strawberries, peaches, and grapes during the winter is convenient, but produce picked too soon, transported an average of 1,900 miles, and warehouse-ripened is more expensive, less flavorful, and less nutritious than those that are tree- or vine-ripened. So, talk to the produce manager if you're confused about *what* and *what not* to buy.

Even if you don't consider yourself a good cook, you'll become one, simply by purchasing freshly harvested produce. To make delicious vegetable dishes, it's far more important to purchase good produce than to follow complicated recipes.

AVOID BRANDED PRODUCE

If you live in a place where fruits and vegetables can't be grown, it's necessary for you to purchase produce that has been shipped. But don't get fooled, as most people do, into thinking that *branded produce* (trademarked fruits and vegetables) is better than seasonal organic. Although branded produce often sells best, it just doesn't make sense to buy Florida oranges if you live in California, or vice versa. Unless you have no other option, why purchase produce that's been sprayed with pesticides, ripened in storage, and shipped?

Perhaps people want to buy Chiquita Bananas for the same reasons they want to show off a pair of Levi's or Guess jeans. But, think about it: Produce ripened in shipping cars couldn't possibly be as flavorful or nutritious as produce ripened naturally. Produce gets its flavor and nutritional contents from the soil, the water, and the warm sunshine.

To purchase fresher, better-tasting, sweeter produce—food that tastes like real food:

- Purchase the *most* locally grown produce available.
- Look for organically grown.
- Buy whatever looks good that's in season.
- Look to lower prices as a clue to what's in season. There's an old saying among people working in produce: "When quality is at its worst, prices are highest; when quality is best, prices are lowest."
- Avoid eating imported, branded, fresh foods on a regular basis.
- Talk to the produce manager if you're still not sure about what to buy.

VEGGIE GAME PLAN

Simplicity is more important than recipes when preparing fruits or vegetables. Take one or two really good vegetables, such as cucumbers, artichokes, and tomatoes, add a complementary fruit and/or dressing, and be done with it! A minimum of ingredients often gets maximum results:

- To guarantee freshness, purchase vegetables that have a firm texture.
- Treat the vegetables gently once you get them home. Don't wash, peel, or cut the veggies until you're ready to prepare or use them, or they'll lose important nutrients.
- Store veggies in the vegetable crisper of the refrigerator (with the exception of tomatoes and potatoes), because they last longest at low temperatures and high humidity.
- When cleaning, rinse well in cool water containing a little dishwashing liquid, rinse again in plain water, and then pat dry.
- Peel fruits and vegetables that *aren't* organic whenever possible to remove pesticide residues. But with organically grown, remember that Grandma-ma always said, "The skin is the best part!"
- When cooking vegetables, it's this simple; the fire goes off when they're cooked to your liking.

VEGGIE DISHES THAT WORK

PUREED CAULIFLOWER

Make this, and your guests will think they're eating mashed potatoes. Steam a large head of cauliflower until it's soft. Puree in a blender, adding a little salt and pepper while it's still hot, and serve immediately.

EGGPLANT PARMESAN

This dish is delightful, served on an open-faced bun and topped with sautéed mushrooms, or over pasta. Slice eggplant one quarter inch thick. Dip the eggplant first in beaten egg whites and then in a mixture of bread crumbs, Parmesan cheese, and any dry herbs you prefer (basil, thyme, garlic).

Pour some ready-made marinara or spaghetti sauce in a shallow baking dish (see chapter 5, page 129, for suggestions). Then place breaded eggplant slices on top, and top with more sauce. Bake at 350 degrees. Top with mozzarella cheese, and heat until bubbly.

TOMATO AND GREEN BEANS ITALIAN

When beautiful fresh string beans are available, try this. Rinse the beans, cut the steam, and remove the string by pulling it along the edge. Leave the beans whole or cut them in half, depending upon the length. Sauté a sliced onion and some minced garlic in a saucepan sprayed with a little oil. Add the beans and a jar of your favorite pasta sauce, enough to coat the beans well, and cover. If you want a richer tomato taste, add tomato paste. Add water if you want a milder sauce. Simmer about forty minutes, or until tender. This is a simple dish to make, and easy to transport to a potluck dinner. (You've come a long way from canned string beans and mushroom soup!)

SESAME CABBAGE AND ONIONS

Make this on a day you're doing other things around the house. Sauté yellow onions and garlic in a skillet with a little oil until onions are brown and caramelized. Add one head of shredded white cabbage (shred by using a sharp knife or shredder). Cook until the cabbage picks up the flavor from the onion and becomes soft and tender. Sprinkle in some soy sauce, or a little red-wine vinegar, add the toasted sesame seeds, toss and serve. (I toast the seeds in the dry pan, before caramelizing the onions.) This is delicious served alongside turkey and mashed potatoes, or as part of a vegetable plate. Try it on Thanksgiving.

EASY RATATOUILLE (VEGETABLE STEW)

"Ra-ta-too-ee" is a little like salsa or stew—delicious alone or as an accompaniment to grilled meats or poultry. It's also wonderful in omelets.

Combine canned stewed tomatoes (or Italian peeled tomatoes, without the core), sliced zucchini, yellow crookneck squash, patty squash, eggplant, onions, garlic, bell pepper, mushrooms, and olives. Omit, of course, any ingredient you don't like. Add garlic, basil, thyme, oregano, marjoram, soy sauce—or whatever you *do* like. Cover and bake, for an hour or so, at 350 degrees, until the vegetables are soft like a stew. Don't worry if you cook it too long; the vegetables are supposed to be tender. Ratatouille is delicious in a crepe or over pasta. Add some cheese, bake until bubbly, and you've got a meal.

EASIER RATATOUILLE

Place thick slices of zucchini, yellow squash, a chunk of eggplant, onion, a sliced fresh tomato, and peeled garlic cloves on a large piece of foil. Drizzle with olive oil, add salt and pepper to taste, and wrap tightly. Broil or grill for thirty-five to forty-five minutes, turning occasionally. *Always, always, always,* give yourself permission to invent!

CARROTS GRAND MARNIER

Sauté garlic and about a half bunch of scallions in a deep skillet that has been sprayed with oil. Add raw shredded carrots—

about three quarter pound per person—and shredded fennel bulb or seeds to taste. When the vegetables are soft, splash with Grand Marnier, sprinkle with pepper, toss, and enjoy.

STUFFED VEGGIES

Some vegetables taste even better when stuffed with chicken or tuna salad, grains, ground meat, pasta, avocado, shrimp, or literally anything that tastes good. Next time you're in the mood for eggplant Parmesan, why not serve it inside a baked eggplant? I think pasta primavera would be delicious baked inside a big red-ripe juicy tomato, or in a big bell pepper. If something works for you, then do it, no matter what experts or everyone else is doing. Your taste is all that matters.

I don't suggest stuffing *overgrown* vegetables, however. Once I had a huge zucchini growing in my garden that I decided to stuff and serve to guests. It was a disaster. After baking the zucchini in the oven for over an hour and fifteen minutes, the seeds I sautéed with the rest of the stuffing remained almost as hard as unshelled sunflower seeds. Thank goodness I had made other dishes, too.

STUFFED EGGPLANT

Cut a large eggplant in half lengthwise. Scoop and cube the flesh, leaving a ½-inch wall on the sides and bottom of each shell. Add a few drops of olive oil to a skillet and sauté the eggplant cubes, diced onion, garlic, snipped cilantro, parsley, and cooked rice or bulgur wheat. (This mixture, or any variation thereof, is great for stuffing cabbage, grape leaves, bell peppers, and zucchini.)

Fill the shells, top with your favorite cheese, and bake in a 350-degree oven for about thirty to forty minutes. For variety, add seasoned lean ground beef, diced tomatoes, and sliced mushrooms before baking.

STUFFED ARTICHOKES

If I were only allowed to eat one vegetable for the rest of my life, it would be the artichoke, and this is how I'd prepare it. Clean artichokes—I usually make two or three at a time; they keep well in the fridge for about a week. Use scissors to snip off the tips of the leaves, and using a spoon and a curved grapefruit knife, clean out the purple leaves and fuzz from the insides. Then I'd boil what remains until I could pull out one of the leaves relatively easily.

Meanwhile I'd cut some stale or toasted bread into small cubes and toss into a mixture of virgin olive oil, minced garlic, a squeeze of lemon, diced organic tomatoes, salt, and lots of herbs.

I'd allow the artichokes to open on a plate, like the beautiful flowers they are, spoon the mixture throughout, and enjoy every bite. The poet Wil Hastings says, "Eating an artichoke is like getting to know someone really well."

STUFFED GRAPE LEAVES—DOLMADES

These are expensive if you buy them ready made, but inexpensive and easy to prepare yourself. Purchase prepared grape leaves from the market. Drain, and cut off the stem. Prepare a mixture similar to the one suggested above, without the eggplant. (Add ground meat instead if you like, or simply use leftover rice.) Place a couple of teaspoons of the mixture in each leaf, fold sides over mixture, and roll as tightly as possible. Steam these for about ten minutes and enjoy eating them hot or cold.

STUFFED CABBAGE

For stuffing cabbage, remove all imperfect leaves, then steam, covered, for about twenty minutes, or until the leaves are flexible. Remove the larger leaves from the cabbage. Place two to three tablespoons of the mixture suggested above (for stuffed grape leaves) in the center of each cabbage leaf. Fold sides over mixture, and roll loosely. Place in an oiled, shallow Pyrex-type dish. For the sauce, add brown sugar to taste to a healthful, ready-made marinara-type pasta sauce. (You'll find suggestions in chapter 5, page 129.) Spoon the tomato mixture over the rolls, and bake them, first covered, then uncovered, until they're heated thoroughly.

STUFFED BELL PEPPERS

Using the same tricks and a little sleight of hand, you can make another similar yet special dish! In a skillet, sauté chopped onion and garlic in a bit of hot oil. Add lean ground beef, chopped basil, cilantro, and cooked rice.

Cut the tops off bell peppers. Remove the seeds and membranes, and rinse well. Stuff the mixture into each pepper, or add bulgur wheat, kashi, or kasha. (See chapter 9, page 241, for more information about these grains.)

Place one quarter inch of marinara sauce in a baking pan and arrange bell peppers on top. Bake covered at 350 degrees, thirty minutes or so. Add cheese if you like, and cook uncovered until done.

STUFFED ZUCCHINI

Slice zucchini lengthwise, scoop out the flesh, and sauté with rice and the other ingredients you enjoy. In other words, fill several zucchini with a mixture similar to the one that's suggested above. (Remember to use medium-sized zucchini rather than one that's huge; when zucchini grow large, their seeds become extremely tough.) Pour tomato sauce on the bottom of the pan, place the zucchini on the sauce, top with more sauce and grated cheese, cover with foil, and bake.

POTATOES

There are as many varieties of potatoes as there are salads. Fortunately—like salads, which are either tossed or composed —potatoes can also be divided into two large families:

There are either dry, starchy baking potatoes, such as Idaho or Yukon Gold—my favorite—or moist, waxy boiling varieties, like Rose potatoes. The boiling potatoes have smooth skins, and the baking potatoes are russet, or coarse skinned. We used to think they weren't interchangeable, but I often boil Yukon Gold and bake the little round red-skinned ones. Both types, however, like tomatoes, should not be refrigerated. They thrive at a higher temperature and humidity, and do best when stored in a cool, dark spot, such as a pantry in the kitchen.

A three-ounce potato contains only 150 calories. Made into French fries, the same potato contains a whopping 300 calories!

It's best not to bake potatoes in foil; this steams the potato and gives it a mushy, boiled texture. In addition, a foil-wrapped potato takes longer to bake.

Mmm-Mmm Potato Chips

Preheat oven to 450 degrees. Slice baking potatoes into ⅛-inch slices, and arrange in one layer on an oiled baking sheet. Lightly spray with oil, sprinkle with salt, and bake until crisp. This takes approximately fifteen minutes. For variety, sprinkle the uncooked potatoes with soy sauce, or the baked chips with Parmesan cheese. The same cooking technique also works well with sweet potatoes!

Twice-Baked Potatoes

I looked forward to eating Aunt Vicki's creamy, double-baked potatoes until I learned that she had been preparing them with butter, cream, and sour cream. Now, copying her basic procedure, I make equally delicious double-baked potatoes healthfully.

Bake one potato for each person, scoop out the insides, and whip the contents with a little nonfat milk, nonfat yogurt, nonfat sour cream, plus a little fat-free mozzarella cheese and several cloves of baked garlic. Refill the shells with this mixture, sprinkle a little cheddar cheese on top, and heat the refilled shells again. Aunt Vicki looks forward to double-baked potatoes at my house now.

ANOTHER TWICE-BAKED IDEA

In an oiled skillet, sauté chopped bell pepper, onion, mushrooms, and marinated artichoke hearts. Scoop out the insides of a baked potato and add the contents to the sautéed mixture. Refill the shell and top the potato with any type of cheese—nonfat, regular, or a combination of both. Broil until crispy.

COOK'S TIP

To turn plain baked potatoes into something fancy, combine fat-free cottage cheese, nonfat sour cream, or plain fat-free yogurt with cut scallions, chives, or Lawry's season salt. This mixture also tastes delicious on baked yams or sweet potatoes. For a nice change, drizzle a little olive oil on baked potatoes, sprinkle with salt and you'll be surprised how good it is. Yum!

OVEN-FRIED POTATOES

Cut scrubbed, unpeeled Yukon or baking potatoes into strips, chunks, or rounds. Place single-layered onto a baking sheet and spray with olive or canola oil. Bake for forty-five minutes, or until done, at 350 degrees, turning occasionally. Sprinkle lightly with salt, paprika, soy sauce, balsamic vinegar, Tabasco, Cajun spice, or Parmesan cheese. Yams or sweet potatoes, alone or combined, work well, too.

HOME FRIES

Heat a little olive or canola oil in a skillet. Brown some onion (green, brown, red, or a combination of the three). Add cilantro,

bell pepper, if you like, and lots of cut-up, leftover baked potatoes. Yukon Gold, purple, or red-skinned potatoes make delicious home fries. Since the potatoes have already been baked,
this technique won't take long.

POTATO & VEGGIE OMELET

Diced leftover potatoes and vegetables make a delicious
omelet. Spray a skillet; pour in three or four beaten egg whites,
the diced veggies and potatoes, and a little avocado and fat-
free cottage cheese if you're in the mood. Fold or flip and it's
done! This also works with whole eggs, if you also enjoy the
yolk.

REFRIGERATOR OMELET

Clean out the fridge and at the same time make an omelet
with whatever you like. For example, sauté onions, purple cabbage, potatoes, apples, and corn. Add beaten eggs or egg
whites, a little cheese, and salt and pepper to taste. This omelet
will be cooked and ready to serve without turning it over.

Try This

Grate potatoes and whatever vegetables you like into an
oiled skillet. Whip three eggs, or four egg whites, and pour
them into the skillet. Top with cheese and roasted sunflower
seeds, and serve.

PAULA'S POTATO SALAD

My friend Paula isn't always a flop in the kitchen. We had
lunch at the beach the other day, and the potato salad she
brought was absolutely scrumptious.

She mixes low-fat ricotta cheese with a little olive oil and
crushed garlic. Then she cuts up any type of boiled potatoes
(with or without the skin), red bell peppers, red onion, olives,

scallions, lots of cilantro, parsley, and basil, and mixes everything together.

As Paula was serving everyone second helpings, she unfortunately dropped the bowl into the sand. We made her promise to make her potato salad again!

PAULA'S POTATO SALAD VARIATIONS

Paula did make potato salad again, with a slight variation. You won't be able to resist this one, and it's easy!

She cut boiled potatoes into chunks, and added chopped onion, bell pepper, celery, salt, pepper, cilantro, olives, and radishes.

Paula drizzled this mixture with her favorite salad dressing, and says you can also add a little fat-free mayonnaise, which has been mixed with a bit of curry and honey for flavor, color, and sweetness.

Another option is to dress this salad with plain nonfat yogurt mixed with a little Dijon mustard. (Without much trouble, you've made potato salad much better than you can buy; yams can be substituted, too!)

INTERESTING TIP

People often confuse cilantro with parsley because they look similar, but cilantro is actually more spicy, peppery, and tingly on the tongue. (While parsley is good, it's bland by comparison.) People seem to loathe cilantro, or love it! I use it in salads, vegetables, salsas, and stir-fry dishes. If you're like I am, you'll want to sprinkle it over most everything.

SPINACH CASSEROLE

In a bowl, mix a pound of nonfat cottage cheese, three egg whites, and a couple of tablespoons of water. (There's no need to beat the egg whites first.) Add two bunches of washed and chopped spinach, some cilantro, basil, bread crumbs, and salt to taste. Spoon into a pie pan or baking dish—the mixture will be a little runny. Bake at 350 degrees, an hour or more, until brown.

NUTRITION TIP

Spinach is rich in folic acid, vitamins A and C. It's high in calcium, potassium and magnesium. Toss it into green salads, omelets, or sauté with garlic and an array of mushrooms.

MARINATED BROCCOLI

This makes a refreshing side dish or salad. Discard ends and, if necessary, peel broccoli stems. Steam the broccoli in a pot with a little water until just tender, and if you quickly rinse it with cold water, you'll maintain its beautiful green color. Drain the water, slice the broccoli spears lengthwise, and place them in a bowl. Combine olive oil, minced garlic, lemon juice, salt, and a little Dijon mustard to taste. Pour this mixture over the broccoli, and chill. At serving time, place the broccoli on greens and garnish this dish with lemon slices, pimentos, olives, or whatever you please.

COOK'S TIP

If you haven't tasted tender, young, succulent broccoli from a home garden, you don't know broccoli. Unfortunately, supermarket broccoli leaves something to be desired. Usually it's overgrown, so the flavor coarsens, and the peel gets leathery. If you have room in your yard, grow your own!

ORGANIC GARDENING

If you have a patch of land, a patio, or even a flower box, you may want to supplement the produce, herbs, and spices you purchase by growing your own. I remember watching my dad grow an abundance of the best-tasting tomatoes on a lit-tle patio in the San Fernando Valley by weaving them through a trellis. Everyone should grow tomatoes sometime in life, and taste a "real" tomato.

There are four simple steps necessary for successful gar-dening:

- Planning
- Soil preparation
- Planting
- Gardening Maintenance

To plant a garden, begin by determining the proper location. It's of prime importance to select the sunniest area of your yard. Next, make sure you're planting in loose, rich soil that has the correct pH balance. A pH test kit, which costs 99¢, indicates whether or not you have the high nitrogen, low phosphorous, and high potassium levels needed for planting. (If you don't, you'll need to nourish the soil before planting, as outlined below.)

Once you've established soil that drains well, think about the vegetables you most enjoy. Depending upon the planting sea-son, purchase *seedlings* (little plants) at your local nursery and plant them in the ground. You can also purchase organic seeds and place them in the ground according to the package direc-tions.

The Two Planting Seasons

The gardening year is divided into a cool and warm season. During the fall or cool season, plant cool-season crops that re-quire cool weather to mature to perfection, such as: lettuce, spinach, and other leafy greens, broccoli, cabbage, root veg-etables, and peas.

And, for best results, vegetables such as tomatoes, peppers, beans, corn, melons, eggplant, and squash should be planted during the spring or warm season.

Once your garden is planted, give it lots of love. Water it in the morning and evening, when there's no sunshine. And, be sure to remove the weeds and bugs regularly.

SAFETY TIP

Be careful not to use any chemical products in or around your organic garden. (That would defeat the whole purpose!) Look at the ingredients in all gardening products to be sure there isn't anything going into the soil, or on the vegetables and fruit, that you wouldn't want inside your stomach.

Compost Pile

Start a compost pile if you have a large backyard and want to recycle your vegetable peelings and yard wastes so you can make your own fertilizer. It's an easy way to give back to the earth, rather than just taking away. But choose your spot carefully.

Find a location that's not too far from the kitchen, yet away from the window because decomposing compost creates a sight and fragrance most people can't stand after six to eight weeks. Like most things, it's a matter of perception, because some folks say it smells like good earth, and looks like black gold.

Paula has become an enthusiastic gardener and since her husband has no sense of smell, she located the compost pile behind his office. (I keep wondering what clients think, especially new ones, when they meet him at his office.)

A good compost is naturally made up of one third carbon and two thirds nitrogen. To keep that balance, collect green and brown items such as vegetables, grass clippings, ashes, and coffee grounds, and add them to your compost pile in a one-to-two ratio, carbon to nitrogen. Generally speaking, brown matter such as fallen leaves and sawdust give off carbon, and green matter such as grass clippings and weeds are high in nitrogen. Mix the compost occasionally, and add some earthworms;

they'll help you do the job. Add water if your compost is too dry, or cover the pile if it's receiving too much water, and you'll eventually have the makings to grow the best fruits, vegetables, and herbs you've ever tasted.

Of course, even for people with green thumbs, gardens can get costly. Andy Rooney, in his book *Word for Word,* writes about the zucchini his wife grew. "There are few things in life more satisfying than saving money by growing your own vegetables in a little garden. Last night, we had three small zucchini for dinner that were grown within fifty feet of our back door. I estimate that they cost somewhere in the neighborhood of $371.49 each."

But, then again, there's so much joy, maybe cost doesn't matter when it comes to gardening. You simply can't put a dollar value on some things.

Alice B. Toklas had it right. She said, "The first gathering of the garden in May of salads, radishes, and herbs makes me feel the way a mother feels about her baby—how could anything so beautiful be mine?"

Maybe it's easier and less expensive to have a peach tree than to purchase peaches at the market, but it just didn't work out that way for me.

Two years ago my daughter, Chelsea, and I wanted to grow our own fruit. We purchased an apple, a peach, and an apricot tree. I thought there was no way to fail, since the trees were already bearing fruit when we transferred them from their cans into the ground. We faithfully watered our orchard and watched the fruit grow and ripen on each tree. But on the day the fruit was finally ready to be picked, the deer and squirrels got to it first each time! Last year, we covered the fruit with mesh netting but the squirrels simply reached through. We're investigating a protective fence to keep them away next year.

Regarding the deer, my hairdresser says that if I put hair clippings around the edges of my garden, the deer will think people are around and stay away. I haven't tried it yet.

In some cases because of these animals, it's also a lot easier to purchase fresh herbs than to cultivate an herb garden. But I guess, for me, it's that minty, fruity, peppery fragrance coming from the herbs through my kitchen window on a summer evening that says it all. I love cooking with fresh herbs, and I adore tossing freshly picked cilantro, basil, mint, and thyme into my salads.

Herb Garden Tips

- Plant herbs in a small area; even a flower box will do.
- Protect your garden. (Try the hair clipping if you have deer!)
- Water regularly.
- Harvest herbs early in the morning before the sun evaporates their oils.
- Rinse the herbs well, and lay them on paper towels to remove the excess water.
- To dry herbs, when you have more fresh herbs than you can use, tie small bunches together at the stem and hang them upside down in a place that's warm, dark, and well ventilated. A large closet works well. (See chapter 4, page 106, for more information about herbs.)
- Microwaving also works well for drying fresh herbs. Rinse the herbs, pat dry, and place a few sprigs between paper towels. Microwave on a low setting for a couple of minutes or until the herbs are completely dry.
- Store dried herbs in glass containers with tight-fitting lids. Label and date.
- Your herbs will retain their flavor for several months, sometimes up to a year.

KITCHEN TIP

Fresh or dried herbs, such as basil, parsley, chives, tarragon, and mint, can be frozen in freezer-safe plastic bags and then used as fresh. There's no need to thaw them first.

TRANSITIONAL PRODUCE

If you are unable to have a garden, or purchase organic produce, locate *transitional produce* in the market or farmer's market. Transitional produce is grown on farms where pesticides were previously used. The requirements vary from state to state, but time must pass without the use of potentially harmful additives before the produce is considered transitional. And then another period of time must elapse before it's considered certified organic.

If you can't buy transitional produce, look for fruits and vegetables grown by farmers who reduce pesticide use by at least fifty percent. Billions of dollars are spent on pesticides annually, but most of the pesticides used never affect the pests. Instead, they go directly into our soil, water supply, and food chain.

Fortunately, farmers who realize that more pesticides are used than needed are cutting back and saving money without losing crops.

SAFETY TIP

Remember to wash all produce well by adding a drop of dishwashing liquid to the water. The soap removes more pesticides than water alone. Peel all nonorganic fruits and vegetables that have a wax coating.

To find out the health effects of pesticides and the safety precautions to take, call the National Pesticide Telecommunications Network hot-line at 1-800 858-7378. They are open from 9:30 A.M. to 7:30 P.M. Eastern time, Monday through Friday.

IRRADIATION

Until we figure out a way to supply the nation with organic fruits and vegetables, or at least transitional produce, irradiation (a process that exposes food to small doses of gamma rays) may be another answer that allows us to safely avoid the harmful effects of pesticides. Gamma rays are high-energy light rays—but why would anyone irradiate food?

Irradiation delays ripening and spoilage of produce, destroys the insects and parasites in beans and grains, and rids fresh meats and seafood of disease-causing microorganisms. Finally, with this technique, we can stop suffering the debilitating effects and sometimes deadly illnesses caused by food-borne organisms.

DESIGNER PRODUCE

Designer produce, otherwise known as *genetically engineered* produce, offers more health benefits from smaller portions than traditional foods; it's genetically engineered to contain more nutrients to fight diseases such as cancer, heart disease, and osteoporosis. Examples are carrots with more beta-carotene than usual, and fruit with extra vitamin C.

One day, dietary specialists and physicians may use designer foods to customize diets for people predisposed to specific diseases. Look for designer produce at your local supermarket and natural-food stores. It will be designated as such. Even if you can't find it—or organic—it's important to include more produce in your daily diet.

EAT PRODUCE REGULARLY

Although eating fruits and vegetables containing potentially harmful pesticides over a long period of time is a concern, *don't avoid produce* for that reason. Always remember that the benefits of a diet high in produce outweigh the ill effects pesticides may cause.

Include More Fruits and Veggies in Your Diet

Add fruit to your cereal for breakfast, drink a glass of juice, or put fruit on top of your pancakes or yogurt to include more produce in your daily diet. Fruit is always convenient and delicious to eat on the run.

For lunch, try a salad topped with grilled vegetables. A veggie and avocado sandwich, or pasta primavera (pasta with sautéed vegetables) is satisfying. Try one, or have them all!

It's always fun to begin dinner with an appetizer of raw veggies and dip, or a cup of vegetable soup. Top a baked potato with salsa and broccoli, enjoy stir-fried veggies, or turn a salad into the main event of the meal.

For dessert, liven up frozen yogurt or angel-food cake with your favorite fruit, or enjoy fresh berries. Be creative. It doesn't matter when, or in what order, you eat. Perhaps you'd like to ignore food traditions and have vegetarian pizza for breakfast and cold cereal with fruit for dinner.

Fortunately, for good health, there's no particular fruit or vegetable you *must* eat, since another similarly colored item contains analogous nutrients. It's important to eat citrus fruits in addition to yellow and green fruits and veggies regularly. If you don't like grapefruit, then oranges, lemons, or limes substitute nicely. If you don't enjoy yellow squash, eat carrots or cantaloupe instead. Even former President Bush won't be deprived nutritionally for not liking broccoli, if he eats plenty of other green veggies instead.

AN (ALMOST) EFFORTLESS VEGETARIAN DINNER

For a Fourth of July pool party, I invited my favorite tennis partner, who's a part-time vegetarian (the one who enjoys tuna sandwiches once in a while), some friends who don't eat red meat, and another family who has teenage daughters who don't eat eggs or dairy products.

After hanging up the phone I began wondering how I got myself into such a mess. Fortunately, I came up with an easy menu while looking around the farmer's market and bought just about everything I needed.

On the day of the party, when everyone started arriving, I served wedges of Camembert and Bel Paese cheese on large wooden trays alongside whole nectarines and peaches. It was a do-it-yourself service with cheese cutters and sharp knives placed nearby.

My husband served drinks while our daughter, Chelsea, made guacamole. She added fresh, hot salsa to mashed, ripe avocados, and had to make a second batch right away since she and her friends ate most of the first batch while making it. She served the dip next to a big basket of oven-roasted chips.

Later in the day, my husband began grilling large bulbs of garlic wrapped in foil and drizzled with a little olive oil and basil. He put skewers of onions, mushrooms, zucchini, and bell pepper on the grill that had been sprayed first with canola oil and then brushed them with his favorite barbecue sauce. (Make sure you put the skewer through the center of the veggies; some of ours slipped off into the coals.)

We also grilled Japanese eggplant, fennel, potatoes, tomatoes, and corn on the cob. (Garrison Keiller once said, "Sex is good, but not as good as fresh sweet corn.")

Before grilling the corn, we peeled back the husks and carefully removed the silk. We rinsed the corn in water, and then brushed the ears with a mixture of olive oil, cumin, paprika, Lawry's season salt, cilantro, cayenne, and garlic powder which flavored it just right! We replaced the husks, tied the ends with twine, arranged the corn on the grill, and roasted it until the husks started to scorch. But be careful, it can burn fast! The corn *was* incredible.

By the time the other succulent veggies were done, the individual cloves of garlic were as soft inside as butter, so we began smearing the puree over slices of warm, crusty Italian bread.

The adults were kicking back with low-fat brownies and coffee, and the kids were lighting sparklers when I overheard someone say, "There's no place like home for a great night with friends!"

So, let's do something else that's exciting—with another favorite of vegetarians and meat-eaters alike: sinfully delicious grains.

CHAPTER 9

◆

Sinfully Delicious Grains

"I have been so well nurtured throughout my life that I'm sure to die completely cured."
—Fernand Point

When my daughter Chelsea was seven, I remember her telling me, "Compared to a lot of my friends, I sure learned to eat well!"

"How, honey?"

"We have delicious food in the fridge that's good for us."

What you do in life truly is a matter of habit, so eating healthier means getting hooked on good nutrition. You eat high-octane "nutrient-dense" foods, and as soon as you begin feeling better, you become dependent upon those foods. Healthful food, when prepared well, starts tasting better than unhealthful foods; you even crave it.

One of my favorite chefs (and friend), Kathy Diamond, from Basalt, Colorado, (the one who made the eggless eggnog) cooks and eats more delicious, high-octane foods than most people I know. She's the executive chef at a hiking resort/health spa, and on her days off she often snowboards for eight hours at a time. Since she can't afford to get fatigued, she always takes her lunch along. I was talking to her yesterday when she said something that stuck with me, "There's no way my body can perform at peak performance on mountain-restaurant Cokes, candy bars, and fries (which, interestingly enough, is all they sell). Some of my friends expect to ski all day long on a bagel, and then wonder why they end up feeling exhausted and get hurt." (See chapter 6, page 171, for Chef Kathy's eggless eggnog.)

MAKE GRAINS PART OF YOUR DIET

Most nights there's a grain dish on our dinner table, and it's not only because they're good for us that I make them. My family couldn't care less that grains are the staff of life. And, the fact that grains are economical doesn't impress anyone in my family, either. When I tell my husband and daughter that a cup of cooked grains has only 200 calories and not enough fat to mention, or that grains are high in magnesium, iron, protein, complex carbohydrates and fiber, I barely get them to look up from their food. The only thing that truly impresses my family at dinnertime is a sinfully delicious dish!

Every country has a president, a flag, and—probably more important—a grain. A healthy diet can't stave off death, but it can make you healthier, so you'll feel better while you're alive. People have lower rates of heart disease, cancer, and obesity in countries where more grains are eaten.

Fruits and veggies are essential to good health (we know to eat Five a Day), but shouldn't we have a slogan to remind us to include more grains in our diet, too? Grains are good sources of essential fatty acids, vitamin E, and all the B vitamins except B-12. I suggest you make more sinfully delicious grains, and eat them often.

Grains Are an Intricate Part of Life

Essentially, all of the food people eat comes from *grass seeds,* otherwise called grains. Even the farm animals eat grains, so without plants there wouldn't be anything at all for anyone to eat! Grains have always been precious to society. Writing was initially invented to keep track of grain sales rather than to record and transmit expression.

In America, however, eating a bowl of pasta with a slice of bread is about as close as most people get to consuming grains. In fact, more barley is eaten by American farm animals than by American people. That's unfortunate, since refined products aren't nearly as flavorful, nutritious, or fibrous as whole grains.

FIBER

A diet high in fiber helps prevent constipation and reduces your risk of colon cancer and intestinal problems. Fiber also helps you control your weight, regulate your blood sugar, and lower your cholesterol level.

The National Cancer Institute and The Food and Drug Administration recommend that we each have thirty-five to forty grams of fiber per day, but the latest word from the National Health and Nutrition Examination Survey is that the typical adult consumes only about half that amount.

The easiest way to obtain more soluble and insoluble fiber in your diet is to eat more fruits, vegetables, beans, and—you guessed it—whole grains.

FORGET TRADITIONAL GRAIN RECIPES

Most people want to include more grains in their diet, but run into problems. They don't know where to find barley, quinoa, oats, couscous, bulgur wheat, and kasha. And, they don't know how to prepare these delicious grains quickly and simply.

Actually, grains are as easy to prepare as pasta. In other words, if you can boil water, you can prepare grains. Besides being healthy, grains have a satisfying taste, interesting textures, and versatility. They're delectable when made into dishes of their own, added to salads, or used to thicken soups.

GRAIN GAME PLAN

Grains such as white rice, brown rice, and bulgur wheat are found in the rice and pasta aisle of your local market. Others, like quinoa, amaranth, and millet, require a visit to the health-food store where these and other grains are often sold in boxes and by the pound from bulk bins. Grains aren't seasonal, so they're available and convenient all year long. Purchase the ones that interest you and you'll learn to cook as you go!

Most grains are simmered or cooked over a low flame with a lid on the pot for about thirty-five minutes in a 2:1 ratio, two parts liquid to one part grains. The cooking time varies depending upon the absorption of the liquid due to the coarseness of the grain. Quinoa, couscous, and bulgur wheat are more delicate and therefore can be cooked quickly, or just soaked in boiled water. Check the chart below for exceptions:

COOKING TIMES AND PROPORTIONS CHART

Grain	Grain-to-Liquid (Cups)	Cooking Time
Amaranth	1–3	25 min.
Barley	1-3½	45 min.
Brown Rice	1–2	40 min.
Buckwheat	1–2	15 min.
Bulgur	1–2	35 min.
Couscous	1–1¼	5 min.
Jasmine	1–2	25 min.
Kasha	2–4½	15 min.
Kashi	1–2	25 min.
Millet	1–2½	25 min.
Polenta	1–4	25 min.
Quinoa	1–1½	15 min.
Risotto	1–2	35 min.
Wild Rice	1–3	45+ min.
White Rice	1–2	25 min.

In addition to being boiled, the following grains can be eaten after they're soaked.

COOKING TIMES AND PROPORTIONS CHART (cont'd)

Grain	Grain-to-liquid (Cups)	Soaking time
Bulgur	1–2	45 min.
Couscous	1–1¼	15 min.
Quinoa	1–1½	15 min.

NEED ENERGY? EAT RICE!

Rice is a staple for over half the people in the world. In addition to being delectable, rice is vitally important to people. It's possible to produce more rice per acre than any other food, so it's the very soul of the people living in Japan, India, Thailand, and China.

Rice in Chinese means "agriculture," and Chinese farmers eat it at least twice a day, usually for lunch and dinner, because they believe without rice they wouldn't have strength. They even feed it to their dogs and cats, mixed with a little fish or meat for flavor (to fool them). Since the starch in rice is easier for the body to break down, it's important to include rice in every healthful eating plan for its quick source of energy.

Go with the Grain

I recently met a woman named Frances, while hiking. We were talking about cooking, and Frances told me she always takes rice along when she goes camping. She had just returned from a trip in Peru and explained that with water, a few seasonings, and dehydrated veggies and mushrooms, she and her hiking partners made incredibly delectable grain dishes, on an open fire, that provided the fuel they needed on long treks.

Rice is naturally low in fat and high in fiber, and each little nugget, or grain, contains a gold mine of nutrients. White rice is also the perfect dish to eat if you have diarrhea, or if your stomach is bothering you. At approximately a nickel a serving, it's the perfect way to slim down your food budget, too.

What Type Should You Buy?

More varieties of rice are available today than ever before due to the increased consumer demand from the influx of people from Asia and Latin America, so the main problem with rice is knowing which type to buy. It's confusing to stand in the supermarket aisle staring at brown rice, black rice, white rice, wild rice, basmati, texmati, jasmine, arborio, carnaroli, and baldo lined up on the shelf.

To keep the subject simple, let's think in terms of two main classifications, short- and long-grained rice. Both types of rice contain two different starches (amylose and amylopectin) but since short grain contains more amylopectin, the grains stick together more. The rice used in risotto, sushi and *sticky rice*— my personal favorite—are short grained. Asian people also prefer short-grain rice, because it's easier to handle with chopsticks.

Long grain is any rice that's at least three times longer than it is wide. Basmati, texmati (a commercial name for basmati), jasmine, and wild rice are good examples because they contain more amylose, which allows the grains to remain separate when cooked.

Of course, there are thousands of varieties within these two categories, including a "round" rice! This rice is often called medium grain, and the rice used in paella is a good example.

And, let's not forget brown rice, which is available in both long and short grain. Brown rice, unlike white, contains a touch more oil, since its fiber-rich bran and germ haven't been removed. That fact also makes it more nutritious, so I recommend using it whenever its nutty flavor complements the dish you're making. (It needs a little longer to cook, too.)

KITCHEN TIP

To prevent rancidity, store brown rice in the refrigerator if you're not going to use it within a week or two after purchase. If there's no room in the fridge, storing rice in an airtight container in a cool, dark place is helpful.

RICE BASICS

Marketing experts say, "Quick-cooking rice turns out perfect every time!" But actually every type of rice cooks flawlessly once you know how long to cook it!

To make rice, bring the liquid (water, soup stock, clear broth, or a combination of the three) to a boil, add the grains, and simmer covered for about 25 minutes, or until tender. Allow the pot to stand with the lid on for about five minutes, fluff, and serve.

Asian people have a slightly different technique. They wash their rice before cooking it by putting it into a bowl and adding water. They stir it in the bowl with their fingers, pour out the water, and add more until the water runs clear. Then they pour the rice into a pot and add enough water to cover the grains by a depth of one knuckle joint, or slightly over an inch. They bring the water and grains to a boil together, boil the rice for one minute, reduce the heat, cover, and simmer it for approximately twenty-five minutes.

COOK'S TIP

If rice, or any other grain, is cooked but all the liquid isn't absorbed, uncover the pan and continue heating until the liquid evaporates.

When you want to add more flavor to plain long-grain rice and keep it from sticking together, add a couple of drops of oil, beef or chicken broth to the cooking water. The flavor turns out full-bodied and richer, and it looks more appetizing and shiny.

WILD RICE

This grain, with its chewy texture and distinctive woodsy flavor, is actually an aquatic seed grass, rather than a rice. It's the only grain native to North America. One could say it's America's claim to fame. Today it's cultivated in man-made paddies in Minnesota and California. It's also more nutritious and "pricey" than ordinary rice, and it's delicious alone, or combined with other types of rice and grains.

Except for the proportions and cooking time (see the chart on page 226), wild rice is cooked like the others. Rinse the rice really well and add it to the boiling water, or broth. Depending upon how the rice has been cured, the cooking time varies between forty-five and fifty minutes. Wild rice is fully cooked when the grains are cracked.

ORZO AND WILD RICE

Last night I made a dish I must tell you about. I boiled orzos (little pasta, the size of rice) and wild rice separately, until done, approximately a pound of orzo and a third of a pound of wild rice. I added cut-up sun-dried tomatoes with some of the olive oil they were soaking in, pitted Greek olives, cut-up marinated artichoke hearts, chopped red onion basil, cilantro, walnut halves, and a touch of balsamic vinegar and salt. I served this cold with barbecued salmon and dill sauce. The meal was a big hit, and so simple.

MEXICAN RICE

Heat a heavy skillet with a little olive oil, and use it to toast a cup of long-grain white rice that you've rinsed. Add two cups of hot chicken broth. Mix in some chopped onion, garlic, cilantro, bell pepper, and tomato. Turn the heat down low, cover the skillet and simmer without lifting the cover for about twenty-five to thirty-five minutes, or until the liquid is absorbed.

JASMINE RICE

This aromatic rice has a natural aroma and flavor similar to roasted popcorn or nuts. Begin by purchasing jasmine rice; it's available in most supermarkets and specialty Asian markets.

Wash the rice until the water runs clear, boil water, and add the rice. Return the water to a boil, cover the pot, reduce the heat to a simmer, and cook for twenty minutes, or so. Allow the rice to stand covered several minutes, fluff with a fork, and serve.

HURRIED, CURRIED RICE

To make curried rice in a hurry, sauté an onion in a little olive oil in a medium-sized skillet or pan. Add the usual cup of rice—but this time quick-cooking enriched—two cups of water, a small handful of raisins or currants, and a teaspoon or more of curry powder (depending upon your palate).

Simmer with the lid on for about ten minutes, or until the rice is cooked. (Rinsing isn't recommended with enriched rice, because the water removes the dusting of thiamine, niacin, and iron added after milling.)

To create a complete meal, sauté chicken, lean meat, or shrimp with the onion, and add it to the rice.

Felicia, the young woman who did some of the research on this book, told me that when she and her friend went to Japan the food was so expensive all they could afford was steamed rice and curry powder. They ate curried rice casseroles, curried rice salads, and curried rice balls. For dessert, they'd add a little milk and dried fruit to make curried rice pudding.

QUICK TIP

I use enriched rice for convenience, occasionally, but do my best to avoid converted rice. Although it's nutritious, since its vitamins and minerals from the bran layer are forced into the rice kernel, I don't like anything about its precooked factory flavor.

Jambalaya

Once in a while I put together a mixture of spices to have on hand for times when I want to become a cajun chef and make jambalaya, or add "fire" to other dishes. The exact proportions don't matter, but here are some guidelines.

Use about one tablespoon of the following spices: chili pow-der, paprika, crushed chicken bouillon. Then add one teaspoon of cumin, curry powder, thyme, and crushed red pepper. Talk about spicy, this will knock your socks off! If it doesn't, add a little cayenne pepper. (Unless, of course, you're making this for people who want you to turn down the heat!)

To make jambalaya, add enough oil to cover the bottom of a large pot, and turn the fire on medium-high. Depending upon how many people you're going to serve, sauté until brown one or two turkey or any other type of seasoned sausage (nitrate and MSG-free). I squeeze it out of the casing and form the meat into little balls.

Add one chopped onion, some diced celery (remove the strings), and bell pepper. Sauté these vegetables with the sausage until the onions are clear. Add a large can of cored canned tomatoes, including the juice. Add four to six teaspoons of the cajun seasoning mix you put together, and cook every-thing together for ten minutes. Add crawfish tails (if you can find them), and shrimp, if you can't. (Skinless, cut-up chicken can also be added.) Cook another ten minutes. Add approxi-mately six cups of chicken broth, water, or a combination of the two. (You can make this dish ahead of time to this point, and finish cooking it after your guests arrive.)

Turn the fire on high, and bring to a rolling boil. Add three cups of enriched rice, and return the pot to a boil. Reduce the fire to low, cover, and cook for approximately twenty-five min-utes—without lifting the lid. Serve with a cold tossed green salad, hot rolls, and a frosty beer. (I love one-pot meals!)

Creamy Risotto

A woman I met at the beauty shop the other day told me she soaks porchini mushrooms in chicken broth and uses this com-bination instead of butter or cream to make creamy risotto. The creaminess results as the starch is released during the cooking process.

She sautés shallots and garlic in a little olive oil, adds risotto (arborio) rice, and then *slowly* adds the mushroom/broth mixture, stirs it, and adds some more.

I tried her method (added artichoke hearts), and it took about thirty-five minutes to cook. You don't have to stand there the entire time, but you do need to stir it occasionally. Add a little turmeric if you want this dish to have a yellow color. Top with Parmesan cheese, serve, and go to heaven!

COOK'S TIP

Turmeric is an inexpensive substitute for saffron. It adds a rich golden color to dishes and has a slightly bitter, peppery flavor. To retain its flavor and color, store this spice out of the light.

LOVE THOSE LEFTOVERS

Leftover rice seems to lend itself to cooking creatively. The other day I looked up from a book I was reading in a restaurant and saw a waitress enjoying a heavenly-looking dish that I couldn't find on the menu. Our eyes met, and I asked her what she was eating.

"Oh, some leftover rice, chicken, and spinach," she said, "just something I concocted. I may even tell the chef to put it on the menu!"

Whenever you make rice, I suggest you cook extra for the refrigerator, so you can artfully create something new from something old. And, every time you go to a Chinese restaurant I suggest you order extra. By adding a few extra ingredients, there's no end to what you can do with leftovers.

Put a Surprise in Every Dish!

In his book *How to Create,* Barry Cooper quotes Beethoven, "Between ourselves the best thing of all is a combination of the surprising and the beautiful."

Beethoven's belief in surprise went hand in hand with his belief that all art should move forward. Progress implied for him a surprise for his listeners, and it's the same with food. The grain dishes you make don't have to be difficult, take a long time, or contain costly ingredients. They only need to amaze! And, since grains are open to every interpretation, it's easy to jazz up any grain dish by adding one or more of the following: *artichoke hearts, almonds, bell peppers, carrots, corn, cheese, dried apricots, dried cranberries, jalapeños, peas, pine nuts, raisins, sautéed mushrooms, sautéed onions, sesame seeds, sunflower seeds, walnuts.* If you put something else in that's okay too! (If it turns out great, let me know.)

RICE AND VEGGIE CASSEROLE

Whenever I cook brown rice, I prepare extra so I can make this dish.

Lightly oil an oblong Pyrex dish or lasagna pan. Spread a thick layer of leftover cooked rice. Both white and brown, short and long grain work beautifully, but I prefer the brown, short-grain variety.

Cut on the diagonal and steam four of your favorite vegetables. I like to use zucchini, bell pepper, tomatoes, and carrots. Layer them in the dish with a jarred, ready-made spaghetti sauce. (See chapter 5, page 129.)

Now add a layer of sliced mushrooms on top and two of your favorite cheeses; I prefer Jack and mozzarella. Top with a layer of raw sunflower seeds, and bake until the cheese melts. Cut this vegetable casserole into lasagna-sized squares, and serve immediately. *Yum!*

REFRIED RICE

Refried rice is a well-known Asian dish that requires cold, leftover long-grain rice—freshly steamed rice doesn't work as well! If you don't have any leftover rice on hand, you can cook some rice and let it cool awhile.

Begin by heating oil in a large skillet or wok, then scramble a couple of eggs (or egg whites) in a skillet. Transfer the egg to a plate and cut the chunks into smaller pieces. Sauté an assortment of fresh or cooked leftover veggies. Add soy sauce, precooked rice and a little sesame oil. (Fried rice becomes a main dish when you add pieces of lean meat, chicken, or shrimp.) Add some salt, pepper, the egg, and finally more soy sauce if necessary. (Use lightly colored soy sauce if you don't want the rice to turn brown.) Top with green onions, chopped nuts, and serve immediately, while it's hot!

PAULA'S REFRIED RICE

The other day Paula made refried rice at my house. She had been to a Thai restaurant and brought over the leftover white rice. She sautéed diced bell pepper, scallions, and carrot in a little oil, then added the rice and a little soy sauce to taste. She added two raw eggs to the mixture, and tossed everything together. It turned out so mushy that my dog, Shiva, ended up with a side dish in addition to her kibble that night.

Paula's intentions were good—egg is an integral part of refried rice—but the egg *must* be scrambled and cooked before it's added to the rice and veggies!

SPANISH RICE

Sauté leftover brown rice in a skillet containing a little oil. Add turmeric, cumin, diced red bell peppers, frozen peas and corn.

QUICK TIP

It's exciting that there are so many organic packaged products available today! Cascadian Farm and Sno Pac are two of the many good brands of organic frozen veggies.

If you can't locate an organic brand, any package of frozen veggies without sauce works!

Try This

Heat a can of cored whole tomatoes in a saucepan or skillet, including some of the juice. Add some diced bell pepper (any color) and any type of leftover rice you have on hand. Sauté until you've obtained the consistency and color you prefer. Snip some basil, cilantro, chives, or another leafy green on top. (If it's too "soupy," allow some of the liquid to reduce.)

Tofu and Rice

Some say tofu was discovered while the Japanese were trying to make Styrofoam, but I don't think so! Actually, it originated in China around 500 B.C. Tofu is plain, like pasta and rice, so it picks up the flavor from anything it's soaked in and must be highly seasoned. It will also pick *you* up if you're feeling physically low, since it's highly nutritious, particularly when combined with rice.

I like to treat tofu like chicken and keep it in the fridge, marinating in barbecue sauce, or Italian or oriental salad dressing. Then, when I'm in the mood for a quick and healthy meal, I sauté tofu in a little olive oil, tamari (soy sauce), or Bragg Liquid Amino Acids and serve it over leftover, "microwaved" hot rice. Marinated tofu also makes a good sandwich. I know it sounds pretty awful, but add a slice of cucumber or tomato and you'll see how wonderful a marinated tofu sandwich actually tastes! Bragg Liquid Amino is available at most health-food stores. I use it because it provides the *essential* amino acids (those that our body cannot make), and because it tastes a lot like soy sauce.

VALUABLE TIP

Tofu spoils, so plan on keeping it in the refrigerator for only about a week. If the tofu is soaking in water, instead of a marinade, it will keep best if the liquid is drained and replaced with fresh water every day to avoid bacteria buildup.   .

Tofu is available in soft, regular, and firm. I prefer firm tofu, except when I'm using it in the blender. (See chapter 11, page 281.) Tofu can be frozen right in its container, but its soft texture becomes a bit spongy.

GRANDIOSE GRAIN DISHES

There are so many grains, let's not stick to rice! Here are a few ideas for preparing a few of my favorites, and not so favorite, grains:

Quinoa

Quinoa (pronounced Keen-wa), with its light pleasing taste and texture, is often used as a substitute for rice or bulgur. This ancient sacred grain of the Incas is also grown in the Colorado Rockies today. And since it's high in fiber and contains all the essential amino acids our bodies need, unlike most other grains, it's a perfect addition to every diet, particularly vegetarian.

Quinoa that's sold in the United States is usually prewashed, but wash it again before cooking to make certain the *saponin,* an insect repellent often put on its outer layer, has been removed. (Quinoa is ball shaped when it's raw, and light and fluffy when it's cooked.)

Bring water or broth to a boil. Add quinoa and a few finely chopped red bell peppers, or whatever vegetables you like. Simmer for about fifteen minutes, or until all the water is absorbed. Use a clean pair of scissors to "snip in" your choice of fresh herbs, and then fluff everything together.

Bulgur

This Middle Eastern grain, which began growing around the southern border of present-day Turkey, is essentially wheat berries that have been steamed, dried, and then cracked. Since it has already been "cooked" when you purchase it, you only need to reconstitute it in hot water.

In most supermarkets, this easy-to-prepare grain is available in a red box in the rice section under the brand name Ala. Purchase Ala, make tabbouleh and you'll be doing yourself a favor. I promise you'll enjoy the distinctive nutty flavor and chewy texture of this remarkably easy salad. (You can make much better tabbouleh from scratch than from a preseasoned package.)

Tabbouleh

This is a delicious, refreshing, satisfying dish. It takes some chopping but otherwise it's simple to make. Pour two cups of hot water over one generous cup of bulgur wheat, and allow it to sit for forty-five minutes, or until the water is absorbed. Now the options are almost endless:

Add cut-up or snipped cilantro, parsley, watercress, mint, radish, cucumber, onions, scallions, and any other vegetables you prefer. (As you know, there are no rules!) Sometimes I add torn basil leaves, cherry tomatoes, or sliced mushrooms to this dish. They're all good; simply vary the proportions to your taste. Season with lemon juice, olive oil, salt, or a little of your favorite vinaigrette, and chill. If you don't add the dressing until serving time, this salad will keep well in the refrigerator for five to six days.

QUICK TIP

Try substituting quinoa for the bulgur in tabbouleh. It's your love of adventure that makes you a great cook!

I took a tabbouleh salad to a party recently, and Robin, one of the other guests, asked me for the recipe. I explained that I hadn't written down what I had done, but would be happy to tell her. As I began tossing in a few variations here and there, Robin said, "I'm really not good at improvising. Without a recipe, how will I know which ingredients to add?" "It's about using your senses," I said. "Smell seasonings. Look at the color of the dish you're making, think about the texture, the ingredients you like, and you'll know what it needs. You already have some knowledge about what tastes go well with certain foods."

Robin called a week later to say she had made tabbouleh "her way," and stuffed it into pita bread. She also created another dish by adding a few simple ingredients she had on hand to cooked bulgur. Robin made a *pilaf!*

ROBIN'S BULGUR PILAF

Heat a little oil in a skillet. Add diced onion (listen for the sizzle), and sauté until soft. Add about one half teaspoon of curry powder and cook the onions a little longer. Now add one cup of cooked bulgur, and stir. Add a cup of grated carrots, some slivered almonds, and raisins to taste. Robin said this dish is good hot or cold, and that next time she may try substituting cashews for the almonds, and dates or currants for the raisins.

VEGGIE BURGERS

These veggie patties are great when you feel like eating a sandwich, yet don't want to eat meat. In a Teflon-type skillet, sauté a chopped yellow onion in a little olive oil until translucent. Place it in your food processor assembled with the standard metal blade. Do the same thing with a carrot and a couple of pounds of sliced mushrooms. If you'd like, add some minced garlic, and grated zucchini, too.

Now, to the processor, add about two cups brown rice to

one half cup cooked bulgur and one half cup cooked lentils, plus an egg white or two, depending upon the desired consistency. If it's too runny, add raw oats and sunflower seeds.

Season with a little salt and pepper, garlic powder, dried basil, and plenty of chili powder—start with one half teaspoon and add a pinch at a time—to taste. A handful of grated mozzarella cheese adds more flavor. Form into patties. Add a little oil to the skillet you used previously, and pan-fry as many burgers as you need. Another way to cook these is to sear the patties on both sides, and then bake them in the oven on a low heat for about ten to fifteen minutes. (The leftover uncooked patties can be frozen between waxed paper for future use.)

Try This

Bring chicken broth to a boil in a medium-sized pot. Add bulgur wheat, plus a handful of dried cranberries or cherries—pits removed. Simmer until the liquid is absorbed. Stir in some nuts and a little olive oil and serve hot or cold. I like this mixture stuffed into Cornish game hens.

Barley

This grain is a good source of niacin, thiamine, and potassium. Barley takes a longer time to cook than most other grains, but its rich nutty flavor is worth the wait! Whole barley is exceptionally rich in fiber and nutrients, but it's usually processed into smaller round granules known as pearl barley, which makes delicious desserts. Fortunately, this process does not destroy the nutrients!

Try This

To make an unusual barley casserole, add some pine nuts or slivered almonds to a medium saucepan containing a little olive oil. Stir-fry the nuts until lightly toasted and then transfer them to an oiled casserole dish.

Add a little more oil to the pan and sauté whole barley, a diced onion, a little chopped parsley, green onions, salt, and pepper to taste.

Spoon everything into the casserole. Heat some chicken broth to boiling, pour it over the barley mixture, and bake in a moderately hot oven, about 350 degrees, for about an hour or until the barley is tender and the liquid is absorbed.

CULINARY SECRET #9: Almost every dish you put into the oven can be baked to perfection at 350 degrees for 45 minutes to 1 hour. *That's how uncomplicated cooking is!*

Buckwheat

This grain is also called by its Russian name "kasha" and is available roasted or raw, whole or cracked. When raw, it's called buckwheat; roasted, it's kasha. This grain can be boiled like rice, but to bring out its rich flavor, the secret is to seal the kernels with an egg before adding the hot liquid.

KASHA VARNISHKES

Stir-fry uncooked kasha with two egg whites in a skillet containing browned onions. Add chicken broth, and then mix everything together with cooked bow-tie noodles (or any shape pasta you prefer). I recommend dressing this dish with a little olive oil.

Omit the noodles, add veggies instead, and you've made a pilaf.

Kashi

Not to be confused with kasha, *Kashi* is a mixture of seven whole grains and sesame seeds that can be used to make dishes for breakfast, lunch, and dinner. The manufacturer of this product sure came up with the perfect name: In Chinese, it implies "happy food"; in Hindi, "spiritual food"; in Japanese, "energy food"; in Hebrew, "pure food"; and in Russian, Kashi means "cereal."

No matter what you call it, cook Kashi according to the chart on page 226 of this chapter. Allow it to cool, add your favorite cut veggies—mushrooms, bell pepper, peas, tomatoes, sugar peas—and toss with your favorite salad dressing.

Couscous

Couscous (pronounced Kooce-kooce) is actually a pasta that's treated as a grain. It originated in Morocco, traveled to Algeria, spread to France, and now it's in America. The popularity of this dish is on the rise because one cup of couscous contains only 200 calories and less than half a gram of fat. The flavor is plain, however; so, like tofu, couscous needs lots of added flavor.

Add couscous to boiling water or broth, and cover. Turn off the flame immediately and allow the couscous to steam, five to ten minutes or until soft. Uncover, fluff, and from here you can do a zillion things!

ONE OF A ZILLION EASY THINGS . . .

Anything that tastes good with rice or pasta goes well with couscous. Add uncooked couscous to boiling water, cover, bring the water back to a boil, remove the pot from the heat, and let it stand for a few minutes.

After you've cooked the couscous, add garbanzo beans, cooked onion, red and green bell peppers, mushrooms, zucchini, carrots, chicken, and parsley. Now add raisins, red pepper flakes, and a few black olives if you have them on hand. Toss and serve. The leftovers will keep in the fridge for a week. Zap a portion in the microwave when you want to eat it.

MY FAVORITE COUSCOUS SALAD

Prepare couscous using chicken broth instead of water (vegetable broth makes it vegetarian). Add dried cranberries, diced apricots, or both. Put in some quartered tomatoes, garbanzo beans, and chopped parsley (or cilantro), and season, depending upon the desired hotness, with Frank's Original Red-Hot Sauce, or Tabasco. Add the juice from one lemon, a pinch of cumin, a few drops of olive oil, kosher salt, freshly ground pepper, and whatever else sounds good to you. I've tried it with green onion, purple onion, olives, chicken, bell peppers—green, red, yellow, or purple. Carrots and cucumber are nice additions, too.

Toss everything together and refrigerate, so the flavors can marry for a while. This dish is usually served cold, but it's also delicious as a stuffing in chicken or as a base for spicy meat or fish stew.

ANOTHER QUICK COUSCOUS IDEA

Brown some fresh garlic in a skillet containing a little hot olive oil, and add approximately two cups of couscous. After it's browned, add a small can of cored stewed tomatoes with basil, saving the juice. Pour the juice into a cup and add enough broth and water, including the juice, to make a total of three cups. Add it to the pot and simmer covered. It only takes about eight minutes for the liquid to absorb. Season with salt and pepper.

THE QUICKEST COUSCOUS IDEA YET

Add couscous to boiling chicken stock. (See stock ideas in chapter 7, page 176, or simply use canned broth.) Now top the couscous with your favorite store-bought pasta sauce, or experiment and make a homemade sauce with whatever you have in the pantry and fridge!

Polenta

I like to use this traditional Northern Italian grain as a crust on fish. Take your favorite firm fish and *dredge* (or coat) it in raw polenta. Heat a skillet, add a little oil, and pan-fry the fish until it's golden brown. The polenta will provide a tasty crust.

Polenta is also made into a simple cornmeal mush. It's not my favorite dish, but I'm going to explain how to make it because a lot of people love it. Some Italian mamas say it takes two hours of stirring, but it can be made creamy in less than half the time if you do the following:

Boil three cups of water, add a little salt, and one cup of Italian coarse-grained yellow cornmeal in a stream—mix it frequently for forty-five minutes to avoid lumps. (When I beat in some olive oil and grated Parmesan cheese before serving, I like the taste better.)

To serve polenta for lunch or dinner, add hot chiles, pepper flakes, garlic, sautéed onion—any additional flavor you want to the cooked cornmeal. Pour it into an oiled baking dish, allow it to cool and set, and cut it into squares, triangles, rectangles, or whatever shape you prefer. Sauté in oil to brown on both sides, and serve. It's even better topped with ratatouille, a mixture of eggplant, zucchini, and peppers. (See chapter 8, page 205, for suggestions.)

VALUABLE TIP

Polenta is definitely a nutritious and cost-effective dish, but for my taste it isn't *labor effective.* In other words, you don't get enough flavor for the amount of effort you must put in.

With all nutritious foods you should consider the magnitude of the taste, and with fatty or salty foods, it's important to consider the magnitude of the nutrition.

Millet

I don't recommend that you cook millet alone, because although it's easy to make (and extremely healthful), it looks and tastes a lot like birdseed. It has fewer calories than rice, how-ever, and it's used to make porridge in North Africa and *roti,* a flat bread that originated in India. Millet is an excellent source of protein, iron, copper, magnesium, and B vitamins. If it pleases your taste buds, it's available in health-food stores, and it's best when made into a pilaf.

Amaranth

This pseudograin is actually a pale-yellow seed that comes from a broadleaf plant. It is a staple of the Aztec people, who believe it has supernatural powers. Amaranth contains a great deal of protein and, like quinoa, all nine essential amino acids including lysine, which is only found in small amounts in other grains. This grain is particularly good when added to soups, pi-lafs, stews, and cereals.

CEREAL: THE BREAKFAST OF CHAMPIONS

Grains, made into hot or cold cereal—oatmeal, rice, Kashi—with added fruit and nuts is one of the easiest, most delicious ways to include more fiber and nutrients in your diet. Enjoy them in the morning, or anytime you want. Millet, amaranth, and polenta can be made into breakfast cereals, too, but they're not high on my list of what I want to wake up to!

BROWN-RICE CEREAL

It's simple. Add leftover brown rice to some nonfat milk you've warmed in a saucepan. Add raisins, cinnamon-sugar, and top with slices of banana, maple syrup, yogurt, or brown sugar.

BREAKFAST RICE

Cook short or medium-grain white rice. Add nonfat milk and sugar, cinnamon, and raisins to taste, and top with banana.

QUICK TIP

If you have a milk intolerance, or an inability to digest lactose, try granola and other cereals with fruit juice, a nondairy rice and soy beverage (Eden Foods makes a good one), or "Rice Dream," a milklike liquid made from rice, available at specialty markets. Even if milk bothers your stomach, plain yogurt mixed with a touch of maple syrup may not!

This Tastes Better Than It Sounds

Mix raw one-minute oatmeal with unsweetened applesauce to taste. Top with sugar and cinnamon, maple syrup and currants—or any other dried fruit. (Try it. You may be surprised. It's good!)

HOMEMADE GRANOLA

This tastes better than the best dessert—and with granola there's no limitation on your imagination!

Begin by heating your oven to about 350 degrees. Then, in your largest skillet or wok, *dry toast,* roast or brown a small handful of sesame seeds and an equal amount of sunflower seeds, or any type of seeds you have, until they're golden brown. Place them in a big bowl.

Add some canola or olive oil to the same skillet and lightly toast some cashews, and stir frequently. If you don't like cashews, use almonds, walnut pieces, or whatever nuts you prefer. (There's no need to measure.)

In the same skillet, continue to toast some dried coconut until golden brown, and add it to the mixture. Turn up the heat and add about six medium-sized handfuls of old-fashioned raw oats, stirring frequently until brown.

Add the sesame seed/nut mixture back into the skillet along with approximately one third cup honey, and heat the mixture for a few minutes, again stirring frequently.

Now turn the mixture onto a large nonstick cookie sheet, spread evenly, and bake until it turns a rich golden brown. Remove the pan from the oven and stir in some currants or raisins. (Once I added semisweet miniature chocolate chips, too!)

Line another large cookie sheet with paper towels and place it on a wire cake rack. Turn the mixture onto the paper towels, and spread it evenly. Cover the mixture with more paper towels and allow to cool completely. Break the granola apart; if some of the paper towel sticks, pull it off. Store this homemade treat in several airtight storage containers, or give portions to special friends. Everyone will love you for the taste and effort you put into this one!

ADDITIONAL OPTIONS

Dried fruit, such as apricots, dates, apples, and nuts, will add more fiber to your cereal. Fresh berries, bananas, peaches, apples, and nectarines taste delicious with all cereals.

THE BUDDY SYSTEM

Have you noticed that going into the kitchen to fool around by yourself is delightful sometimes, and at other times it's dreary? Sometimes the "right" partner can make dancing, tennis, cooking, writing, painting, parenting or any collaboration more fun!

Many people get upset because their partner (usually their husband or wife) doesn't automatically show up in the kitchen, apron tied, prepared to cook. I've noticed that when I ask anyone in my family to help out in the kitchen, they love cooking, once they begin. But, when I don't ask, they're perfectly happy if I do it myself and call them to the table when it's done.

You may be thinking it's easier to cook by yourself, especially if your cooking buddy is married to recipes. You say to your partner, "This dish needs more water." You reach for it and your buddy says, "Stop, it doesn't say that in the book." "Just

taste it," you reply. "It needs about a quarter teaspoon of salt."
And your buddy says, "Wait, we need to measure!" That's frus-
trating, especially now that you're an intuitive cook. But don't
make it a big problem, because for any collaborative effort to
work, you must believe in your partner. Simply slow down and
give your buddy time to measure. Or, better yet, divide the jobs
equally, so each of you can work comfortably in your unique
way. (One person shouldn't have to do all the cleaning and
chopping, while the other directs!)

My husband, Robert, and I had guests visiting from Seattle
recently, so we decided to make a streamlined paella fiesta instead of running out to an impersonal, costly restaurant meal.
Our friends pitched in too, and eight hands were definitely
more efficient than two!

I began by cleaning arugula leaves, while Robert put them in
the spinner to dry. Robert rinsed and sliced four boned chicken
breasts into bite-sized pieces. Then, he sautéed a thinly sliced
onion and three cloves of chopped garlic in a large skillet.

Once the chicken was cooked, I transferred it to a bowl while
Robert added about 1½ cups of canned chicken broth to the
skillet, two chopped tomatoes with their juice, about one half
teaspoon cinnamon, 1½ cups long-grain rice, and one quarter
teaspoon of the world's most expensive spice—saffron. (Remember, turmeric is an excellent substitute.) Next, he covered
the skillet, brought it to a boil, turned down the heat and allowed the contents to simmer for about twenty-five minutes.

Meanwhile, our friends were preparing dessert. They sliced
a ready-made pound cake, put frozen yogurt in between,
frosted it, and put it in the freezer to set.

I made a balsamic vinaigrette for the arugula salad, added
torn spinach leaves, marinated artichoke hearts, goat cheese,
sliced mushrooms, and tossed it all together while Robert deveined three quarters of a pound of fresh shrimp and added
them, along with the cooked chicken, to the skillet. Everyone
set the table together in about twenty-five seconds.

I poured a cup of frozen, organic peas into the pot, sliced
some crusty French bread, and placed a bottle of chilled rosé
on the table.

We had the most delicious time; you won't believe how easy this dish is, or how good it tastes. Go ahead, make paella, and tell your guests it's your great-aunt's favorite recipe that she picked up on her trip to Spain last summer. (I certainly won't snitch!)

So let's move on now to the next chapter and talk about beans. When rice and beans are combined, they're the best of friends.

CHAPTER 10

◆

Spill The Beans

"The most remarkable thing about my mother is that for thirty years she served the family nothing but leftovers. The original meal has never been found!"

—Calvin Trillin

I can't think of any food that's more nutritious, or more versatile, than beans. When I was a kid, I remember my mom boiling a big pot of beans, pureeing half, adding it back to the pot, and then incorporating this bean mixture into a different dinner several nights a week. Beans are practically a perfect food, and as far as I'm concerned, they should be on every plate in town!

Beans, otherwise known as *legumes,* are vegetables that grow in pods, including beans, peas and lentils. Dating back at least four thousand years, they are one of the oldest foods we know of—a staple in many countries—yet beans play only a minor role in the American diet.

Why do so many people miss out on this delectable, user-friendly, easy-to-store food? Some people shy away from beans because they produce an embarrassing side effect: gas!

It's true, the problems with beans ring loud and clear! But since the gas beans produce can often be eliminated, don't you think beans deserve a higher billing?

THE BENEFITS OF BEANS

Nutritionally speaking, beans are a phenomenal food. Although they're low in fat and lack the artery-clogging cholesterol of animal products, dollar for dollar they contain more protein than any other food. A whopping twenty-five percent of their calories come from protein!

In addition, beans are high in complex carbohydrates, and are a good source of the B vitamins thiamine, riboflavin, niacin, and folacin. They're also rich in several minerals, including calcium, phosphorus, iron, copper, zinc, and potassium. And, at less than a dollar a pound, beans are reasonably priced.

Since beans are extremely high in soluble fiber, one cup contains half your daily needs. Eating beans on a regular basis will lower your blood-cholesterol level, help regulate your blood-sugar level, and keep your intestinal track functioning smoothly which greatly helps in preventing gastrointestinal troubles such as hemorrhoids and bowel cancer. And if that's not enough to convince you to eat more beans, there's more. Beans are also good for dieters because even small quantities provide a sense of satiety.

And finally, beans are beautiful! To me they look more like a bag full of semiprecious gems than something to dump into boiling water.

Long ago, in grade school, I remember making mosaics with beans. And, it was only eight short years ago that Chelsea proudly presented a pencil holder to me on Mother's Day that I will always cherish. She had pasted varying sizes and types of decorative beans on an orange-juice can. It's sitting in front of me right now.

MAKE BEANS A PART OF YOUR DIET

For me, not to eat beans would feel like a major punishment, and it would be torture not to cook with them. By mixing and

matching beans with the best from every cuisine, masterpieces of the highest standards can easily be created.

Some beans are a little sweet; others have a slightly smoky taste but despite their splendid array of beautiful colors, shapes, and interesting textures, you'll find that the flavors are pretty subtle. Like tofu and pasta, however, they're easy to cook with because they absorb flavors readily.

To me, the best beans for pureeing, baking, and adding to thick soups are the ones with a buttery, creamy texture and taste. Examples include garbanzo, pinto, cranberry, and my personal favorite—black beans.

More starchy, grainy, earthy tasting beans, such as adzuki, kidney, small red, and lentils, are better for adding to side dishes. But remember, when it comes to ingredients and their uses, there are no hard and fast rules! Kidney, red, and pinto beans, for example, taste creamy when they're pureed into re-fried beans, while garbanzo, pinto, and black beans are wonderful in salads. Actually, most beans can be substituted for others successfully.

HAVE YOU "BEAN" GETTING ENOUGH FIBER?

The average person who eats cereal for breakfast, a sandwich and salad for lunch, and beef, chicken, or fish with a potato and fresh vegetable for dinner isn't eating enough roughage, or fiber.

If you add to the foods I just mentioned, fruit at breakfast, a bowl of lentil soup or grains—rice, bulgur wheat, or tabbouleh—at lunch, then another fruit as an afternoon snack, an additional vegetable or a tostada, a bowl of chili, or bean burrito at dinner, then you're talking "high-fiber diet."

CULINARY SECRET #10: You'll feel full, you won't be bloated, and you certainly won't need to diet, if you *gradually* increase more beans and other high-fiber foods into your diet. You need up to a total of 35 to 40 grams of fiber per day, or approximately 25 grams for every 1,000 calories you consume. It's amazing, but some people who think they're on a high-fiber diet have never seen a bean!

Many people who want to lose weight consume a lot of fat-free foods without considering whether or not those foods contain much fiber. You'd be eating and enjoying more beans, if only you'd known this information sooner. Right?

Six Tips for Including More Beans in Your Diet

- Use black beans to make soup, dips, and refried beans. (See chapter 7, page 187, and pages 258 and 273 of this chapter.)
- Serve *plant-based foods,* otherwise known as beans, rice, and vegetables, in place of animal protein whenever you're in the mood.
- Discover bean recipes that inspire you, and then vary the type of bean you use. Remember, most are interchangeable!
- Serve beans to complement a main dish.
- Add garbanzo beans, kidney beans, or black-eyed peas to salads. (See chapter 4, page 100.)
- Enjoy tacos, quesadillas, or refried beans with steamed veggies for lunch or dinner whenever you're in the mood.

WHAT CAUSES GAS?

Flatulence, or the discomfort caused from eating beans, occurs because our stomachs do not produce the necessary enzymes to digest the *oligosaccharides,* or carbohydrate molecules, in beans. Then, the bacteria that live in the large intestine feed off these sugars and produce hydrogen, carbon dioxide, and other gases that tend to cause bloating and discomfort.

Paula Got Rid of Her "You Know What"

My dear friend Paula avoided beans for years because she had an enormous problem with gas. She practically convinced herself that she didn't like them. But the fact is, she adores beans!

Paula has tried soaking garbanzos before making hummus, and black beans before making soup, but she has always suffered the embarrassing consequences afterward. After eating even a small amount of beans, she'd need to stay home, or go home immediately afterward if she ate them in a restaurant.

Then, one day she came to me and asked if there was any way she could eat beans and still socialize.

I recommended that she add *epazote* to all bean dishes, a finely minced sprig of the easy-to-grow herb that relieves gas. (It's available in most Latin-American markets and some supermarkets today, see chapter 7, page 185.) You can also purchase a small epazote plant at your local nursery to grow at home, so you can cook with it whenever you want.

I also suggested that Paula try Beano, an over-the-counter liquid enzyme preparation designed to help people digest the sugars that produce intestinal gas. Even though Paula was elated to discover a combination that worked, I couldn't believe what she did.

When her dog Beau had puppies, Paula actually named the smallest, gray and white, spotted male from the litter—Beano!

I explained to Paula that if she'd slowly increase the amount of fiber she eats, her body would adapt to the change and her gas would diminish. Most people only consume between ten and twenty grams of fiber per day, but they need much more.

BEAN GAME PLAN

- Look for packaged beans in the rice and pasta section of your local market, and in bulk bins at the health-food store.
- Purchase beans that are brighter in color. With beans, uniform color is a sign of freshness, meaning they haven't been sitting on the shelf too long.
- Look for whole beans that are uniform in size, because beans of a similar size will cook at the same rate.
- Pick through and rinse dried beans, avoiding those with tiny holes because insects may be inside.
- In a large pot, bring enough water to a boil to cover the amount of beans you're using, approximately six cups of hot liquid per pound of beans.
- Add the beans to the pot. Two cups of dried beans weigh one pound and yield six cups of cooked beans, which will feed seven people comfortably, or provide leftovers. There's no reason to add salt, oil, or anything else but the epazote to the pot.
- Add chunks of peeled onion, then put the lid halfway on the pot.
- Boil ten minutes, reduce the heat, and simmer the beans for about 1½ hours, or until they're tender. There's a chart below to help you estimate the cooking time, but with beans you can never be certain how long they'll take. When fully cooked, beans are easy to crush between your forefinger and thumb. (Make sure the bean is cool, of course, so you don't burn your finger.)
- Add more hot water to the pot if the beans soak most of it up before they are fully cooked.
- Beans stay fresh in the refrigerator for four to five days, or in the freezer for a couple of months.

INTERESTING TIP

Don't bother soaking beans overnight; it doesn't reduce their gas-producing properties, and the cooking time is basically the same. Beans cooked without soaking have a richer flavor and a more consistent texture, too.

Bean Dishes without Recipes

Canned beans are convenient, and I especially like the organic brands. But I still like to boil my own beans for dishes that require a fresh, firmer-to-the-bite taste. Use the following cooking chart as a guide:

COOKING CHART

Beans	Uses	Cooking Time
Adzuki	Soups, salads, pasta dishes	1 hour
Black	Sauces, soups, refried beans, salads, bean dips	2 hours
Cannellinis (White)	Soups, stews, salads, purees casseroles, and baked beans	1½ hours
Chickpea (garbanzo)	Hummus, falafel, chili, salads curries, and pasta dishes	2½ hours
Cranberry	Soups, stews, refried beans, casseroles, and salads	1½ hours
Fava (Broad)	Soups, stews, and casseroles	1½ hours
Kidney	Chili, refried beans, salads, and casseroles	2 hours
Lentil	Soups, salads, purees, dips, burgers, and curries	40 minutes
Lima	Soups, baked beans, casseroles	2 hours
Pinto	Refried beans, burgers, and chili	2 hours
Small Red	Soups, salads, refried beans, chili	1½ hours

COOKING CHART (cont'd)

Beans	Uses	Cooking Time
Soy	Soups, stews, burgers, salads, and baked beans	3½ hours

VALUABLE TIP

When stored in an airtight container at room temperature, dried beans will keep up to a year. Remember, 2 cups of dried beans yields 6 cups of cooked beans.

MEXICAN-STYLE FOOD

Never add lard to beans when preparing Mexican-style dishes, and be certain it isn't in the flour tortillas you purchase. Lard is a saturated, artery-clogging fat, so in Mexican-style food use corn oil instead. For delicious flavor and good health, incorporate a lot of corn, chilies, and tomato into these dishes. And, if you're adding meat, always have stewing beef (or some other inexpensive lean beef) freshly ground.

TACOS

Tacos (Mexico's little sandwiches), are low in calories and, in my opinion, more fun to eat than an American sandwich. I prefer making them with soft corn tortillas, because the ready-made hard shells are fried in artery-clogging, saturated fat.

To make what may turn out to be a favorite dish in your house, sauté lean ground beef with packaged taco seasoning. I usually use Lawry's, because I like its flavor, and it doesn't contain MSG. (If you prefer, doctor a prepared seasoning to your liking, or make Mexican-style foods more appealing by adding individual spices such as cumin, turmeric, chili powder, cayenne, and red pepper flakes, salt, and Frank's Original Red-Hot Sauce.)

Corn tortillas can be softened in the toaster oven, microwave, or in a skillet containing a few drops of one of the healthful oils.

Add the seasoned, cooked meat to the shell and, so your friends can assemble their own tacos, provide bowls of shredded lettuce, tomato, taco sauce, olives, avocado, and cheese (my family prefers cheddar, Muenster, or mozzarella).

To round out this meal, I like to serve refried beans on the side, topped with *queso seco,* a hard, somewhat salty cheese available in Latin American specialty markets.

INTERESTING TIP

Burritos, tacos, tostados, fajitas—and chili, for that matter—can all be made with prepared seasoning packages. I don't think twice about using them because, to me, it's like hiring a group of professionals to concoct the perfect blend! Chili and curry powder are prepared blends so, think about it, professional chefs cook with pre-blended or packaged seasonings all the time!

MEATLESS TACOS

Make vegetarian tacos by filling heated corn tortillas with avocado, diced fresh tomatoes, shredded lettuce, grated cheese, olives, vegetables, nonfat sour cream.

For something more unusual, add stir-fried veggies, corn, roasted bell peppers, sautéed eggplant, or Mexican rice (see chapter 9, page 230). Then make some refried beans to serve on the side, using the technique that follows.

REFRIED BEANS

This dish is simple to make, low in fat, satisfying, and versatile! In a large pot bring to a rapid boil enough water to cover the beans. In the meantime, wash and pick through a package of beans. Pinto and black beans are best for making this dish, but kidney and red are also delicious.

Pour the beans into the water and add chunks of onion. Boil the beans until they're tender—about two hours. If necessary, add more hot water to cover the beans.

Now puree the beans and onion, and some of the liquid, quickly in your blender. The amount of liquid you use determines how thick or thin the puree will be, but the quantity of liquid you need to get the blade moving usually makes the consistency perfect.

Just before you're ready to eat, pour the amount of beans you're planning to use into a Teflon-type skillet and *refry* the beans, allowing a little of the liquid to reduce (you don't need to add oil, and, although I never do, you may want to add salt).

If the beans are too thick, add more of the liquid left over from cooking the beans. If they're too thin, cook them a little longer. If you don't puree the beans, you've made whole beans, *frijoles de la olla,* or pot beans.

Both *frijoles de la olla* and refried beans provide a lovely foundation for all sorts of dishes. Take a look at the ideas that follow to stimulate your improvisational juices, and I'm certain you'll come up with more.

NACHOS

Spray a Pyrex pie plate or some other ovenproof dish with oil, and spread refried beans on the bottom. Top the beans with a layer of canned corn (drained), and then sprinkle a layer of cheese on the top. Bake a few minutes in the oven until the cheese melts. (This works in the microwave, too!)

Take the platter out of the oven, place chips around the edge, and sprinkle with cilantro. Serve alongside a large bowl of oven-baked tortilla chips, available in most markets, or roast your own. Cut corn tortillas into triangles, baking five to ten minutes (in a 400-degree oven), turn, bake a few minutes more, and remove when crisp. Salt and enjoy.

WAISTLINE TIP

Oven-baked, each whole tortilla contains 60 calories, compared to 150 when they're fried.

Vegetarian Burritos

Put refried beans in a large flour tortilla that you've heated in a lightly oiled skillet. Add some diced tomatoes, olive slices, a little shredded cheese, and some salsa. Roll, and serve hot with a tossed green salad on the side.

Simple Variations

For variety, make burritos using *chapati,* an unleavened whole-wheat pancake like Indian bread, available in most supermarkets today. Spread refried beans on the bread, add a little nonfat sour cream, avocado, hot sauce, diced tomatoes, and whatever you like. With chapati, it's easier to fold than roll.

NUTRITION TIP
Remember to avoid all brands of flour tortillas containing lard. Lard is a saturated fat that can clog your arteries. Look for labels that say "contains no lard."

Bean and Meat Burritos

If you're not a vegetarian, simply add shrimp, seasoned lean ground beef, shredded white meat turkey, or diced turkey to the burrito idea above. I also like Mexican rice, steamed vegetables, barbecue sauce and mozzarella cheese added to the beans and meat in the burrito.

Tantalizing Tostadas

To make this dish, prepare the tortillas first in one of the following ways:

- Pan-fry tortillas flat in a skillet sprayed with canola oil.
- Lay tortillas flat on the oven rack, in a pre-heated 450-degree oven, and turn occasionally until they're browned.
- Or fry tortillas, one at a time, in one inch of oil in a pot.

No matter which method you select, the tortillas will taste better than the boxed, store-bought varieties that contain saturated fat.

Now, layer the tortilla with leftover refried beans, shredded lettuce, cilantro, tomato, avocado, and cheese. Place slices of olive, nonfat sour cream, and scallion on top.

QUESADILLAS

If you like grilled cheese sandwiches, you'll love quesadillas. Heat an oiled skillet and add a flour tortilla. Top with a thin layer of cheese, cooked vegetables, and refried or pot beans. Add taco sauce and diced tomatoes. Place another tortilla on top—like a sandwich—flip it over, and heat until the cheese melts. Slice it in triangles as you would a pie, and serve it hot with cilantro sprinkled on top.

QUICK & EASY CANNED BEAN DISHES

If you don't have the time to boil dried beans, or you're feeling a little lazy, or if you're making a dish that doesn't require the fresh, firm (al dente) taste of boiled beans, canned beans are the perfect solution!

There are many brands of canned beans on the market, such as Hunt's, Heinz, S&W, and Sun-Vista. Health-conscious manufacturers such as Eden Foods, Westbrae Natural, American Prairie and Trader Joe's put out organic varieties. Don't hesitate to use canned beans, but if you find any dented, swollen, or punctured cans throw them away immediately! (They may be spoiled.)

Although some of the vitamin and minerals are lost in the processing, canned beans are still a good source of nutrition and the right consistency for the following dishes.

BLACK-BEAN BURGERS

To make these delicious burgers, sauté approximately one half cup of chopped onion and a little garlic in a non-stick skillet. In a food processor, mix a can of drained black beans (or whatever kind you prefer). Add a handful of your favorite crackers or matzah. (I've used pretzels, and they worked fine!) Now add the sautéed onions and garlic, an egg white, a pinch of cumin, and chili powder to taste. This mixture should be thick. If it's too runny to form patties, add more crackers.

Spray a nonstick skillet with Pam, or coat it with a little canola oil. Once the pan is hot, spoon a rounded tablespoon of the bean mixture into the pan. When the sides of the patty congeal, flip the burger. It's cooked when both sides are brown.

These burgers look amazingly like hamburgers. Serve them plain, or top them with salsa on a mound of steamed rice.

QUICK BEANS

Cook some onions and garlic until soft in a skillet containing a little oil. Add fresh, diced tomatoes and your favorite vegetable—I like zucchini. Drain a can of your favorite beans and add them to the pan. Season with cumin and basil, cilantro, or your favorite fresh herbs.

VEGETARIAN BEAN LASAGNA

In a big bowl, mix a can of drained beans, frozen organic corn, fresh diced tomatoes, black or green pitted olives, sautéed onion, green onion, cumin, a few dashes of hot sauce, and a can of chopped green chilies.

Meanwhile, preheat the oven to 350 degrees and spray an oven-proof casserole dish with any nonstick spray.

Now line the pan with fresh corn tortillas (cutting them if necessary). Alternate the bean mixture with more tortillas, and then grated cheese, until you reach the top of the pan. Bake this casserole for about thirty minutes, or until the cheese bubbles. Cut into squares, as you would lasagna, and place a sprig of cilantro, parsley, or nonfat sour cream and olives on top of each serving.

Try This

For a change of pace, dress beans simply with a combination of olive oil, herbs, and balsamic vinegar. It's a delicious dressing on all beans!

NEW ENGLAND STYLE BAKED BEANS WITH PEARS

I tasted incredible beans at a party recently and decided to modify them for a potluck I was attending, using pears instead of sweet butter. I thought they were wonderful and so did everyone else, since the serving dish was empty five minutes after everyone started eating.

Oil the casserole dish you want to serve in (rinse the top of the cans), and add the following three items: canned vegetarian beans (do not drain), large white lima beans (drained), diced canned pears (retain juice), and about one half cup of dark brown sugar. (Fava, kidney, pinto, navy, and white beans can be substituted for the lima beans.)

Combine and bake about two hours at 325 degrees. Stir occasionally and cook until bubbly. As the beans begin to dry out, add a little of the pear juice you put aside. Serve hot!

QUICK TIP

Make sure your brown sugar still has flavor. If you've had it a long time it loses its rich maple taste.

GARBANZOS

These beans are known as *garbanzos* in Spanish, chickpeas in English, and *ceci* beans in Italy. These versatile beans, with their soft texture and buttery flavor, are a staple in India and

north Africa and often sautéed like a stew with onion, coriander, ginger, curry powder, cumin, diced tomatoes and potatoes.
They also appear prominently in the Middle East in soups, salads, and hummus—my favorite dip (see chapter 6, page 149).

Dried garbanzo beans take longer to cook than most other
types of beans, so in America canned garbanzos are used most
frequently. It's rare to find the fresh beans in their small, fuzzy,
green, oval pods.

Mix canned garbanzos, kidney beans, and green or waxed
beans together. (Navy, pinto, or black beans work, too.) Add
cut cucumbers, tomatoes, slices of Bermuda onion, and diced
cilantro, parsley, watercress—anything you like.

Toss with red-wine vinegar, olive oil, salt, and pepper to
taste. If possible, allow this dish to stand overnight in the fridge.
Serve on individual plates in lettuce cups.

GARBANZO NUTS

Drain canned garbanzo beans. Spread them on a nonstick
cookie sheet, sprinkle them with a little salt, and bake them at
400 degrees, or until roasted and crunchy. You may need to
roll them around by shaking the pan a few times to get all sides
salted and browned. (These garbanzo nuts contain 80 calories
for half a cup, compared to 425 calories for the same amount
of salted, roasted peanuts!)

Try This

Drain a can of your favorite beans and heat. Add a little paprika and chili powder to taste and serve over leftover rice,
potatoes, or with heated tortillas on the side.

CHILI

Chili has become another one of my family's favorites, because for us it epitomizes a satisfying spicy dish. And due to

the texture and infusion of flavors going on, chili is one of those dishes that actually tastes better made with canned beans than fresh. So, it's hassle-free!

At a comedy club I heard a comedian say, "Chili is a hearty dish that represents your three types of matter—solid, liquid, and gas." (But that's only true if you forgot to add the epazote!)

Everyone has a different idea about chili. Some people say chili must contain tomatoes, while others say it shouldn't. Some chili connoisseurs add beans while others say chili is only good without them.

I've tasted chili made with beer, tomato juice, beef, stock, or water, and they've all turned out just fine.

CHILI BASICS

No matter what type of chili you like, I suggest you begin—as you have with so many dishes—by sautéing a diced onion and garlic in a little hot oil. (Remember to listen for the sizzle.) This dish can be made in any large pot or skillet. The only requirement is a lid!

After the onion and garlic have cooked awhile, you must decide if you're going to add lean ground beef or turkey, to make **Meat Chili with Beans,** or if you're more in the mood to make **Meatless Chili.**

MEAT CHILI WITH BEANS

If you've decided to add meat, sauté it in the same pot as the onion and garlic. The amount and type of meat you add (one or two pounds of ground turkey, chicken, or beef), depends upon the proportions and taste you and your friends prefer.

It's time to add seasonings, and as usual there are several options. You can add Lawry's chili seasoning—it's a healthful option—or another brand of chili spices (be certain it contains no MSG). Or, you can put chili powder together with spices you like, such as cayenne pepper, salt, ground coriander, cardamom, cumin, and marjoram. (If you leave something besides the chili powder and cumin out, that's okay!)

Select from canned kidney, pinto, garbanzo, chili, and black beans. (Canned organic black and kidney or pinto and black beans also make good combos. No one will ever get bored with chili if you vary the beans each time.)

Drain the water from all the beans, but don't toss out the thick, rich sauce or juice from the chili beans or canned tomatoes. These liquids are flavorful, so dump them right into the pot!

Add the epazote. I also like to add a large can of cored Italian tomatoes. Add the juice, water, or beer, if the chili is too thick, and allow the chili to reduce to a simmer awhile if it's too thin.

It's fine to use beans you've boiled but, remember, I recommend saving your time and bean-boiling skills for other dishes.

MORE-BEANS-THAN-MEAT CHILI

My family likes More-Beans-than-Meat Chili best, so I add lots of beans and tomatoes and only a little lean meat.

CHUNKY MEAT CHILI

If you're making Chunky Meat Chili, add large-diced chunky veggies (I like corn and red peppers). Add them instead or in addition to the meat.

EASY MEATLESS CHILI

If you prefer to make Easy Meatless Chili, sauté plenty of veggies rapidly in a separate skillet and omit the meat. When I make this dish I usually add seeded bell pepper, a few stalks of celery, frozen organic corn, a handful of sliced mushrooms, fresh, cubed tomatoes, and a large can of cored, peeled tomato. (The next time I omit the meat, I'm planning to add steamed new potatoes, butternut squash, and a small can of diced green chilies.)

CREATIVE GARNISHES

Delicious toppings, for all types of chili, include: diced avocado, chives, shredded cheese, nuts, chopped onion, nonfat sour cream, cilantro, jalapeño peppers, or a few shakes of red or green Tabasco Sauce.

Serve all types of chili with crackers, sourdough bread, or cornbread. Or, maybe you'd rather serve this versatile dish over rice, or even on top of tortillas, French bread, or pasta.

Serve it over spaghetti and you've made Cincinnati chili (see page 271 of this chapter). A pot of chili will spice up your life!

SPICE UP YOUR LIFE!

In addition to making your food more interesting, the *capsaicin* in hot peppers can make you feel "high." It's because the burning on the tongue excites the brain to excrete endorphins—the same chemical credited with the "runner's high." But be easy with this spice, it's not necessary to go overboard!! You can definitely obtain the following benefits by making your food *mildly* hot.

The Therapeutic Benefits of Chili Peppers

- Chili peppers act as an expectorant, loosening up chest congestion.
- Chili peppers act as a decongestant in case of the common cold.
- Chili peppers kill pain. Hot pepper extract was once used as a local anesthetic for toothaches. Today it's used for pain in creams and lotions.
- Hot peppers induce a feeling of euphoria in the brain.

What's Hot and What's Not?

Certain chilies are much hotter, milder, or sweeter than others. Generally speaking, pointed chilies are hotter, and those that are rounded are milder and sweeter. But whether you prefer hot or mild, it's best to purchase smoother, straight chilies because it's more difficult to remove the indigestible skin from the crooked, crinkly ones.

Depending upon the "heat" you desire, purchase the following chilies, available in most supermarkets.

CHILIES

Hot	Mild	Sweet
Cayenne	Anaheim	Hungarian Chili
Jalapeño	Green Chili	Red Chili
Yellow Jalapeño	Pascilla	Mulato
Serrano	Pepperocini	
Poblano	Ancho	
Habeneros		

SAFETY TIP

When cooking with the hottest chilies, it's a good idea to wear plastic gloves and discard the seeds. Don't accidentally rub the capsaicin into your eyes, nose, or lips until you've discarded the gloves or washed them off with warm soapy water.

Chilies can be minced, chopped, sliced, or halved, and then steamed, blanched, fried, broiled, or grilled. They're a vegetable that add flavor, color, and texture to food (in addition to adding the heat).

Learning to Like It Hot!

If you want to build up your taste and tolerance to hot food, start with the milder chilies, and add a little of them to your food at a time.

When my husband and I started dating, and I began cooking for him, his eyes would water and his cheeks would turn red if I put even a little black pepper in our food. If I added a sprinkle of chili powder, he needed a box of Kleenex by his side at the dinner table. With a couple of shakes of cayenne, you'd think he would have run into the arms of another woman, but instead he asked me to marry him. (My lucky day!)

Once we began cooking together we gradually added more spice and hot sauce to the dishes we made. He built up his tolerance to heat, and now, he likes everything hot!

BEANS & RICE HOLD HANDS

Beans and rice are like a perfect marriage. Separately, their proteins are incomplete, but when combined they're the perfect match since their protein content is as complete as meat. For example, the combination of kidney beans and rice provide 56 percent more protein than those two foods eaten separately on different days.

It was once thought that to obtain complete protein, beans had to be eaten at the *same meal* as rice—or some other type of grain—seeds, or a small amount of animal protein. But, now we know differently. If you merely eat legumes (dried peas, beans, and peanuts) with nuts, seeds, grains, bread, or anything made with flour on the *same day,* you'll obtain all of the essential amino acids, or complete protein. Of course, that doesn't mean that beans and rice aren't still delicious in the same dishes. Here are a few favorites.

ARROZ CASADO

Black Beans and Rice is a dish that's both good for your body and simple to make! In El Salvador it's called *Arroz Casado,* which literally means, "married rice," referring to marriage of the rice with the beans.

Making this dish entails cooking black beans with chunks of onion in water until they're tender, then rinsing white long-grain rice and cooking it separately in the dark purple—almost black—liquid that remains after cooking the beans. These two foods are then served side-by-side in a bowl with Parmesan or queso seco cheese on top, (see page 258 of this chapter). If you prefer, dark red beans, and any type of cheese may be substituted.

BEANS & RICE SIDE DISH

Combine approximately one cup of cooked adzuki beans with one cup of cooked rice and one cup of diced tomato. Add grated cheese, snipped parsley, cilantro, basil, ginger, chives— or whatever fresh herbs you have on hand. Toss with vinaigrette, lime dressing, and serve cold.

Try This

Fill a large pot with water, turn the flame on high, and bring the water to a rolling boil. Add rinsed, packaged black beans and diced onion, then turn the flame down and simmer for about an hour.

Meanwhile, in an oiled skillet, sauté until tender: garlic, tomatoes, more onion, ginger, green peppers. Add black pepper, cilantro, and cumin, or whatever spices you like, to taste.

Add the cooked beans and a little of their liquid to the vegetables in the skillet. Stir and simmer until the beans are tender and the juices thicken. I like to serve this with low-fat sour cream, cheese, rice and tortillas on the side.

LESS TRADITIONAL BEAN DISHES

Too often beans are thought of only in the context of Mexican or Latin American cooking. But they're a versatile food ideal for every creative cook. Make a big pot of beans and your gastronomic eyes, brain, and tongue will tell you what to do!

CINCINNATI CHILI

My friends think it's because I was born in Ohio that I enjoy Cincinnati chili so much, but I make it because it's as satisfying as pasta and as hearty as stew.

Cincinnati chili is not that different from other types of chili, except that it's served over plain hot spaghetti. (Avoid the packaged Cincinnati chili seasonings, however, because they contain saturated fat.)

Many people make this dish with meat that is processed to a finer consistency than when it's made into meat sauce. Cinnamon is usually added to the seasonings, and sometimes chocolate is too. Shredded cheddar or grated Parmesan cheese is often sprinkled on top. Fool around with this dish. You'll be surprised how good it is, even if you're not from Cincinnati!

VEGETARIAN LENTIL CHILI

Bring water to a boil in a large pot. Rinse about two cups of lentils, removing any stones or shriveled beans you find. Red, green, brown, or pink lentils are good combined, or they can be made separately.

Add the beans to the water, then turn down the flame and simmer about one hour, or until the beans are tender. Add a package of chili seasoning, red pepper flakes, garlic, and cored canned tomatoes (if you want this dish to be thinner, include the juice too). Diced veggies would be delicious too! Top with nonfat sour cream and chopped cilantro.

SOYBEANS

The protein in soybeans is almost as good as that of beef, and they contain only 1 percent saturated fat, as compared to the 10 percent in hamburger. The colors of these beans vary from brown and black to pale-yellow, red, and green. These nutritious beans are commonly used to make tofu, tempeh, oil, flour, miso, soy milk, and tamari. I encourage you to try these healthful ingredients in your cooking.

A FINE FIESTA!

Whenever I think of beans, I'm reminded of the surprise birthday party my dear friend Leslie and I gave our friend Brian at his beach house many years ago. He's always pulling practical jokes on everyone else, so just once we wanted to fool him.

Since some of the guests were vegetarians, fitness buffs, dieters, and representatives of the meat-and-potato generation, we didn't have a clue about what to serve.

We wanted to serve something out of the ordinary, and wanted the party to have a theme, so, remembering that Brian's favorite cuisine is Mexican, we thought a "Healthy Mexican Fiesta" would fit the bill!

Since his birthday was only two weeks away, we jumped on the phone to call his friends and hire a mariachi band. (Forty-five people responded favorably!)

Three days before the party, Leslie and I shopped for everything, and, except for the guacamole, we made all of the food at Leslie's house the next day.

On the day of the party our timing couldn't have been better. Two of Brian's best friends coaxed him into the ocean for a swim just before Leslie and I sneaked in. (Fortunately, Brian never locks his side door!)

We let the band in, assembled a gorgeous buffet overlooking the ocean, and as the guests arrived we made the guacamole, and heated the bean dip and enchiladas.

Everyone hid in the bedroom until Brian walked in wrapped in a towel. He almost fell to his knees in disbelief as we all sang *Happy Birthday* as the band played along.

The Fiesta Menu

Once Brian recovered, we served Cervesa Mexicana, sodas, and watermelon agua fresca, watermelon juice with water and ice. Salsa was available alongside bowls of oven-roasted and blue corn chips.

We also had two versions of Leslie's black bean dip, two

types of my guacamole, enchiladas, and Mexican rice (see chapter 9, page 230).

After Brian blew out his candles, we served a gorgeous chocolate sorbet birthday cake, (see chapter 11, page 282). The band members liked the cake so much we had a hard time getting them to go back to playing after their break.

SOUTHWEST SALSA

Since salsa can be added to Mexican food for flavor without adding excessive fat or calories, Leslie and I tossed the following fresh, organic ingredients into a bowl and mixed them together to make a spicy salsa: diced onion, seeded tomato, jalapeño, cilantro, lime juice, kosher salt and pepper.

Our friends like a lot of heat, so we added a couple of jalapeño peppers, and after tasting it, we added some RedHot Cayenne Pepper Sauce. But you be the judge, depending upon the flavor you and your guests prefer.

BLACK BEAN DIP #1

Leslie boiled black beans and chunks of onion until the beans were tender. While the beans and onion were still warm, she blended the beans, liquid, onion, tomato paste, and cilantro together to a thick consistency. She served the dip warm, with tortilla chips on the side, but Leslie says this is also good cold.

SAFETY TIP

Remember, when blending foods that are extremely hot, there is the risk that the accumulation of steam will cause an explosion. To avoid this, open the steam vent or feed cap (located on the center of the lid) and release some of the steam before blending.

EASY BLACK BEAN DIP #2

We wanted to be sure we had enough food, so Leslie opened cans of black beans, drained the liquid, poured the beans into a bowl, and added an equal amount of the Southwestern Salsa we had already made. (Prepared salsa works, too!) Leslie added diced tomato, RedHot Cayenne Pepper Sauce, chopped cilantro, salt, pepper, cumin, bell peppers. You can stop there, or add any ingredient that tantalizes your taste buds.

GUACAMOLE #1

To make the guacamole, I scooped avocado out of its shell, into a wooden bowl, and, to prevent it from becoming brown I squirted lemon juice on it. I added chopped onion, diced tomato, hot sauce, cilantro and a couple seeded and chopped serrano chilies.

After Leslie and I did our taste test, we added a little salt and pepper to the dip. (I added the avocado seed for decoration, but it won't prevent anything from turning brown.) Almost as soon as I put a bowl of chips next to the dip they were both gone! (I don't think any of the dieters showed up at the party that day.)

INTERESTING TIP

Half an avocado contains 150 calories and 15 grams of fat, but don't panic. Most of the fat is monounsaturated, or healthful. (If you're storing leftover "guac" in the refrigerator, plastic wrap pressed directly onto its surface prevents discoloration.)

"MOCK-O-MOLE" #2

To make this "guacamole," I mixed a bag each of Cascadian Farm Organic Sweet Corn and peas. Next I mixed in diced, red onion, cilantro, garlic, salt, and pepper. (From making this dish I learned that whenever you cut or snip cilantro, you'll get more flavor if you use both the leaves and stems.) This dish was good, but the guacamole went faster.

EASY ENCHILADAS

Most enchiladas take a long time to make and they're high in fat because they're fried and stuffed with cheese, but ours were easy to make and healthy!

Leslie began combining and mashing well-drained, canned pinto beans, finely diced onion, and skinless, shredded white meat turkey using a potato masher, so it would all adhere. Meanwhile, I mashed canned kidney beans with a fork, added chopped onion, and soft tofu (pretending it was cheese).

We made the sauce in a skillet by bringing a cup of water to a boil. I added green pepper, garlic, and chopped onion, and simmered the mixture until the onion softened. Leslie added cans of tomato sauce, diced green chilies, oregano, pepper, and RedHot Cayenne Pepper Sauce to taste. (I buy it by the gallon so I never run out!)

We oiled shallow baking dishes and began dipping corn tortillas one-by-one into the simmering, savory sauce, to make them flexible. We filled each softened tortilla with either the turkey-bean-onion, or tofu-bean mixture—rolling and placing each enchilada seam side down in the baking dishes. (It took us less than an hour.)

We poured the remaining sauce over the enchiladas, sprinkled them with diced green onion, and put out nonfat sour cream and yogurt, so whoever wanted to could spread it on top.

Everyone ate well and had a fantastic time at the party, some of the guests stayed until midnight, and Brian said it was the best birthday he had ever had.

In the next chapter you'll learn just how easy it was to make Brian's gorgeous chocolate sorbet birthday cake, and other exciting, climactic opulent desserts too.

CHAPTER 11

◆

Opulent Desserts

"People can live just so long on a sugarless, saltless, fat-free diet, and then they turn mean."
—Erma Bombeck

My maiden name is Baker, and although my *mother* makes the most delicious deep-dish apple-crumb pies—*I* will never be a traditional baker! It's not that I don't indulge in pastries once in a while. I do. But I'd rather buy than bake, for two significant reasons: Most dessert recipes require more time and attention than a complete meal. And wonderful desserts—cakes, cookies, frozen yogurt, ices, and pies—are available in bakeries, markets, and every "Baskin-Robbins, Starbuck-Häagen Dazs" corner in town.

I guess you could say I feel the same about baking that I do about assembling mail-order exercise equipment, reading my computer manual, or programming the VCR. I hate following all types of complicated directions, especially when there's little hope for success! I've made soufflés that didn't rise, pies that run over, pineapple upside down cakes that stuck to the pan, and all that was after I'd endured the torturous process of measuring, creaming, and combining everything precisely.

Instead of conventional baking, I prefer using store-bought convenience items to quickly create splashy-looking, sinfully delicious, guilt-free, healthful desserts that require only a few simple procedures. And fortunately, like others who have eaten healthfully for a long time, I'm not in the mood to inhale saturated fat too often. But . . . once in a while, I still add a little semi-sweet chocolate to my masterpieces—it's my favorite kind. (Milk chocolate or carob just don't satisfy me.)

To decide what you'd like to serve for dessert, I suggest you select the menu first, and then think of dessert as a continuation of the meal. For example, if you've prepared a low-fiber meal, offer rice pudding or oatmeal cookies, so you and your guests can include the nutrients the meal lacks. If you haven't had enough dairy products or fruit lately, create a dessert that includes frozen yogurt, strawberries, peaches, or watermelon. If you're not obtaining enough calcium or protein, add nonfat milk, milk powder, or egg whites to your favorite dessert ingredients in tempting ways that satisfy your urge to splurge. It's refreshing to realize that as a nation, we've become as obsessed with nutrition as we've always been with dessert!

GIVE UP NOTHING

Although dessert is often considered the climactic moment of the meal, to be good it should *not* steal the show. Instead, a good dessert should finish off the meal and render it "just right." In other words, as the hors d'oeuvres set the tone, the dessert creates the memory. But I have a surprise for you: The most revolutionary meals and memorable desserts are simple, and they don't require recipes!

CULINARY SECRET #11: With little or no cooking, it's possible to put together thousands of dramatic desserts that are healthful and take practically no time to assemble. In fact, you can create delectable, custom desserts without using measuring cups or spoons, following directions, or turning on the oven with this easy 4-step plan.

Custom Dessert, Easy 4-Step Game Plan

1. Use ready-made items to put together delicious desserts effortlessly.
2. To save time and energy, improvise special, uncomplicated desserts from baked goods you purchase from bakeries, markets, and other specialty stores.
3. Check the labels, or ask the clerk, to make sure the cookies, cakes, and pies you buy don't contain saturated, hydrogenated, or partially hydrogenated fat.
4. And, remember: to taste good, desserts don't have to be floating in a pool of crème fraîche that's surrounded by a fancy design.

Desserts from Store-Bought Items

Depending upon your favorite flavors, I'm confident you'll come up with your own custom-made desserts. Allow me to stimulate your imagination with the ideas that follow:

TRIFLE

English Trifle is made by using a trifle of this and a trifle of that. Here's my version; adapt it to your taste.

I cut store-bought angel food cake into large cubes. Then I prepare Jell-O brand instant vanilla pudding, using skim milk, according to package directions, and chill it in the fridge for about five minutes. Finally, I alternate layers of the pudding, cake, and fresh-cut strawberries into a large clear bowl. Here are a few options:

- Make this dessert, instead, in individual sorbet glasses.
- Peel and slice kiwi fruit and spread it out beautifully like a peacock's open tail.
- Top the trifle with fresh blueberries or raspberries.
- Sprinkle it with chocolate shavings, miniature marshmallows, or chocolate chips.

Try This

Pour canned apple pie filling into a pie plate and spread it around. Sprinkle uncooked yellow cake mix over the top and then a little canola oil. Bake at 350 degrees until the top is brown. Serve this cake in pretty bowls with a scoop of your favorite frozen yogurt on the side. Dessert is often thought of as a reward, and with this one you won first prize!

ANGEL FOOD CAKE: THE SKY'S THE LIMIT

For a filling and refreshing low-calorie treat, place a big scoop of rainbow sherbet over a healthy slice of angel food cake and top it with chocolate or multi-colored sprinkles.

Or slice a piece of angel food cake in half, widthwise. Then use a thin layer of preserves (apricot, marmalade, or any flavor) to put the two halves back together. Cover half with fresh fruit, the other half with a dusting of powdered sugar, and serve a scoop of sherbet, or yogurt, on the side.

HASSLE-FREE HOME-BAKED CAKE

Purchase a box of cake mix, follow the directions, and add your unique signature by adding your own touches, such as blueberries, raspberries, raisins, dried cranberries, chocolate chips, diced apple, nuts, cinnamon, granola, or a combination of your favorite ones. (See chapter 9, page 246 to learn how to make incredible homemade granola.)

Try This

Cut angel food cake into slices and top with whipped topping over fresh blueberries, raspberries, pineapple, bananas, or the traditional strawberries. Sprinkle with a fruit sauce or powdered sugar and you've made an easy, impressive dessert.

Decadent Chocolate Desserts

On my death bed, I don't want to be wishing I'd eaten more dark chocolate, so I'm always sure to include a little—without it I'd definitely feel deprived! But don't use that excuse too often, or eat too much chocolate, because it does contain saturated fat.

LITE CHOCOLATE MOUSSE

With a spoon, slowly blend a pint of aerosol fat-free whipped topping (Kraft makes a good one), with one small can of Hershey's Syrup. Do not stir too much or it will separate. Add a hint of orange (Grand Marnier) or mint flavored (Baileys) liqueur and refrigerate.

When you're ready to serve this dessert, top it with chocolate sprinkles. If it's too runny, set it in the freezer for a while.

Try This

Cover a bowl of semi-sweet mini chocolate chips with plastic wrap and melt them in the microwave for about thirty seconds. Mini chips melt quicker and more evenly, but if the chocolate isn't melted in that amount of time, stir, and put it in for another ten seconds.

Dip *chilled* strawberries, dried apricots, almonds, your fingers, or whatever you'd like into the chocolate. (When the food is cold, the chocolate adheres better, but it must be dry or the chocolate won't solidify.) Place the dipped fruits and nuts on parchment or waxed paper and chill again, allowing the chocolate to harden before serving. Or, set up everything for your guests, and invite them to have fun in the kitchen, too.

PUT TOGETHER TOFU PUDDINGS AND PIES

Blend soft or silken tofu in a blender with a little Hershey's Syrup to the consistency of pudding. Pour the mixture into dessert bowls, shave chocolate on top—or make a pie by pouring it into a graham cracker pie crust. Cover with plastic wrap, and refrigerate.

I also make pumpkin pie by blending soft tofu with canned pumpkin, and pouring it into a crust. Or, you could whip soft tofu with chocolate pudding and eat it straight out of the mixing bowl, serve it in individual bowls, or make a chocolate cream pie. (See page 291, to find out how to make a healthy graham cracker crust.)

NUTRITION TIP

To build strong, healthy bones and prevent osteoporosis, you need approximately 1,200 milligrams of calcium a day.

Tofu and dairy products are excellent sources of both calcium and protein. The key to good health and a slim waistline is to choose dairy products that are nonfat and low fat.

Gorgeous Chocolate-Sorbet Birthday Cake

Slice a pound cake (lengthwise), and spread chocolate, or any flavor, sorbet in between each layer (I'm hooked on every flavor of Häagen-Dazs sorbet). Put the cake together again and frost it with ready-made nonfat, chocolate frosting. Set it in the freezer until you're ready to slice, and serve. As Gilda Radner once said, "When all else fails, let them eat cake!"

Felicia's No-Guilt Brownies

This is one dessert that I'll take out my measuring cup and spoons to make. Indulge yourself, because these incredible brownies are fat-free. They're delicious, healthy, and take practically no time to make!

Begin by spraying a shallow baking dish with nonstick spray. Combine about one half cup of pureed prunes in a saucepan with about two ounces of cocoa powder and stir them together over low heat until warm. (You can use baby food pureed prunes to save work and time.) Turn off the fire, add a cup of sugar or honey, four egg whites, and a big dash of vanilla, and stir.

In a separate bowl, sift three fourths cup all purpose flour and a teaspoon of baking powder. Incorporate the flour and wet mixture slowly, and at this point improvise as you please. I've tried adding a handful of mini chocolate chips, chopped nuts, raisins—it's your call. Bake in an oiled cake pan at 325 degrees for about twenty-five to thirty-five minutes, or until a toothpick inserted in the center comes out clean.

BROWNIE ALTERNATIVES

Usually, I make a double batch of the No-Guilt Brownies, because there are so many alternatives:

- Put hunks of these brownies in chocolate yogurt and serve over vanilla cake.
- Slice the brownies in half to make something like ice cream sandwiches. Put vanilla or cherry frozen yogurt in between.
- For an unusual punch, add a pinch of chili powder to these brownies, or to your favorite chocolate cake mix.
- Serve the brownies with frozen vanilla yogurt and your favorite dessert topping or sauce. (See page 284, of this chapter.)

CHOCOLATE YOGURT BALLS

Make extra brownies and allow them to sit around for four to five days. (You might have to hide them so they don't disappear before they become stale.) Put them in the food processor to make fine crumbs, and then place them in a small bowl.

One by one, put a scoop of frozen chocolate yogurt or sorbet into the bowl and coat it. Place the coated scoops onto a piece of waxed or parchment paper and put them back into the freezer to set. Serve these dessert balls with a mint leaf or fresh raspberries on top and a cookie on the side.

Create Your Own Dessert Toppings

These easy-to-make sauces can be served warm or chilled. They frame poached fruit exquisitely and dramatically complement brownies, cakes, and parfaits.

Leftover fruit sauce tastes good over grilled meats, pancakes, or on top of hot or cold cereals. Their intense flavors and vibrant colors eliminate the need to add heavy cream or butter sauces.

EASY STRAWBERRY SAUCE

To make this intense strawberry sauce, heat one half box of fresh strawberries in a saucepan containing about two tablespoons of water, two tablespoons of white wine, and sugar to taste. Strain this mixture through a fine-holed strainer and serve over vanilla yogurt, pancakes, or whatever you like.

Try This

Combine plain or vanilla yogurt, a can of ready-made apple pie filling, orange juice, a little honey and cinnamon to taste. Serve over chocolate brownies, waffles, or have fun letting your imagination run wild!

FRUIT TOPPINGS

Unsweetened strawberries taste great crushed or sliced. Peaches are wonderful, sliced or pureed. Canned cherry or blueberry filling tastes good over just about—anything.

BERRY SAUCE

In a blender, combine a couple of handfuls of washed, fresh strawberries and blueberries. Add the juice from half a lemon, puree, add sugar to taste, and blend again. I like this over grilled meats, or whole wheat dessert waffles with more berries, bananas, and nonfat whipping cream on top.

HONEY SAUCE

Mix honey and hot water, in a two to one ratio, until dissolved. Mix a little corn starch or arrowroot with some of the liquid to thicken the sauce. I enjoy baked apples and vanilla yogurt topped with this sauce.

NUTRITION TIP

Sugar isn't the "tooth villain" it's been made out to be. It's the bacteria in our mouths interacting with sugars that causes cavities. All types of sugars contain empty calories, however, so only eat sugar in moderation, and always brush your teeth afterwards.

Dessert Parfaits

Parfaits are cold desserts made of layers of fruits, syrup, ice creams, and whipped cream. They first appeared in 1894 as flavored custards containing whipped cream and syrup that were frozen without stirring. Parfait literally means "perfect," from the Latin *perfectus. Parfait* means perfect in French, too.

NO-COOK OUTRAGEOUS PARFAIT

Alternate slices of banana with two types of fruit spread in a fancy wineglass or dish, and top with grated coconut, your favorite dessert sauce, or a fresh mint leaf.

Try This

Using skim milk, make a package of instant vanilla pudding. Scoop a layer into pretty glasses, alternate with your favorite fruit, and then a sprinkling of Grape Nuts cereal. Add more pudding, fruit, and so on until you reach the top.

Try This

Make a package of instant pudding and layer with your favorite flavor of nonfat frozen yogurt, crumbled cookies, sliced bananas, or any fruit—on top.

Sweet Liqueur Desserts

Every dessert becomes a little fancier if you add a touch of Kahlua, Creme de Menthe, Grand Marnier, Amaretto, Baileys, Framboise, Frangelico, Cointreau, or one of the many others.

APPLE-COINTREAU SUNDAE

This dessert is amazingly easy and surprisingly good. Peel and core a crispy Red Delicious apple. Slice thinly and arrange it beautifully around a plate. In the center, add a large scoop of nonfat yogurt, and drizzle with Cointreau. Top with almonds, diced cherries, a little whipped topping—or your favorite fantasy.

CHERRY SUNDAE

Heat cherry pie filling in a saucepan. Add a few sprinkles of cinnamon, allspice, and orange juice. Then a splash of Amaretto, Frangelico, or Cointreau, and bring it to a boil, stirring constantly. Scoop frozen vanilla yogurt into individual parfait dishes, top it with this cherry sauce, and serve immediately.

SENSATIONAL STRAWBERRIES

Mix one pint of fresh, washed strawberries, and slice all but a few in half. Mix the halved berries with a little lemon juice, sugar, and Cointreau to taste, and refrigerate.

At serving time, alternate frozen vanilla yogurt, the strawberry mixture, and refrigerated nonfat strawberry yogurt in sherbet glasses. Top with a whole strawberry, and your favorite type of cookie. Yum!

ORANGES IN COINTREAU

Peel fresh oranges (removing the white) and seed. Cut across into slices, and drizzle with Cointreau or your favorite liqueur.

NUTRITION TIP

The American Heart Association recommends 1 to 2 drinks a day to protect your heart. They're speaking of wine or beer, but if you can afford the extra sugar, a little liqueur once in a while won't hurt.

There are, however, many contraindications for alcohol. Check with your doctor if you're unsure.

Fat-Free Desserts

As you've seen, desserts don't have to be fatty to be good. And don't be fooled: some manufactures put chunks of buttery cookies and brownies in "nonfat" yogurt, or chocolate in "nonfat" cookies, cakes, and muffins. I want to know what I'm eating!

PAULA'S OUTRAGEOUS "NONFAT" CHEESE CAKE

Paula made an incredibly delicious nonfat cheese cake that she shared with me and several other women after we played tennis one day. She made it by blending together a large package of fat-free (room temperature) cream cheese, eight egg whites, lemon juice, three fourths cup sugar, and nonfat sour cream. She poured the mixture into a prebaked graham cracker crust and baked the cake for twenty minutes at 350 degrees.

When she told us how she had made the cheese cake, I

thought Paula had truly invented an amazing fat-free wonder
. . . . . . until she got to the last ingredient in the *crust:* 1 pound
of butter!

I nearly gagged, just thinking about what I was putting into
my body, especially after three long and hard sets of doubles.
Honestly, Paula actually thought the cheese cake she made was
fat-free! (See my healthy pie crust on page 291, of this chapter,
and create your own nonfat cheese cake just like Paula's, but
with a fat-free *crust.*

BAKED APPLES

Core an apple with a grapefruit knife or melon baller for each
person you're serving. I've done this with Pippin, Rome Beauty,
Golden Delicious, Mcintosh, Gala, and Granny Smith apples—
some taste sweeter or tarter, but they're all delicious!

Place the apples in a Pyrex-type baking dish and pour a little apple juice and orange juice over them. Sprinkle with
cinnamon-sugar, a little nutmeg to taste, and bake at 350 degrees for about an hour, or until soft.

POACHED PEARS

Slice fresh pears in half, lengthwise. Peel, and remove core
and seeds. Place pear halves in a large skillet, and add Zinfandel or Chardonnay, cinnamon sticks and cloves. Bring this mixture to a boil, reduce to a simmer, and poach about forty
minutes or until tender.

Remove the pears, throw away the cinnamon sticks and
cloves, and reduce the juice to a flavorful syrup. Place the
pears in a beautiful dish, top with a mixture of fresh berries,
and serve hot or cold.

BAKED APPLE AND POACHED PEAR ALTERNATIVES

I never tire of these desserts, because there are so many exciting variations:

- Serve with frozen, nonfat vanilla yogurt.
- Replace the Zinfandel with cherry soda or fruit juice. Orange juice with a splash of lemon is delicious.
- Add an added pinch of allspice, cinnamon, sugar, and nutmeg; tastes great!
- Pour warm caramel sauce on top.

Try This

Dip slices of pineapple or pear in beaten egg white, then granola, or 1-minute Quaker Oats. Bake for ten to fifteen minutes, at whatever temperature you think best. Test food as it's cooking and you won't go wrong.

DESSERT PIZZA

Try pineapple, apricots, peaches, or bananas on pizza with a little brown sugar and cinnamon sprinkled on top. (See chapter 3, page 72 regarding the crust, but add a little extra sugar to the crust when you make dessert pizza.)

TWO FRUITS ARE BETTER THAN ONE

It's amazing, but any two fruits go together, and, when cut beautifully and spooned into a clear fancy dish, they make a refreshing dessert. Watermelon and kiwi, peaches and raspberries, or mango and seedless grapes. Imagine the flavors of your two favorite fruits together, and add a splash of lemon or lime, or a hint of liqueur. Or leave well enough alone. Mother Nature is such a good cook you don't have to do anything to enhance fruit.

Filo Dessert

Most chefs don't make filo dough from scratch because it's fragile and time-consuming. To hold the dough together, a ton of butter is generally used in filo desserts, such as *baklavah,* a Greek pastry layered with spices, ground nuts, and honey syrup. But a spray can of canola oil makes the results healthier and the job a lot easier and quicker.

Flaky, filo dough made primarily of flour, egg, and water is available in the freezer section of most markets. When you're working with this dough, it dries out fast, so always keep it covered with a clean, damp cloth. Store leftover dough in the freezer.

FILO POCKETS

Defrost a box of filo dough and carefully unroll a sheet. Cut into squares—5″ × 5″ is usually a good size. Lightly spray each sheet, starting from the outside and working your way in, until you've put together about four sheets. Fill with canned apple, peach, or berry pie filling, fold into triangles, a little like a diaper without the baby inside. And, then, press the edges together and spray once more. Place the pockets on a cookie sheet, seam side down, and sprinkle with granulated sugar. Preheat the oven to 350 degrees, and bake until golden brown.

You could also fill filo with chocolate chips and walnuts, or white chocolate and pecans, and top with sugar and cinnamon.

Freezer Desserts

ICE-CREAM PIE

To make one of the best desserts, an ice-cream pie, begin by making a fat-free graham cracker pie crust. Fill it with coffee sorbet, frozen coffee yogurt, or your favorite flavor. Stick it in the freezer, frost it with fat-free fudge sauce, and then freeze it again. Defrost for a few minutes, and then slice as you would any other pie.

Healthy Pie Crust

Grind about one and a half cups of fat-free graham crackers in the food processor. (I use fat-free, because most regular graham crackers contain that nasty saturated fat!) Mix the graham cracker crumbs with one third cup of warm water. Then spray a pie tin or glass dish with canola oil, and press the crumbs on the bottom and sides of the pan. Bake at 300 degrees for about ten minutes, and make a nonfat cheese cake. (Or, fill it with whatever you prefer.)

If you have graham cracker crumbs leftover, save them for another dessert topping.

Fruit Sherbet

If you're in pursuit of something refreshing, cut an orange, grapefruit, cantaloupe, or any type of fruit in half. Scoop out the insides and fill the shell with the same flavored sherbet. Freeze, and serve when hardened with a little shredded coconut or a mint leaf pressed on top. (The scooped out fruit can be used to make fruit sauces.)

DECORATING TIP
Desserts are visually more appealing when you sprinkle spices or place sprigs of fresh herbs—mint, basil, rosemary, sage, or thyme—on top.

Low-Fat Banana Splits

Scoop balls of various flavors of sorbet and frozen yogurt into a beautiful crystal bowl. Place them in the freezer until you're ready for dessert, and then encourage your guests to make banana splits by adding the following toppings: nuts, cherries, nonfat whipping cream, bananas, and sauces (butterscotch, caramel, strawberry, the others described in this chapter, and—of course—chocolate).

Sorbet Sundae

You don't have to wait until Sunday, because this dessert is good any day of the week. Spoon two scoops of sorbet, or vanilla nonfat yogurt into a fancy glass. Top with a few spoons of cherry, apple, or blueberry pie filling, or a squirt of chocolate sauce. Place a fancy little cookie on the plate, or insert one into the sundae.

Comfort Desserts

I consider certain dishes to be "comfort desserts" because just making or eating these standards brings back warm childhood memories. Using your artist's palette, and excellent taste, take poetic license to update and lighten the basic methods that follow:

Try This

Whenever I eat apple crisp, I think about the sixth grade because it was served in the cafeteria every Friday when I was fifteen. Then, it was on the menu every Monday, when I taught the sixth grade. I still enjoy apple crisp today.

Depending upon the number of people you're serving, peel, core, and slice six to eight apples into a bowl. Toss them with a mixture of one tablespoon cornstarch and the juice of one lemon. Now place the coated apples into an oiled pie plate.

Make a topping by mixing equal amounts of flour, brown sugar, and granulated sugar. Add some cinnamon and a little ground cloves to taste. Drizzle some canola oil into the mixture and toss slightly until the topping clumps together. Spread the topping over the apples and bake for about fifty minutes at 350 degrees, or until the apples are tender and the top browns. Serve hot or cold with frozen vanilla yogurt on top.

RICE PUDDING

I remember as a young kid going to my Aunt Sara's house each week and eating "Crunchy Pudding." I thought that was the formal name for the dessert, but it turns out that it was rice pudding—but Aunt Sara never cooked the rice enough. Who knew it wasn't supposed to get caught between my teeth?

In an oiled baking pan, combine Italian Arborio rice—the one that's used to make risotto—with a little milk, sugar, and nuts. To improvise this dish, add dried cranberries, raisins, or currants *plumped* (or soaked) in pineapple juice, Frangelico, or some other sweet liqueur. This pudding becomes extremely rich, thick, and "comfortingly" creamy as it slowly bakes in the oven. Remember, if it's crunchy it hasn't been cooked enough!

THE PROOF IS IN THE BREAD PUDDING!

For a comfort food that's easy to make, begin by beating together some milk and egg whites. Add some cinnamon, nutmeg, sugar, vanilla, raisins, currants, chocolate chips, or chopped walnuts. (Add the spices, and the nuts, chips, raisins, and so on a pinch at a time, so you can make sure they don't smother the flavor of the dish.)

Remove the crust from stale bread, dice the inside into large cubes, and add it to the mixture. Pour everything into an oiled Pyrex dish, spread evenly, and bake it in a *water bath* so it doesn't burn. That entails putting the bread pudding dish into a larger dish containing a couple of inches of water. Sprinkle cocoa, nutmeg and cinnamon on top, and bake for about forty-five minutes at 350 degrees, or until a knife inserted in the center comes out clean.

Serve this dish straight from the oven, or top it with yogurt, nuts, or granola. (See chapter 9, page 246, for an incredible technique for making homemade granola.)

A No-Recipe Dessert Buffet

None of my friends enjoys long meals in crowded restaurants with poor service, especially on New Year's Eve when the prices are doubled.

Last year, while blowing whistles, wearing stupid-looking hats with feathers coming out of the tops, and eating a cold, over-cooked meal, one of the other women promised to host a dessert buffet next year.

My husband and the other men volunteered to make pancakes and omelets. And I promised to bring assortments of organic grapes, pears, and apples alongside platters of brie, cheddar, and goat cheese. We'll toast the new year with champagne or fine wine.

Then, after leaning back in our chairs, or walking around a bit, for the seventh-inning stretch, it'll be time for a special treat, or surprise, and I don't mean more food.

Dessert comes in many forms, so perhaps we'll have a little entertainment. We'll have someone teach us to play the Congo drums, or we'll hire a psychic, or maybe a palm reader. Who knows, we might even get up and dance!

We'll leave for home with bittersweet sorrow in our hearts, torn between wanting to rest before the next day's festivities begin, and not wanting to leave the party because of the magnificent time we've had with our friends.

And now as I'm adding the final touches to this book, I'm experiencing bittersweet sorrow once again.

BITTERSWEET SORROW

I keep thinking of what my dear Grandma-ma told me when I asked her how she learned to cook without recipes. Remember the story? She said it happened in an instant one day after an artist had told her how he had created his painting.

"This piece," the artist said, "started out with a splash of white that asked to be red. Then it solicited a black line through its center. The painting was finished when it didn't ask for anything more."

This book isn't asking for anything more, either. I have given you the best of my heart, so it has all the feelings, seasonings, and information that it needs. But I have a lot of mixed emotions about ending, because I've thoroughly enjoyed imagining you playfully creating—and tasting—in your kitchen. In fact, many of the ideas for *Cooking without Recipes* came to me while thinking of *you*. So, let's just say, "So long for now."

I've planted the seed for my next book idea, and trusting in the creative process, it's percolating. So, we'll meet again soon! And, meanwhile, let me know if this book has made you as hungry as it has made me, or if you have any other comments, please write, or visit my web site:

Cheryl Sindell
c/o Kensington/Zebra 850 Third Avenue
New York, New York 10022
or http://204.108.87.140/sindell/book.html

More Food for Thought

Food is essential to life, fundamental to our health, and also a tremendous source of pleasure. It can make us sick or help us get well, yet most people are baffled about what to eat because they only hear sensational or extreme views from so-called experts. Read the newspaper or watch the nightly news and you'll find yourself confused—at least three times a day.

If you eat right, you feel good. You have the energy you need to lead an active life. Your bones, teeth, and nails are strong, and you even look better because you have shinier hair and a brighter smile! There's a contradiction in our society, however. Health authorities encourage us to nourish our bodies, yet the models in magazines and on TV are 10% taller and weigh 25% less than the average person.

We're fortunate to live where food is abundant, yet we treat food like the enemy. Andy Rooney put it best when he said, "The two biggest sellers in any bookstore are the cookbooks and the diet books. The cookbooks tell you how to prepare the food, and the diet books tell you how not to eat any of it."

In an attempt to become model-thin, we skip meals, eliminate entire food groups, and avoid complex carbohydrates, or protein. If the $35 billion that is annually spent on dieting were donated instead to those in need, we could put an end to world hunger!

Even people who weigh exactly what they should purchase diet pills, herbs, and other aids to help them eat less. They put themselves on diets restricting their fat intake—eating fat-free this, and fake-fat that. But being concerned only with fat is nothing more than the nation's latest fad diet that isn't working. And, consequently, more people than ever are overweight today!

So, what *is* the answer? Eat well because you enjoy it, and because you like the way taking care of yourself makes you feel. Fortunately, to become lean, fit, and healthy, you don't need to exercise until it hurts or carry around a calculator tabulating the number of grams or calories in every food and drink you consume.

All you've got to do is exercise moderately for about 30 minutes, four times a week, and balance the ratio of carbohydrates, protein, and fat you consume—toward the ideal of a 40:30:30 ratio. And, most important, see how *you* feel eating that way! The only concept I'm married to, for basically healthy people, is limiting calories coming from saturated fat to no more than 7 percent.

Add olive oil to your salad, or marinades and low-fat sauces to your meat, if you'd like. And if there are foods such as pizza, tacos, or desserts that you enjoy, incorporate them into your eating plan too. But, eat them for pure pleasure and to nourish your body when you're hungry, rather than for comfort when you're lonely or upset. Most people are overweight simply because they eat too much, so pay close attention to your appetite, so you can eat when you're hungry and stop eating before you're uncomfortably full.

So, now that there's no confusion whatsoever about your diet, I hope *Cooking without Recipes* has stimulated you to cook and have more fun in the kitchen. Remember, you are a gifted cook with an extraordinary talent for creating easy and delicious, healthy meals. And since you're not a slave to recipes anymore, you're free to cook in the style you prefer and entertain more often.

Where else but at home can we kick off our shoes and laugh freely with the people we love? And, there's no better place than around the dinner table to teach our children about wholesome foods, good morals, and family values. Our children are the future!

As a nutritionist and a mother, I believe that each and every one of us must do everything we can to bring the people we care about together. And absolutely nothing draws people together faster than a sensuously, satisfying home-cooked meal!

ACKNOWLEDGMENTS

I've learned that nothing creative is ever accomplished without inspiration from other artists. I'm extremely grateful to all the people who have written about cooking, creativity, spirituality, and nutrition because I have been influenced by so many of them.

And, no worthwhile project is ever completed without the help of a talented team, so I send my love and appreciation to each and every one of the following geniuses who breathed their creative energy into *Cooking without Recipes*.

I send a warm thank-you to my Grandma-ma Sultana Sadacca for teaching me to break the rules and cook from my heart, the way an artist paints or a musician plays. I will always remember her and her innovative ways.

I am eternally grateful to the thousands of clients I've counseled who have inspired me to come up with creative methods for attaining better nutrition and health, without sacrificing taste.

My appreciation goes out to Gerry Schick, M.S.W, for encouraging me to become a writer and express myself. My thanks to Wolfgang Puck for inspiring me to write about cooking in the same way chefs create recipes.

Thank you Sara Mitchell for believing a book about cooking without recipes could not only be written, but sold. I truly appreciate your creative contribution to this project!

Thanks to the best agent in the world, Mike Hamilberg, for teaching me about unique ideas, selling this book with passion, never running out of patience, and always returning my calls promptly. (Joanie Socola, I adore you, too!)

My thanks to Beth Lieberman for embracing this concept and taking it to Kensington Publishing Corporation.

My love and appreciation goes out to Nomi Kleinmuntz. (Nomi, the way we met makes me certain that everything in life happens for a reason!) Thank you for your editorial genius and for prodding me to become the writer I am today.

My heartfelt thank-you to the following people, who shared their unique cooking techniques with me: Susan Baker, Kathy Diamond, Anita Reedy, Sue Chapman, Laura Heller, Linda Pushkin, Dorothy Katona, Ruth Heller, Janet Cahana, Debbie Kaplan, Melba Silva, Marina Hernandez, Manuella Zelaya, Francis Ross, and Robin Thaler.

A huge thanks to Felicia Zigman for doing some of the research and trying out the cooking procedures.

My love and thanks to my dear friend Paula Derrington for allowing me, from the bottom of her humorous heart, to share some of our private moments. Thanks, Paula, for reading my manuscript, always encouraging me to write, and for adding your creative touch to this project. (Paula now cooks like the talented artist she is!)

Thank you to the writers who allowed me to quote them, and to the generous people who endorsed this book. My love to Steven Heller for sending me "food" quotes whenever he came across good ones.

A big hug to my dear friend Leslie who is always there when I need support and is also there when life calls for a celebration!

My thanks to David Heller, Barry Baker, Lara Longo, Linda Ellis, and Lisa Heller for your love and encouragement, and a big hug and kiss to my parents, Sue and Harold Baker, for cultivating my love for good food when I was a child.

My thanks to Annmarie Dalton and Mona Daly for their creative artistry. And to Mindas for his photography.

My love to Joan Carry and Steve Nelson for their positive energy and creative P.R. And, my gratitude goes out to Lisa Ekus for her guidance over the years.

Several people helped to make this dream of mine a reality by trying out the cooking strategies, sharing their comments, and urging me on. Thank you Maxine and Eliot Finkle, Dyanne Aponte, and Julia Knight.

My deepest appreciation goes out to the talented team at Kensington. This book wouldn't be what it is today without my editor, Ann LaFarge. Thank you, Ann. You made this a stronger book. And thanks to all the other players on the team who contributed their expertise and good taste. And a special nod to Kensington copy chief Debbie Babitt, for doing an extraordinary job.

And, from the bottom of my heart, I'd like to send a big hug and kiss to my wonderful friend and husband, Robert. Thank you for supporting me in every way, raving about most of my creations, your expertise, and especially for your patience during the many months I sat at the computer pounding away. I will love you forever!

Chelsea, thanks for being on my creative team. I know you and Dad had to fend for yourselves more than usual, and I promise to make it up to both of you!

And, finally a big scratch behind the ears to my dog, Shiva. Food never goes to waste in our house because of her, even when I make an irreversible kitchen blooper. And, Shiva, thanks for sitting so patiently by my side; I believe every writer and every cook should have a faithful dog exactly like you.

INDEX

ABOUT THE AUTHOR

Cheryl Sindell is the foremost media-nutritionist in Los Angeles. She is a noted clinical nutritionist, author, restaurant consultant, and radio and TV personality. Cheryl triumphed over adversity by earning her degrees in public health, journalism and writing, at the University of California at Los Angeles, to begin a new career after a miraculous recovery from a four year paralysis caused by a debilitating illness known as Guillian-Barré Syndrome.

Currently she shares her opinions about food and nutrition on both national and local radio and TV shows. In Los Angeles, she is the nutrition reporter for KABC TALKRADIO, ABC's Eyewitness News, and she teaches chefs at the Epicurean School of Culinary Arts in Los Angeles.

Ms. Sindell solves her clients' nutritional issues by providing them with individualized eating plans that are practical, safe, and satisfying.

Cheryl Sindell is the author of *Not "Just a Salad"* (Pharos Books), which shows the reader how to eat well and stay healthy when dining out! The foreword was written by Wolfgang Puck.

Ms. Sindell resides in Brentwood, California with her husband Dr. Robert Heller and their fifteen year old daughter, Chelsea. She is writing an innovative weight loss book.